By MARTIN KILSON

Political Change in a West African State

Political Awakening of Africa (co-editor with Rupert Emerson)

By WILFRED CARTEY

Islands in the Sun

Black Images

Whispers from a Continent

COLONIAL AFRICA

The Africa Reader:

COLONIAL

AFRICA

Edited and with Introductions by

Wilfred Cartey and Martin Kilson

VINTAGE BOOKS

A Division of Random House • New York

CONTENTS

Part II: Methods of and Adaptations to Colonial Government

Part III: Emergence of the Masses

Part IV: Elite-Mass Nexus: Formation of National Institutions

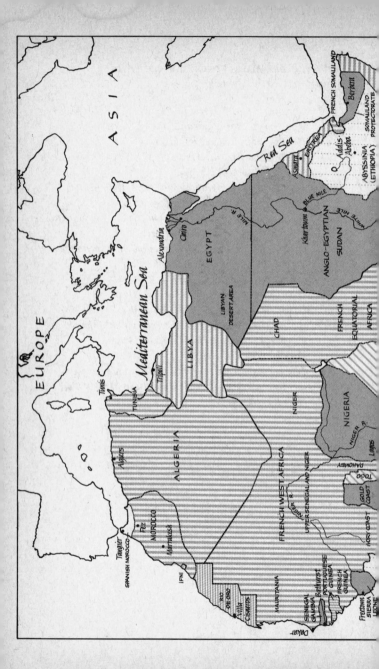

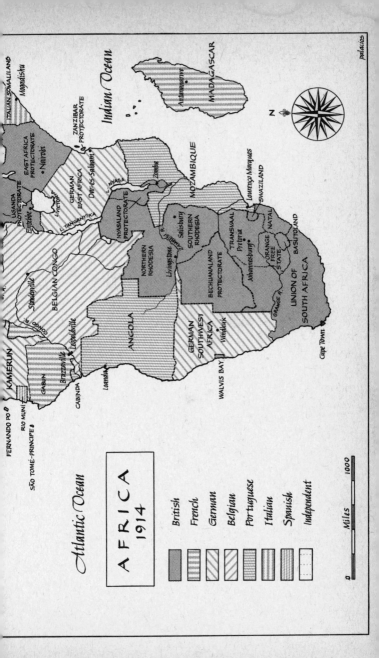

INTRODUCTION

Our purpose in the first volume of *The African Reader, Colonial Africa,* is to put into relief the different kinds and levels of institutional transformations that characterized the emergence of modern Africa. Inevitably, we have been somewhat arbitrary in our determination of which institutional changes to emphasize in this volume; but our hope is that we have at least focussed on those institutional changes that have been basic in shaping political relationships and power in modern Africa.

One important theme we hope will emerge from these pages is that whatever modern Africa has become politically is as much a result of the decisions and actions of Africans as of European colonial regimes. The decisions and actions of both Africans and European colonial rulers were historically conditioned, and both the successes and failures of the colonial era in Africa must be seen in this context. Thus, insofar as the primary purpose of colonial regimes in Africa was to make the continent's natural and human resources available to the capitalist power systems of the West, these regimes pursued only that measure of political development necessary to realize this purpose.

This meant, in the matter of the local administration of African communities, that colonial regimes pursued the line of least resistance: traditional African ruling groups were sought out and invested with limited authority in order to pacify African communities in face of modern economic changes perpetrated by European capitalists, technicians, and officials. In performing their function in the colonial administration of local African communities, the traditional African rulers were not, however, mere automatons of European officials. They were able to exert, legally and illegally, a certain autonomy over a wide range of daily decisions and actions. Often this was done more in the interest of African traditional rulers than of other segments of the population, with the result that by the 1930's African chiefs throughout colonial Africa were in possession of a disproportionate share of modern benefits.

Those Africans who were fortunate enough to have early access to the education provided under colonial regimes were the only other segment of the African population who obtained a disproportionate share of modern benefits. But the effort of these educated Africans to realize and consolidate their share of modernity had a much greater impact on political development in colonial Africa than that of traditional rulers. The educated elites could realize their modern ambitions only by seizing the leading roles in government and the economy held by Europeans. It is this situation that gave rise to African nationalist movements, first in the 1930's and later, at a more mature stage of transformation, after World War II. Through the nationalist parties the new elites mobilized popular support, which in turn convinced the colonial regimes of the need to transfer greater political power to Africans. Though this process occasionally entailed violence (especially in the colonial territories in East and Central Africa where sizable numbers of white settlers established themselves), for the most part this stage of political development in modern Africa was relatively peaceful.

As in all situations of the rise of modern power, the masses in colonial Africa experienced a difficult and haphazard route to modernity, and still do so in the emergent independent African regimes. In the colonial era, the popular forces in rural areas and in the towns often resorted to riotous outbursts as the best means for articulating their needs and interests. Occasionally, some popular elements gained a more institutionalized avenue for realizing modern advancement, like trade unions, mutual benefit associations, and separatist Christian churches. These institutions were usually led by semi-educated Africans who had enough experience with modern society to function as a subsidiary or para-elite.

By the end of World War II, these para-elite leaders of organizations that served popular needs were available for the many secondary leadership roles in the nationalist parties. In a few African states, leaders who fit the description of para-elite actually obtained political power at independence (e.g., in Ghana in 1957), though for the most part the leading political positions went to the well-educated segments of the African elites. Currently, the pattern of contest for influence among the segments of African elites, as well as between the elites and popular forces, display much instability. This political instability is reinforced by profound ethnic, religious, regional, and class cleavages in most African states, and it will be many years before a more predictable pattern of politics will obtain.

It is our hope that the following pages help the reader to grasp the historical basis of the current structure of politics in Africa. No claim of perfection can be made for the writings and documents we have selected as aids to this end; we can only say that to our understanding of the rise of modern African politics, these selections appear eminently suited for this purpose.

WILFRED CARTEY
MARTIN KILSON

PART **I**

Reactions to Conquest

INTRODUCTION:

Types of African Reaction

The selections in Part I are examples of the kinds of initial reactions of traditional ruling groups in African societies to the attempts of European powers to establish colonial hegemony over Africa in the late nineteenth and early twentieth century. It is often assumed that European colonial control of the African continent was achieved without warfare, other than that between the European powers competing in the scramble for Africa in the nineteenth century.[1]

Not only did all European powers participating in the scramble for Africa in the nineteenth century confront some armed resistance from the African traditional rulers, but, in some cases, the resistance was substantial and of some duration. This was markedly so in the wars between the British and the Ashanti Kingdom in the nineteenth century. The British began to assert authority over trade, especially the slave trade, on the Gold Coast (now Ghana) in the early nineteenth century, and met fierce resistance from the well-organized Ashanti Confederacy which had established widespread influence in slave trading to the Western hemisphere in the eighteenth and nineteenth century.[2] With the aid of

---

1. Cf. William L. Langer, *The Diplomacy of Imperialism 1890–1902* (New York, 1951).
2. For an account of the character of Ashanti power in the

guns and ammunition gained as items of exchange in the
slave trade, the Ashanti met British forces (often made up
of African soldiers as well as British troops) in battle seven
times before British authority ultimately prevailed in 1900.
These battles occurred in 1806, 1811, 1814–1815, 1823–
1826, 1863, 1873–1874, and 1895.

The resistance of the Malinke Chief, Samori Toure, to
the penetration of the Western Sudan portion of West
Africa was also substantial and extended. So too was the
attempt of Hehe rulers in East Africa to foil German seizure
of that area in 1891–1898. A unique feature of the resistance of Samori Toure and his Malinke army was the local
manufacture of firearms, though, as in Ashanti, the major
supply of arms was gained as exchange in the slave trade or
through trans-Saharan trade with Arab states in North
Africa.[3] The Ethiopian Emperor Menelik II was perhaps
the only African ruler in the nineteenth century who syste-
matically purchased arms from Europe. He was also the
only African ruler who succeeded in preventing the colonial
subordination of his state.

The selections in Part I illustrate the kinds of issues that
led to organized armed resistance to European penetration.
In the Ashanti wars and the French wars with Samori Toure,
the traditional rulers were seeking to protect their position
in the slave trade and in the trans-Saharan trade, which also
included African slaves. The Ashanti and Malinke rulers
were also in possession of well-organized states, based on
agriculture and limited iron-working, and desired to maintain the sovereignty of their political institutions. The same
desire to maintain sovereignty characterized the rather
limited resistance of Benin rulers in Nigeria. The Benin
Kingdom had played an important part in the slave trade

nineteenth century, see Ivory Wilks, "Ashanti Government," in
Daryll Forde and P. M. Kaberry, eds., *West African Kingdoms in
the Nineteenth Century* (London, 1967).

3. On the origins of guns in eighteenth- and nineteenth-century
West Africa, see J. D. Fage and Roland Oliver, *A Short History
of Africa* (London, 1960).

and had enjoyed large-scale influence in western Nigeria
before the nineteenth century.

The traditional rulers of Buganda, a traditional political unit within what became the colony of Uganda,
were equally concerned with maintaining their sovereignty. But rather than meet the colonial intruder on
the battlefield, they negotiated the terms of British occupation. Baganda rulers had experienced rather extensive exposure to Christianity and Western education before the late
nineteenth century, and this exposure no doubt influenced
their decision to negotiate a settlement with the British.
Negotiated settlements of one sort or another—usually
quite unfavorable to African rulers, compared to the Baganda settlement of 1900—were, in fact, a more common
form of response to European penetration than was armed
resistance. Thus the decision of Baganda's ruling class to
negotiate British occupation was not unusual. Only the
sizable benefits accruing to many Baganda chiefs as part of
the settlement was rather exceptional. Seldom was freehold
land transfer to African rulers used as means to allay their
fears in regard to European colonial occupation: if anything, land transfer as part of a colonial settlement involved
only Europeans, which was the case in Kenya, Southern
Rhodesia, Northern Rhodesia, the Congo, and elsewhere.

The Mende Rising in Sierra Leone in 1898 was a more
limited form of resistance than the Ashanti wars and Samori
Toure's wars with the French. The Mende rulers and masses
were resisting less the fact of British occupation (to which
they had peaceably acquiesced in 1896 when the British
established protectorate authority over the Sierra Leone
hinterland) than the mode of exercising colonial hegemony.
Mende chiefs resented the method of local taxation employed by the British, especially the failure to make special
concessions in the matter of taxation to the chiefs themselves. The Ndebele and Shona rulers in Southern Rhodesia
also resented the method of British occupation, and the
religious leaders of the Ndebele and Shona articulated this
resentment in terms of a glorious political past.

Limited and ad hoc issues like taxation, forced labor, land alienation for European use, etc., were at the basis of other violent forms of resistance to European colonialism in the first two decades of colonial rule. Occasionally, these more limited outbursts covered large areas of a colonial territory, like the Maji-Maji Rebellion in Tanganyika (now Tanzania) in 1905. But usually those outbursts or risings based on ad hoc issues were rather localized, seldom involving more than a group of villages or a district. For the first three decades of this century, there were innumerable outbursts of this sort, of infinite variety, in colonial Africa. It was with the rise of educated and semi-educated new elites, who formed modern organizations as a means of dealing with colonial development, that rebellious outbursts or risings tended to subside. From the 1930's onward, the modern organizations formed by the new elites proved the most effective means of African response to the problems of colonial society.

M.K.

British Advance in Ghana Halted by Ashanti, 1873

W. W. CLARIDGE *

The year 1873 witnessed the commencement of the sixth Ashanti war, a war that is noteworthy for several reasons. In the first place, it absolutely justified the predictions made by Governor Pine ten years earlier, and it was proved once and for all that it was possible to employ European troops on the Gold Coast for short periods, provided due precautions were observed; and further, this was the first occasion on which a British force had ever attacked the Ashantis in their own country, thereby dispelling their belief in their own invincibility and laying the foundations for the overthrow of their kingdom and empire.

In considering the causes that led to this war, it must not be forgotten that, though generally regarded as a separate invasion, it was in reality a continuation of the war of 1863, since which no peace had been made. Governor Pine's refusal to surrender the fugitive Janin was, therefore, the primary cause; for although ten years had elapsed and various circumstances had contributed to defer further action on the part of the Ashantis, this grievance had never been forgotten; the policy of Ashanti had undergone no change; Kofi Karikari, when he succeeded to the stool in 1867, had sworn his "business should be war."

* From W. W. Claridge, *A History of the Gold Coast and Ashanti* (London, 1915).

The king was inclined toward peace for the present, though several of his chiefs were clamoring for war, and in all probability further action would have been deferred until the losses of men and stores in Krepi could have been made good, had not the transfer of Elmina brought matters to an immediate head.* This, therefore, must be regarded as the actual cause of the resumption of hostilities. The king undoubtedly believed that Elmina was a portion of his kingdom and had repeatedly protested against the transfer, and since there is good evidence that this contention was perfectly correct, and that the so-called renunciation of his claim was not all that it purported to be, this second cause must also be considered a just one.

Apart from the contention that Elmina really belonged to the Ashantis, the transfer affected them in other ways. The abolition of the slave trade had been a serious matter to them, for they had thereby been deprived of the ready and remunerative means of disposing of their prisoners of war that had been their principal source of revenue. The kings had frequently complained of this, and the departure of the Dutch, who had still bought a certain number of slaves—nominally as soldiers for service abroad—had finally closed even this limited market. The abolition of the slave trade may therefore be cited as one of the more remote causes of the war.

In earlier times the Ashantis had traded largely at Accra; but for the past half-century they had been dependent upon free intercourse with Elmina, and its possible closure to them was, therefore, a matter of vital importance. It was absolutely necessary for them to have free access to the sea, or they could find no outlet for their own trade and no means of obtaining a direct supply of powder, rum, salt, and other articles that they needed. Their friendship with the Dutch had secured them hitherto; but once Elmina passed into the hands of the English, they knew that the

---

* Elmina, a Dutch trading center, was transferred to Britain.—
Editor's Note.

roads might be closed against them at any time, forcing them to use the distant market of Assini, and indeed striking at the very root of their power and independence: it is small wonder, therefore, that they objected to the transaction. The unwillingness of the Fantis to allow the Ashantis to trade directly with the Coast, and the desire of the latter to avoid the large profits of these middlemen, had in fact been a contributing element in nearly every dispute with Ashanti.

To recapitulate, therefore, this war was merely a continuation of that of 1863, which was now resumed because of the occupation of Elmina; but had the Dutch never left the Coast, or had the English declined to take Elmina, the invasion would have taken place just the same, if not at this particular time, then at some future date. One of the principal objects of the English in acquiring Elmina and the other Dutch Settlements had been to put an end to the warfare on the Coast, but now the common fate of would-be peacemakers was theirs and they found themselves seriously involved.

No matter what its actual exciting causes were, this war was inevitable from the Ashantis' point of view, and it was equally inevitable from the point of view of the British government. Whether or not matters might have turned out differently if a wiser policy had been adopted by the trading companies half a century earlier, it is now impossible to decide; but it is deeply to be deplored that the Ashantis were not more fairly treated then and the experiment at least made of trying to gain this fine race as the friends instead of as the declared enemies of the English. Could this have been done, they would have proved invaluable allies. The time for such an experiment, however, was now long past, and the mutual feelings of distrust that had grown up had put it outside the range of practical politics; while the conditions of life in Ashanti, the barbarous and despotic nature of its government, the enmity between its people and the British-protected tribes, and the losses involved by the frequent quarrels and disputes consequent thereon, made some decisive measures necessary. The longer such measures were delayed and a weak and temporizing policy adopted, or any stronger policy was unbacked by the power to enforce compliance with legitimate demands, the greater the difficulties became and the more did the Ashantis learn to despise the power of the English and have increased faith in their own supposed invincibility. So far had this process already gone, and so peculiar and difficult would have been the situation, even if a treaty could now have been made between two nations so widely separated in the scale of civilization, the more barbarous of which was locally the more powerful, that the definite conquest of Ashanti would no longer be deferred.

The Ashanti army crossed the Pra on January 22, 1873. So soon as the Chief of Yankumasi Assin heard of its approach, he had sacrificed three women and fourteen men to the god of the river to induce him to prevent the passage of the enemy, and when the Ashantis tried to cross at Prasu a few days later and some forty of their men, among whom was a subchief of Bantama, were drowned, their loss was attributed by both parties to this sacrifice. The Ashantis then made further sacrifices, and, abandoning Prasu, went about half a mile higher up the stream to Atasi, where they succeeded in crossing without further loss. The strength of this army was estimated at 12,000 men; it took five days to cross the river, using two ferries of two canoes each and sending thirty men over at each trip. The Ashantis then plundered and burned several Assin villages, and a skirmish took place between a portion of their force and a body of a thousand Assins, in which one Ashanti was taken prisoner and two more were killed, their heads being sent down to King Anfu Otu at Abakrampa as proof of the actuality of the invasion. It was from a letter from him and a message from Chibu the King of Assin, both of which reached Cape Coast on January 31, that the government learned the first definite news of the invasion, though there had been a number of vague rumors afloat for several days.

The Ashantis had so completely succeeded in blinding

the authorities to their real intentions that Colonel Harley*
was even now disinclined to believe that an Ashanti army
had really entered the Protectorate, and instead of immediately calling the tribes together and providing them with
arms and ammunition for the defence of their country, wasted valuable time in sending Dr. Rowe as Special
Commissioner to Anamabo, Abakrampa, and Assin to see
how far these reports were correct, and, if true, to impress
upon the kings the necessity for united action.

Chief Bentil of Mumford, who had been elected Commander-in-Chief by the Fanti kings during the last war,
offered to collect an army of 20,000 men and was requested
to do so; the Cape Coast Volunteers were called out, and a
proclamation prohibiting the sale of arms and ammunition
to the enemy was issued. The Accras were not called up, but
the eastern tribes were loyal with the exception of the
Akwamus.

The Ashantis had caught the government in its habitual
state of unpreparedness. There were but 160 officers and
men in the whole country, and even these were broken up
into small detachments and scattered along the coast as
garrisons for the various forts, while the reserve store of
arms available for distribution among the protected tribes
amounted to only 190 Enfield rifles and 381 flint muskets.
Even after the administrator had received convincing information that the Ashantis were marching toward the coast,
Governor Hennessy, to whom everything was referred, refused to believe that the conciliatory policy that he had
adopted could possibly have failed.

The Assins collected at Yankumasi Assin and made a
gallant attempt to check the enemy's advance; but it was
obvious that they could never hope to do so unaided, and
though every effort was made to stir up some fighting spirit
in the other tribes and cause a general advance to their
support, the allies proved so dilatory in their preparations
and acted with such a complete absence of cooperation, that

---

* Commander of British forces.—Editor's Note.

the Assins were left to face the enemy alone, with the natural result that, when the Ashantis attacked them on February 9, they were defeated and driven back and the enemy then camped in Yankumasi. Thus the old story of the earlier invasions was once more repeated and the enemy were allowed to engage and defeat the several tribes one after the other, driving before them the fugitives from the first battles to demoralize those whom they next had to encounter. Nothing, indeed, showed the impracticability of the scheme devised by the promoters of the Fanti Confederation more than this total absence of concerted action or agreement among the different tribes; for the Confederation at best could only have existed by the suppression of all intertribal quarrels and disputes and the union of the whole Fanti race for one common purpose. It was this policy that was the real secret of the power of Ashanti. The Fantis, however, even in the face of this great, common danger, were not only slow to combine, but were even quarrelling among themselves. Never a fighting race, but willing enough to do their best when necessary and then often fighting well, they never gave themselves a fair chance to repeat their victory at Dodowa, but by their own inaction and disunion constantly placed themselves in positions from which retreat was their only course and thus largely contributed to the growth of a belief, that is not altogether justified, that they are quite useless as soldiers.

This defeat brought the Ashantis to within thirty miles of Cape Coast and was the principal cause of a most disgraceful outrage in that town. A proclamation had been issued on February 17 setting forth that the government would not guarantee the safety of any Ashantis living within the protectorate, and warning them that if they remained they would do so at their own risk. It seems, however, that an exception was made in the case of those who had been living on the coast for any length of time,[1] provided, of course, that they behaved themselves.

---

1. *Vide* letter from Civil Commandant, Elmina, dated March 2, 1873, *Ashantee Invasion,* 1873, part ii, p. 336.

The allies had now formed a new and very extensive camp at Dunkwa, where about 25,000 men had been collected by the end of the month, and on March 20 a reinforcement of an officer and 100 men of the West India Regiment had arrived from Sierra Leone. The new camp had a frontage nearly seven miles in length, and the bush had been so well cleared that the enemy would be forced to cross a large stretch of open ground if they attacked it. Nothing, however, would induce the allies to make an immediate attack on the Ashantis: they preferred to think about it, and kept putting it off for two or three days at a time, thus enabling the enemy to receive a steady stream of reinforcements and several convoys of ammunition from Kumasi.

The allies hesitated so long, that in the end it was the Ashantis who attacked them at about seven o'clock on the morning of April 8; but they then fought extremely well, and in a battle lasting five hours fully held their own all along the line. The firing was very heavy, and enormous quantities of ammunition were used. The Fantis always fire recklessly, and frequently overload their guns, seventy of which burst in this action alone, so that it is difficult to keep them supplied with powder and lead. No prisoners were taken on either side, and the wounded were often most barbarously mutilated. The Hausas lost 17 men killed and wounded, and the allied tribesmen, whose strength was estimated at over 56,000, had 221 men killed and 643 wounded. What the losses of the Ashantis were is unknown, but they must have been considerable. The Ashantis, however, had been greatly astonished at the amount of determined resistance that had been offered, and it was not until the fourteenth that they once more advanced and attacked along the whole length of the line. This battle lasted throughout the whole day, from nine o'clock in the morning till seven at night, but when darkness at last brought it to a close neither side could claim a victory. Most of the fighting took place in a thickly wooded valley to the north of Dunkwa, near Tetsi. Into this the enemy poured in great numbers; but the allies advanced boldly, although they were at a distinct disadvantage in having to cross the open ground that they had cleared from their camp nearly to this valley. A rocket battery did good service in the center of the line, and the losses on both sides must have been fairly heavy, although no figures are given.

The Ashantis were so disheartened after fighting these two hard battles and gaining nothing, that they destroyed a great deal of their baggage and began a retreat. Had the allies then fallen on their rear with but half the determined spirit that they had shown on the previous day, they must have inflicted a most crushing defeat, and the war would practically have been at an end. They knew nothing of this movement at the time, however, and having themselves had quite as much fighting as they cared for, also began to retire. News of this movement soon brought back the Ashantis, and the retreat became a rout as the allies neared Cape Coast.

Malinke Chief Samori Toure Delayed French Occupation in French West Africa, 1882–1898

R. GRIFFETH *

Samori's long career is usually divided into three phases. The first phase includes his years as a growing boy and young man (1830–1852) which he spent learning to become a trader. During the latter years of this part of his life he traveled extensively in the far western part of the Sudan.

Somewhere around the year 1852, a new phase began. His mother, Masorona, has been taken as a captive by Sori Birama, the chief of Bissandugu. In order to gain her release Samori voluntarily became a soldier in the army of this king. His life was thus transformed. From the peaceful life of a trader he was introduced to that most tempering experience for a young man, the rigorous training of the warrior. And it was also at this time that his obvious leadership talents came to the surface. Samori quickly rose to an important position in Sori Birama's army.

This second phase of Samori's career (1852–1882) was taken up with the great tasks of construction. First he gathered a large following of ambitious young men and allies. With these followers he set out both by force and by diplomacy to build up from among the many small and independent communities of the Upper Niger region a

* From R. Griffeth, "Samori Toure," *Tarikh*, 1967, No. 4.

strong and unified state. These years witnessed the fulfil-
ment of Samori's manhood. He created an empire of which
he was the unquestioned leader.

While this monumental task of state-building could easily
stand as an achievement worthy of our undivided study,
it is the last phase of his career, from 1882 to 1898, which
has attracted by far the greatest attention. For during this
decade and a half Samori was locked in a desperate struggle
with French military forces who were slowly transforming
the Western Sudan into a French colony. In this long and
drawn-out conflict Samori's one great purpose was to save
from destruction the empire into which he had poured the
enormous energies of his life.

Sanankoro became the main town of this new army. From
there it began to push out in all directions. Throughout the
late 1860's and 1870's the ever-growing Samorian armies
campaigned regularly, so that by 1879 the limits of the area
under his rule extended from Sierra Leone in the west to
Ivory Coast in the east, and from a point near Bamako in
the north to the Liberian frontiers in the south. When in
1879, Samori finally placed the major trading center of
Kankan under his direct rule, he held sway over all the
major groups of Malinke peoples.

As more and more territory and ever-growing numbers of
people were brought within the jurisdiction of Samorian
rule, new forms of organization were developed in order
to make the state run smoothly. Previous states, like old
Mali, had not paid much attention to everyday affairs on
the local level except in the central territory of the capital
and in important trade centers. The technique used to control local rulers was to require them to pay an annual tax,
or "tribute," to the king's treasury. But in the Samorian
state (which was smaller and thus more easily governed)
even local matters came under the direct supervision of
Samori and his appointed officials. It was in this sense, then,
that the Samorian state represented something quite new
for the Malinke peoples.

The army was the most important element of Samori's

authority. This fact remained unchanged throughout the life of the state. While Samori had the undoubted prestige which surrounded his religious title of almami, his power finally rested upon his command of an intensely loyal army.

The most striking feature of the Samorian army was that its ranks were filled mostly with captives—young boys who had been trained to serve as professional soldiers. Unlike the Fulani troops in Sokoto and Macina, these soldiers were infantrymen who carried rifles. They were called *sofa*, and very few among them owned horses. Even though the *sofa* were recruited by the provincial commanders, they owed their first loyalty to Samori himself, for the commanders were frequently changed and moved about from province to province. During times when major campaigns were undertaken, this standing army of professional *sofa* could be greatly expanded by calling upon a conscripted reserve (one man in ten in every village was required to answer a general call for more soldiers), a volunteer "militia" consisting of those who owned horses and who could become the cavalry force in a large army corps, and other troops sent by chiefs who were outside the central state but under Samori's protection. The size of the army thus depended upon the military needs of the moment; and in periods of intense crisis as many as ten to twelve thousand fully equipped soldiers might be available for duty.

This growing and prosperous new state met its first challenge from the French in 1882. The year before, a Samorian army had laid siege to the village of Keniera (near the modern city of Siguiri in Guinea). Since the French were, at that time, attempting to secure their lines of communication by establishing a series of fortified posts of which Siguiri was one, they saw the presence of Samori so near their line as a definite threat. The commander of the French forces, Lt. Col. Borgnis-Desbordes, sent an emissary to Samori asking that the siege of Keniera be withdrawn. The request was refused by Samori, and when the emissary returned to his chief and reported the outcome of his talk,

Borgnis-Desbordes decided to employ a show of force. He
sent out a column of some two hundred infantrymen, accompanied by a section of artillery, in hopes that Samori
might thus be forced to withdraw from Keniera. The first
shot was fired when this column made contact with an
advance cavalry reconnaissance element from Samori's
army. This mounted force was successfully repulsed by
the French, but Borgnis-Desbordes' orders prevented him
from following up this minor victory by pursuing Samori's
main army.

A second encounter took place in 1883, after one of
Samori's commanders had led a raid in which the telegraph
line between the forts at Kita and Bamako was cut. At the
same time a number of captives were taken from villages in
areas which the French declared were under their protection. The engagement took place a short distance from
Bamako where, at first, Samori's troops seemed to gain the
upper hand. Borgnis-Desbordes was forced to order his
troops back into the fortifications of the city. In a series of
subsequent actions the French succeeded in demonstrating
the superiority of their firearms as against those possessed
by the *sofa* armies, and Samori reluctantly faced the pros-
pect of having to alter his military tactics from those of
direct confrontation with the main body of French troops
to the more limited ones of planned raids by small numbers
of highly mobile soldiers. This became the pattern of warfare for the future. Samori was able to preserve a partial
advantage by the means of never overcommitting his forces.

The French were now coming to see that their task was
not to be a simple one. Around the end of 1885, a large con-
centration of troops was built up at Niagassola. Their main
goal was to contain Samori, since they saw that defeating
him outright was not possible with the forces at hand, and
to limit his sphere of operations to the area south of the
Tinkisso branch of the Niger. At the same time Samori saw
that he was faced with a similar problem, for the French
with their superior weapons could not be decisively beaten.
So the almami sent messengers to the French, indicating

that he would like to open negotiations for a treaty of peace and a delimitation of territories.

Emissaries from both sides finally met at a place called Kenieba-Koura where a treaty bearing that name was signed. By its provisions Samori was granted sovereignty over the lands south of the Niger where it joined the Tinkisso. North of that boundary was to be the sphere under French protection. Samori clearly rejected the French suggestion of any form of protectorate over his state, a matter which troubled the French sufficiently to cause them to seek a re-negotiation of the treaty two years later.

But while the treaty itself gave Samori a period of respite from French interference, it also checked the drive to expand his army. He was now forced to redirect his efforts, and so turned eastward into areas which seemed by the treaty to fall within his guaranteed sphere. His first main object was to bring the important town of Sikasso under his control. In this ambition Samori probably made a grave strategic error, for Sikasso, under its own aggressive leader, Tieba, was also well into a period of expansion itself. Sikasso was a well-fortified place and thus Samori had to employ a lengthy siege-and-starve operation in the attempt to overpower it. For sixteen months the pressure was kept up, but to no avail. Tieba held out, partly owing to assistance given him by the French. This instance of French aid to a ruler whose country Samori declared to be within his sphere of influence so angered him that he declared the treaties broken.

Once again bands of the *sofa* began to raid north of the boundary line and the French seized the opportunity to retaliate. The breathing period had mainly benefited the French for they were able to pursue other adversaries free from any worry created by Samori. The almami on the other hand had suffered an important reverse, since the central object of his attention during the same period had resulted in no gain. Now that the battle was once again joined a last attempt at negotiations was made. The new French commander, Archinard, sent representatives to

Samori in 1889. One last treaty, called the Convention of
Niako, was dutifully and solemnly signed by both parties.
But the issue was already clear: the French would tolerate
no independent state anywhere within the Western Sudan,
so that whatever treaties were signed were temporary by
their very nature. It was equally clear to Samori that the
means of an independent existence were being badly undermined by the French presence. By 1891, therefore, an un-
relenting and implacable hostility came to characterize the
attitudes of these two adversaries.

By 1893 Samori had been forced to retreat from the
major centers of his empire and had, as a consequence, re-
built his capital at Dabakala (in the northeastern Ivory
Coast). Elements of the *sofa* now scattered to the east where
they raided numerous communities. Frequently there were
encounters with the French, but none of these amounted
to a large-scale battle. Back in the Upper Niger valleys the
French continued to push on in spite of the terrible difficulties created by Samori's land-ravaging retreat. At the
same time the French were planning a massive campaign
which was designed to encircle Samori completely, cutting
off any possible escape route. Columns were to advance
from bases in the Sudan and others were to be dispatched
from the Coast to join them, in an all out effort to run
their adversary to ground.

This grand operation got under way in 1894. From all
areas of West Africa under French occupation detachments
were sent to assist. Numerous columns from the French
Niger forts converged on the newly created posts of the
upper river valleys. Others came by way of Sikasso in the
northeast. Yet a third column was sent up from Grand
Bassam under the command of Colonel Monteil, who had
recently brought a large contingent of seasoned forces from
Equatorial Africa to that place.

As the isolation increased, military needs became more
and more acute. In order to acquire goods for trade, Samori
redirected his forces northward. In April of 1895 he
launched a vigorous attack against Kong. In spite of his

former profession of friendship to the town's rulers, his *sofa* pillaged the territory, burnt the city, made captives of its able-bodied men, and took the rest to be sold as slaves or to be executed. It is to this deed, particularly, that those critics of Samori who have regarded him as a cruel fanatic have pointed. In this instance, his critics appear to have the better of the argument. But one must not forget the extreme pressure which was being applied to Samori from all sides at this time. Survival had become by now a matter lived out day by day.

The last three years of Samori's history as an independent ruler form a record of desperate resistance and overwhelming frustration. French attacks upon his *sofa* were met by counterattacks, though there were also occasional attempts to reopen peace negotiations. When three emissaries were sent forth to petition the French, the French interpreted their arrival to mean that at long last Samori was willing to accept a protectorate. The ambassadors, on the other hand, insisted that their instructions were only to sue for peace and the establishment of a new set of boundaries. The almami was still to be guaranteed an area over which he alone would exercise sovereignty. But the French would have no less than their protectorate. Disheartened, the emissaries were forced to convey this bitter news to their leader.

Hehe Chief Mkwawa Foiled German Seizure of East Africa, 1891–1898

ALISON REDMAYNE *

The Hehe won fame by defeating a German expedition at Lugalo on August 17, 1891, and maintaining their resistance for seven years, until Chief Mkwawa[1] shot himself. This struggle, which was extremely costly to both sides, so impressed the Germans that they acquired a respect for the military prowess and determination of the Hehe. The ambush of the German forces at Lugalo, the destruction of the Hehe fort at Kalenga on October 30, 1894, and Mkwawa's death on July 19, 1898, were key events in the German colonization in East Africa. Romantic descriptions of "these coarse, reserved mountain people . . . a true warrior tribe who live only for war" [2] could apparently find ready readers in Germany, so there is a large amount of published Ger-

---

* From Alison Redmayne, "Mkwawa and the Hehe Wars," *Journal of African History*, No. 3 (1968).

1. This name is an abbreviation of Mkwavinyika, and the way it is pronounced is more accurately represented Mkwava. In the early literature there are many different spellings of this name, including Kwawa, Kuawa, Qwawa, Mkwaba, Mkuanika, Mukwawi Nyika, Kwawinjika and Mkuu wa Nyika. Mkwawa is now the accepted spelling of the name used by his descendants and is the commonest version, and so I have accepted it to avoid confusion.

2. E. Liebert, *Neunzig Tage im Zelt* (Berlin, 1898), p. 24. My translation.

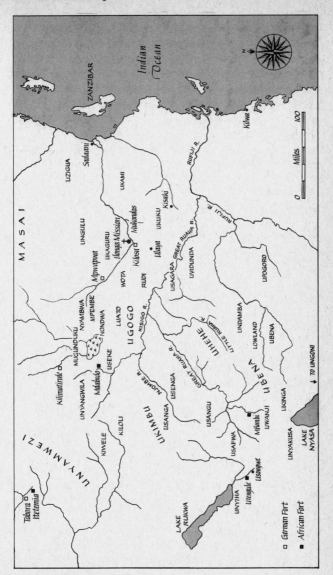

man literature about the campaigns and about the Hehe themselves.

Uhehe lies between the Great Ruaha and Kilombero rivers, in the Usungwa mountains and the plateaux which lie in the northern part of the area known as the Southern Highlands. It includes areas of rain forest, high rolling grasslands, a central plateau of *Brachystegia* woodland and, below the escarpment in the northeast, north, and west beside the Great Ruaha river and its tributaries, dry plains covered with thorn scrub. In the 1957 census, the Hehe numbered just over a quarter of a million, and were the eighth largest tribe in Tanganyika.[3] They speak a Bantu language and their physical appearance does not distinguish them from the neighboring peoples. Their political unity, like the name Hehe, is of relatively recent origin, and their history is obscure until appreciably later than is the case with other Tanganyika peoples of their size and importance, such as the Gogo, Nyamwezi, and Chagga.

When the French traveler Victor Giraud stayed at Kalenga in February 1883, Mkwawa was apparently unchallenged ruler of all Uhehe,[4] and under him the Hehe had extraordinary military success during the next decade.

At the time when the Hehe were expanding toward the coast, the Germans were moving farther and farther inland.[5] After the 1886 Anglo-German agreement, which limited the authority of the Sultan of Zanzibar to a strip along the coast ten miles wide and delimited the German sphere of influence in East Africa, the Germans began to assert their authority on the coast with no concern for the feelings of

---

3. *Tanganyika Population Census 1957* (East African Statistical Department, 1958), I, p. 1. The exact number was 251,624. The area which was officially recognized as Uhehe coincided exactly with the then Iringa District, of which the total poulation was 245,965 of whom 191,655 were Hehe.

4. Victor Giraud, *Les Lacs de l'Afrique équatoriale* (Paris, 1890), pp. 129–144.

5. See G. S. P. Freeman-Grenville, "The German Sphere 1884–1898," in Oliver and Mathew, *History of East Africa*, Vol. I, Chap. XII.

the local population, nor for those of the Sultan of Zanzibar. In 1888, an Arab, Abushiri, led a rebellion which was joined by Africans along the coast and some way inland. Abushiri was finally caught and hanged, but news of the rebellion, and of German activities, spread far.[6]

In 1890, Julius Freiherr von Soden was appointed to be the first governor and, in order to administer the vast area marked on the map as German East Africa, the Germans began to build administrative forts, first at Mpwapwa and then at Kilosa on the caravan route. From their settlements at Wota near Mpwapwa and Ulaya near Kilosa, the Hehe continued to raid caravans and also to punish those Africans living near the forts who had submitted to the Germans. This made the Germans fear that the Hehe might even attack the coast.[7]

The two parties were now bound to enter into negotiations with each other or to fight. Each side knew something of the reputation and activities of the other, but neither can have known accurately the other's strength and intentions. The Hehe stood in the way of effective German control of the territory of German East Africa, and the Germans were becoming an obstacle to further expansion and raiding by the Hehe. The German governor wished to avoid warfare, because his limited financial resources and personnel were inadequate for the tasks of pacification and administration, and because violence would disrupt the expansion of legitimate trade, which he believed to be the best hope for colonial development.

When most of the available German troops had gone to Kilimanjaro in the north, Commander Ramsay was sent to Usagara with a small force of 150 men.[8] He camped at

___

6. Schynse stated that Abushiri fled into the interior to summon the aid of the Hehe, *A travers l'Afrique,* 257.

7. Arning, "Die Wahehe" (1896), 53; Nigmann, *Wahehe,* 15; Tom von Prince, *Gegen Araber,* 79.

8. I give here an abbreviated account of the events during the crucial period 1890–1896. The available published sources vary both in matters of fact and in interpretation. I know of no his-

Mukondoa and, with the help of Arabs and Baluchi, began
to negotiate with Mfaluhenga, the Hehe subordinate ruler
who was in charge of the settlement at Ulaya. After agree-
ing with the Hehe that they should go to the coast to negotiate with the governor, Ramsay returned to the coast in a
hurry because he feared the rains were about to break.
Some days later, a group of Hehe arrived to negotiate with
the governor. It is not clear whether the latter agreed to
the request they had made earlier to Ramsay, that they
might buy arms and ammunition, but when the Hehe departed the Germans assumed that they had left with peaceful intentions.

In June 1891, the Germans received reports that the
Mafiti (Ngoni) were raiding in the hinterland of Kilwa and
that a Hehe chief, Taramakengwe,[9] was taking prisoners.
The Germans therefore organized an expedition under

torian who has attempted to work out in detail the chronology of
the campaign and the reasons for the Germans conducting it as
they did. Much more knowledge could be gained from unpublished
sources in the National Archives of Tanzania in Dar es Salaam
and from the German Archives in Potsdam, East Germany. I am
extremely grateful to Fr. E. Durkin of the Holy Ghost Mission,
Bromley, Kent, for sending me copies of extracts of the *Bulletin
général des Pères du Saint Esprit* from 1890 to 1895. This is particularly valuable, because it is the only contemporary non-German
source I have obtained. My account of the defeat of the Zelewski
expedition, the negotiations between the Hehe and the Germans,
the Hehe attack on Mukondoa and the events leading up to the von
Schele expedition is drawn from these extracts and also from the
German reports published in *D.K.B.* (1891), 409–411, 435–438,
(1892), 609–611, and (1893), 58–60. These are the best contemporary accounts I have found and are consistent with much
that was told me by Ngwadanalamu mwaChula of Image who
fought at Lugalo. Some information is also contained in Rochus
Schmidt, *Geschichte des Araber-Aufstandes in Ost-Afrika* (Frank-
furt a. Oder, 1892), 304–307, 309–311; Arning, "Die Wahehe"
(1896), 53–57; Nigmann, *Wahehe*, 16–19; Dempwolff, "Beiträge,"
120–121; Paul Reichard, *Deutsch-Ostafrika: Das Land und seine
Bewohner* (Leipzig, 1892), 491–502; Tom von Prince, *Gegen
Araber*, many references, especially 288–314; C. Velten, "Suaheli-
Gedichte," *M.S.O.S.* xx, pt. iii (1917), 80–182.

9. I have not been able to find out anything else about him.

Commander Zelewski, who in the Abushiri rebellion had earned himself the Swahili nickname Nyundo, meaning "the hammer." He set out, intending to deal with the Mafiti first and then to go to Mpwapwa by way of Mukondoa, in Usagara, but he did not find the Mafiti, and, having had to alter his original plan because of lack of food on the route, he entered Usagara. The Hehe subordinate rulers of the area fled and, according to Lieutenant Tettenborn's report to the governor, and to the account of the French Holy Ghost missionaries at Ilonga (which in early reports was called Lalonga), the German forces burnt the huts which the Hehe had abandoned.

The expedition then moved toward Uhehe. When they had climbed the escarpment they saw some Hehe at Image. A few were armed with rifles, but most had only shields and spears, so the Germans, not realizing the real strength of their enemy, fired on them and they disappeared. The German forces then destroyed a number of huts in this densely populated area and moved on toward Kalenga, which they knew from the Arabs was a large fortified settlement on the Little Ruaha river. On the night of August 16, they camped at Ilula, and early next morning they set out, with Commander Zelewski near the front, riding on a donkey. Shortly before 7:00 A.M. they halted in order to restore the cohesion of the marching column. They had begun moving toward the side of a hill, where large pieces of rock were scattered about amid dense bush, when a shot sounded and, from the bush only about thirty paces away, a great number of Hehe rushed out to attack the invaders, who had no idea of their presence.[10]

───────

10. The details of this command to attack are interesting. Tettenborn, who was in the rearguard, merely wrote "ein Signalchuß ertönte," but implies that the shot was fired by a Hehe, *D.K.B.* (1891), 435. In an essay written for Dempwolff in 1907, Norbert Chelula wrote "vahehe vakatova huti yimwi, mbevali vakavuka luvilo, vakahomanga na migoha" (the Hehe shot one gun, they all moved quickly and fought with spears): "Beiträge," 121. Reichard's account, written in Germany in November 1891, on the whole fol-

This first Hehe attack decided the battle, but the German rearguard under Tettenborn assembled on a hill where they were able to defend themselves. They remained there throughout the day and night and the following day in order to give other survivors a chance to join them. Having set fire to the dry grass, so that those wounded unable to flee were burnt to death, the Hehe withdrew to Image. Tettenborn decided that it was safest for his forces to retreat by a different route, so he set out at night and went through the hills to the southeast of Ilula, probably passing Ikula and Mdene on the way to Mukondoa. He reported the German losses as follows: ten Europeans (of whom one was Commander Zelewski, three others were officers, and six were N.C.O.'s), about 200 men, as many guns, three cannons, 23 donkeys, 96 porters and most of the baggage. He estimated that the Hehe numbered not less than 3,000, of whom perhaps 700 were killed. These estimates about the Hehe forces may be unreliable, because Tettenborn also stated incorrectly that the chief Kuawa and the Hehe leader Marawatu were killed.[11] However, the losses were sufficient to make

---

lows Tettenborn's report closely, but at this point he adds "als ein Schuß ertönte, worauf die Wahähä unter dem Kriegsschrei, in großer Überzahl . . . auf die Karawane eindrang," *Deutsch-Ostafrika*, 495. This may account for two versions of the story current among the Hehe: the one that they had been instructed to attack when their leader imitated the cry of a bird, a real bird cried and so they attacked sooner than intended; the other that they had been instructed to attack when a gun was fired, by chance Zelewski shot at a bird as he was riding along and so caused them to attack. These stories, which are not necessarily incompatible with German accounts, are used to explain why the ambush was only partly successful in that they failed to destroy the German rearguard. Tettenborn attributed his escape to the Hehe lack of leadership, *D.K.B.* (1891), 437.

11. These numbers are taken from Tettenborn's report, *D.K.B.* (1891), 437, which Reichard quoted with slight inaccuracy, *Deutsch-Ostafrika*, 498. Marawatu must be a Swahili rendering of Malavanu, who had been the subordinate ruler of Image. He died a few years before the battle of Lugalo. Nigmann stated correctly that Ngosingosi, who had been an important subordinate ruler in the Kalenga fort, was killed, *Wahehe*, 16–17.

a deep impression on Mkwawa, who forbade any mourning for the Hehe dead for fear of depressing the survivors.[12]

Soon after the news of this defeat reached the coast, a small German expedition of about 150 men was sent to Usagara to reassure the inhabitants, who feared that the Hehe might attack them. The governor approached Monseigneur de Courmont of the Holy Ghost mission to assist him in negotiating with the Hehe. These missionaries had stations at Ilonga and near Morogoro, and were themselves concerned that there should be peace in the area in which they worked. One of their members, Father Toussaint, traveled into Uhehe many times in order to negotiate with the chiefs, but only managed to return with a depleted Hehe embassy to Ilonga. While these French missionaries were making contact with the Hehe and assuring them that the Germans only wanted to make peace, the Germans themselves were establishing garrisons at Kilosa and Kisaki, presumably intending to protect the inhabitants of these regions and to show the Hehe that, although once defeated, their opponents were not negotiating from a weak position. The Hehe did not make peace, and on October 6, 1892, they attacked and virtually annihilated a large commercial caravan at Mukondoa. The French priests had anticipated the attack and taken the precaution of evacuating the inhabitants of Ilonga mission. The Germans then, because these Hehe attacks on Usagara continued, reinforced their garrison at Kilosa.

When the Germans failed to make peace with the Hehe, they were unable to use force and send a larger expedition against them immediately, partly because of the demoralizing effect of their defeat in 1891 and partly because they had also to deal with other chiefs who resisted their au-

---

12. Nigmann, *Wahehe*, 17. I have a Kihehe text written by Bonifas, son of Mkwawa, in 1933 for Gordon Brown. It describes how Mkwawa forbade mourning until two years later and then he ordered people to brew beer and slaughter cattle for a feast. Most Hehe who know anything about the battle of Lugalo comment that Mkwawa forbade mourning afterwards.

thority. The most famous of these was Isike at Itetemia in Unyamwezi, who, presumably thinking defeat and capture inevitable, attempted to blow himself up and was then killed by the Germans.[13] At the same time the Hehe were threatening the people who had submitted to the Germans, and, in 1893, with the encouragement of the relations of his late father-in-law, Isike, Mkwawa undertook an expedition to Kiwele against the chieftainess Mugalula, who was ruling the territory of her late father Nyungu-ya-nawe, who had been an enemy of Mkwawa.[14]

The inhabitants of Usagara were still fearing Hehe raids in the dry season of 1894 when the new governor, Freiherr von Schele, set out from the coast with a large expedition. There are many summaries of this campaign, of which the best is that of Tom von Prince, who led the storming of the Hehe fort.[15] The Germans hoped that the destruction of the fort would be enough to make Mkwawa come to terms. Once more they attempted to negotiate with him through intermediaries in Usagara, but the Hehe continued to attack the neighboring peoples.[16] In 1896, because there appeared to be no other method of forcing the Hehe to acknowledge German authority and live in peace, the Germans returned

---

13. A first-hand account of this expedition is given by Tom von Prince in *Gegen Araber*, 194–213.

14. Nigmann incorrectly stated that it was the country of Sultaness Mtsavira, *Wahehe*, 18. She had died before 1893. See also Fritz Spellig, "Die Wanjamwezi, ein Beitrag zur Völkerkunde Ostafrikas," *Z. f. E.* (1927), Heft 3/6, vol. LIX, 204. Spellig thought that Mugalula was a man, but Aylward Shorter's Kimbu informants and my Hehe ones all stated that Mugalula was a woman.

15. Tom von Prince, *Gegen Araber*, 298–303. See also "Einnahme der Hauptstadt Uhehe," *D.K.B.* (1894), 621, and "Über den bisherigen Verlauf des Feldzuges gegen die Wahehe," *D.K.B.* (1895), 39–44.

16. Nigmann, *Wahehe*, 18–19. Arning claimed that he raided Lupembe and Chief Mbeyela, "Die Wahehe" (1897), 56. Alfons Adams stated that it was Chief Kivanga's complaints about Mkwawa's raids which brought the Germans back in 1896, *Im Dienste des Kreuzes* (Augsburg, 1899), 48.

with substantial forces and built a garrison town at Iringa
about seven miles away from the fort.[17]

Only a few weeks after von Prince's arrival in Iringa,
Mkwawa gave his consent to, or possibly even ordered, the
surrender of four of his close agnates, Sadangamenda, Mu-
gungihaka, Papande and, most important of all, his young-
est full brother, Mpangile.[18] This gave the Germans hope of
an early settlement, and they attempted to rule the Hehe
through Mpangile. On Christmas Eve 1896, at his installa-
tion as Sultan of Uhehe, the Germans organized ceremonies
which included a shooting match, a procession through
the garrison town and donkey racing. To the great grief of
Magdalene von Prince and the Benedictine priest Alfons
Adams, Tom von Prince believed that Mpangile was responsible for the continued attacks on the German patrols,
tried him, and on February 21, 1897, had him executed
with the other three relations who had surrendered with
him earlier. The Germans did not appoint another Sultan
of Uhehe, but intensified their campaign against Mkwawa,
who was probably responsible for the attacks which had
been blamed on Mpangile.[19]

Over the next eighteen months the resistance of the Hehe
gradually weakened. Worn out by hunger, disease, and
continual warfare, individuals and small groups surrendered

17. In the early sources the site of the Hehe fort is usually called
Alt Iringa, or Ilinga, i.e., Old Iringa, and the German garrison and
the present town Neu Iringa, i.e., New Iringa. Now Iringa is always used to refer to the town and Kalenga to the place of the
Hehe fort. When Hehe use Ilinga to refer to Kalenga they are usually speaking about the fort before it had been destroyed.

18. Mpangile's brief reign is well documented. As well as the
official reports there are accounts by two of his admirers: M. von
Prince, *Eine Deutsche Frau,* ch. III, "Mpangires Sultanat," 63–77,
and Alfons Adams, *Im Dienste,* ch. v, "Sultan Mpangire," 53–62.

19. M. von Prince, *Eine Deutsche Frau,* 75. Adams stated that
just before his execution Mpangile complained that he was a vic-
tim of his enemies' tricks, *Im Dienste,* 59. Many Hehe tell stories
which explain how Mkwawa tricked the Germans into believing
that Mpangile was disloyal to them.

and others who did not do so were killed. By the dry season
of 1898, war and famine were obviously pressing very hard
upon the Hehe, who still held out against the Germans. In
July, the Germans received news that Mkwawa was in the
Pawaga area on the Ruaha plains. A patrol was sent in
pursuit and, after tracking him for four days, on July 19
they came upon his corpse and those of two of his companions only a few hours after his death. He had been
spitting blood and had shot himself in order to avoid capture.[20] This marked the end of all Hehe resistance to the
Germans. Even the toughest German officers had suffered
from nightmares during the campaign,[21] and the hungry,
war-weary Hehe were also relieved, even though some of
them mourned.[22]

---

20. I have discovered two published German versions of Merkl's
account of tracking Mkwawa and finding his corpse; "Bericht über
den Tod des Sultans Qwawa," *D.K.B.* (1898), 645–646, a report
written by Feldwebel Merkl at Iringa dated 22. vii. 1898, of which
an abbreviated English paraphrase is given in Gerald F. Sayers,
The Handbook of Tanganyika (London, 1930), 70–71; another
version of Merkl's report is given in Magdalene's diary for 21. vii.
98, *Eine Deutsche Frau,* 180–181, an English translation of which
is given in Culwick, *Ubena,* 420–421.

21. M. von Prince, *Eine Deutsche Frau,* 93.

22. Ibid., 182–183. In 1965–1966 I recorded mourning songs for
Mkwawa which probably closely resemble those sung in the period
immediately after his death.

Ethiopian Emperor Menelik II
Repulsed Italian Invasion, 1895

RICHARD PANKHURST *

Menelik, who reigned as King of Shoa from 1865 to 1889 and as Emperor of Ethiopia from 1889 to 1913, was perhaps the greatest of Ethiopia's rulers. His reign was of considerable importance in that it witnessed the reunification and modernization of his country, as well as a great increase in its position in world affairs.

Ethiopia, though a powerful state in ancient and medieval times, had in the middle of the eighteenth century fallen on evil days. The powers of the monarchs had been usurped by the feudal lords and centralized government had been replaced by the autonomy of the various provinces whose rulers warred among themselves.

The reorganization and resurrection of the ancient state had first been attempted in the middle of the nineteenth century by the Emperor Theodore (1855–1868) and had later been partially accomplished by his successor the Emperor Yohannes IV (1872–1889). It was, however, left to Menelik to bring this work to fruition, as well as to withstand the pressure of the European powers in the scramble for Africa, and to lay the foundations of a modern state.

Menelik's personality, his innate intelligence and ability, his grasp of world affairs and his interest in modernization,

---

* From Richard Pankhurst, "Emperor Menelik II of Ethiopia," *Tarikh,* 1965, No. 1.

impressed all observers. "During the many interviews I had
with him," recalls the British diplomat Rennell Rodd, "I
formed a high opinion both of his intelligence and his character . . . His energy was astonishing. By rising before
dawn and beginning his day with prayers in chapel at 6:00
A.M. he made time to attend personally to every detail of
the administration in a country constituted of many het-
erogeneous elements. Accessible to all his subjects from the
highest to the lowest, he had succeeded in winning universal
regard and affection."

Menelik was above all a modernizing ruler and, as such,
greatly interested in machinery of all kinds. The foreign
travelers of the time provide many anecdotes, often hu-
morous, to that effect. Thus the missionary Martial de Sal-
viac reports that one of his colleagues once brought Menelik a sewing-machine which had been taken to pieces for
packing. After several attempts at putting it together the
priest confessed his inability to do so. Menelik, however,
spent the whole night with the machine, carefully examined
each of the pieces, tried them together and by the next day
had the whole thing working perfectly. Other travelers describe Menelik carefully examining such varied articles as
an oil traction engine, a circular saw, and a mechanical
stone cutter about which he became "so excited," Hohler
says, that it was "impossible to do business" on other matters. On the arrival of the first motor car the Emperor insisted on being driven in it.

Menelik for his part devoted much of his attention to the
import of arms and was willing to pay very high prices for
them. The French poet Rimbaud, who engaged in the
trade, reports that old rifles could be purchased in Europe
for seven or eight francs each and resold in Ethiopia for
forty francs. An extensive trade in fire-arms soon developed. Menelik is estimated to have obtained no less than
25,000 rifles between 1882, when the arms trade for practical purposes started, and 1887 when he occupied Harar,
thereby rendering easier his contact with the coast. In January of the following year, the Italian Prime Minister, Fran-

cesco Crispi, sent Menelik a gift of 1,000 Remington rifles with the message: "May these increase your power and carry destruction among your enemies and those of my country." Further sales and gifts followed with the result that Menelik soon had by far the best equipped army of any independent African state.

On the death of the Emperor Yohannes in March 1889, Menelik succeeded him as Emperor and was crowned on November 3. The first years of his reign were clouded by difficulties with the Italians who had seized the Red Sea port of Massawa in February 1885, and began to advance on to the Eritrean plateau not long after the death of his predecessor. This was the period of the Scramble for Africa, which had become particularly fierce in 1885. To avoid disputes among themselves the European Powers had devised the General Act of Berlin which was signed on February 26 that year. Article XXXIV stated that "any power which henceforth takes possession of a tract of land on the coast of the African Continent outside of its present possessions, or which, being hitherto without such possessions, shall acquire them, as well as the Power which assumes a Protectorate there, shall accompany the respective act with a notification thereof, addressed to the other Signatory Powers of the present Act, in order to enable them, if need be, to make good any claims of their own."

Notwithstanding growing Italian interest in East Africa, Menelik had been on friendly terms with Italy until his accession as Emperor. On May 2, 1889—less than two months after the death of Yohannes—he signed a Treaty of Perpetual Peace and Friendship with Italy. This treaty, which was destined to be of crucial significance in the history of Ethiopian relations with the European powers, contained articles of benefit to both signatory powers. Menelik recognized Italian sovereignty over the Eritrean plateau including Asmara, while the Italian government recognized Menelik as Emperor of Ethiopia and agreed in Article VI that he was entitled to import arms and munitions through Italian territory. The most important article, however, was

Article XVII, which was soon the basis of a dispute between the two signatories. The quarrel arose from the fact that the treaty had two texts, one in the Ethiopian language, Amharic, and the other in Italian, the sense of which, though identical in other respects, differed materially in the aforesaid article. The Amharic text stated that the Emperor Menelik should have the power to avail himself of the services of the Italian authorities for all communications he might wish to have with other powers. The Italian text, however, made it obligatory for the Emperor to conduct all his transactions with the other powers through the Italian government. Though the Italian formula was soon used by the Italian government to claim that it had established a protectorate over Ethiopia, the time was not yet ripe for an open conflict.

The Emperor's cousin, Ras Makonnen, went to Italy to negotiate further details for the implementation of the Italo-Ethiopian agreement, while General Baldissera, the officer in charge of Italian expansion in Africa, prepared to advance on to the Eritrean plateau in accordance with the Ucciali treaty. On August 2, 1889, Baldissera issued a proclamation for the occupation of Asmara, and on October 1 Ras Makonnen signed an Additional Convention to the Ucciali treaty. By the terms of this new agreement Italy again recognized Menelik as Emperor of Ethiopia, while Ethiopia recognized the sovereignty of Italy over her Red Sea colony on the basis of the frontiers actually in existence at that time.

The Italian government, which was by this time in control of the Eritrean plateau, now felt that it was in a position to proclaim to the world that Italy had obtained a protectorate over Ethiopia. This was done on October 11, over five months after the signing of the Ucciali treaty. The Italian diplomats were to inform the governments to which they were accredited that "in conformity with Article XXXIV of the General Act of Berlin" Italy was serving notice that "under Article XVII of the perpetual treaty between Italy and Ethiopia . . . it is provided that His Majesty the King of Italy consents to avail himself of the Government of His Majesty the King of Ethiopia for the conduct of all matters which he may have with other Powers or Governments."

Britain, which accepted the Italian claim, accordingly entered into three Protocols with Italy, dated March 24 and April 15, 1891, and May 5, 1894, whereby the boundaries between British colonial territory and the alleged protectorate were defined.

The Emperor, however, refused to accept this interpretation of the Ucciali treaty. On September 27, 1890— eleven months after the announcement of the Italian claim —he wrote to King Umberto I of Italy declaring that on reexamining the two texts of Article XVII he had discovered that they did not agree. He added: "When I made the treaty of friendship with Italy, in order that our secrets be guarded and that our understanding should not be spoiled, I said that because of our friendship, our affairs in Europe might be carried on with the aid of the sovereign of Italy, but I have not made any treaty which obliges me to do so. I am not the man to employ the aid of another to carry on my affairs your Majesty understands very well."

Italo-Ethiopian relations had thus reached a deadlock which could only be solved by resort to war. The Italian envoy, Count Antonelli, said to Menelik: "Italy cannot notify the other powers that she was mistaken in Article XVII, because she must maintain her dignity." The Emperor's consort, Empress Taitu, who was present at the interview, exclaimed, "we also have made known to the powers that the said article, as it is written in our language, has another meaning. As you, we also ought to respect our dignity. You wish Ethiopia to be represented before the other powers as your protectorate, but this shall never be."

After a delay of over two years, which he turned to good advantage by importing very large quantities of fire-arms especially from France and Russia, Menelik at length denounced the Treaty of Ucciali on February 12, 1893; a week or so later, on February 27, he informed the Euro-

pean Powers of his decision, declaring: "Ethiopia has need
of no one; she stretches out her hands unto God."

Fighting began in January 1895. The invaders were at
first victorious and succeeded in occupying a large stretch
of territory including Adigrat, Makalle, and Amba Alagi.
Later in the year, however, Menelik moved north with a
large and moderately well-armed force and, himself com-
manding operations, won significant victories over the Italians at Amba Alagi in December and at Makalle at the
turn of the year. The Italians were obliged to fall back on
Adowa.

The first weeks of 1896 witnessed a period of inaction on
either side, neither the Italian nor the Ethiopian army de-
siring to take the initiative. Finally on February 25, Crispi,
exasperated by the delay, telegraphed to General Baratieri:
"This is a military phthisis, not a war . . . a waste of
heroism, without any corresponding success . . . It is clear
to me that there is no fundamental plan in this campaign,
and I should like one to be formulated. We are ready for
any sacrifice in order to save the honor of the army and the
prestige of the Monarchy."

Baratieri's reaction to this telegram was to order his army
to attack; accordingly the battle of Adowa opened in the
early morning of March 1.

The Emperor from the outset was in a relatively good
position. He had the wholehearted support of the local population, whose patriotism was intensified by the fact that
the Italians had been expropriating a sizeable amount of
land in an attempt to settle Italian colonists. The inhabitants
of the area in which the battle was fought were therefore
most willing to show Menelik's troops the best paths and
to bring news of enemy movements. The Italians, on the
other hand, had to face the enmity of the local people and
had no accurate maps to help them. Their army therefore
moved in the greatest possible confusion.

The Ethiopian army moreover was much larger than that
of the Italians. Not counting soldiers with spears he had
well over 100,000 men with modern rifles. The Italians for

their part had somewhat more cannon—56 as against Menelik's 40—but only about 17,000 men, of whom 10,596 were Italian and the rest Eritrean levies.

The result of the battle was the complete defeat and rout of the invaders. Official Italian figures record that 261 European officers, 2,918 noncommissioned officers and men, and about 2,000 *askaris,* or native troops, were killed, and that a further 954 Italian soldiers were permanently missing and had therefore to be presumed killed. Total Italian casualties thus amounted to over 7,560, or nearly 43 percent of the original fighting force of 10,596 Italian and about 7,100 native troops. The Italians also abandoned all their cannon, as well as about 11,000 out of the 14,519 rifles with which they started the battle.

As a result of this battle Menelik gained enormous local and international prestige. On October 26 the Italians agreed to the Peace Treaty of Addis Ababa, whereby they accepted the annulment of the Treaty of Ucciali and recognized the absolute and complete independence of Ethiopia. Menelik, on the other hand, did not consider himself in a position to insist on an Italian withdrawal from Eritrea though he had often expressed a desire of obtaining access to the sea. In the months which followed, the French and British governments sent diplomatic missions to sign treaties of friendship with Menelik; other missions came from the Sudanese Mahdists, the Sultan of the Ottoman Empire, and the Tsar of Russia. Addis Ababa thus emerged as a regular diplomatic center where several important foreign powers had legations.

Ndebele and Shona Risings Against British Occupation, 1896–1897

TERENCE RANGER *

There were so many reasons for the Ndebele and the Shona to take up arms against the whites in 1896 that it is easy to take their uprising too much for granted. We should not forget that it was not easy to organize such a rising. The Ndebele nation had lost its king, the essential focus of all national activity; in any case, even under the leadership of its king it had been swept aside in 1893. The Shona people no longer enjoyed the centralizing influence of the Rozwi empire and had continued their rivalries and feuds even after the arrival of the whites in 1890. So it was remarkable enough that so many of the Ndebele aristocracy and of their old subject peoples and so many of the western, central, and eastern Shona came out against the whites in 1896. It was even more remarkable that their rising was organized, that in each province it was planned to attack whites in all districts at the same time, and that a degree of cooperation was achieved between the various elements on the African side.

We should remember also that the 1896–1897 uprisings were not merely one of a series of similar resistances

* From Terence Ranger, "African Politics in Twentieth-Century Southern Rhodesia," in T. O. Ranger, ed., *Aspects of Central African History* (London, 1968).

throughout central and east Africa. They were in fact by far the biggest challenge to the whites made in the 1890's and in the later period were rivaled only by the Maji-Maji war in Tanganyika. Even in comparison to Maji-Maji the 1896–1897 risings were impressive; they were much more highly organized and they did more damage to the whites. "The settlers lost something like ten percent of their total number, a staggeringly high figure, infinitely greater than the proportion of casualties suffered by white colonists in the Algerian national uprising or the Mau Mau war in Kenya." [1]

As far as central Africa is concerned, these risings were different from resistances elsewhere not only because of their much greater scale and intensity but also because they involved so many of the old agricultural peoples of Southern Rhodesia who had occupied the area before the upheavals of the nineteenth century. In Malawi, for example, the old agricultural peoples of the Malawi confederation did not resist the coming of the whites; resistance rather came from the intruders of the nineteenth century, the Ngoni, Yao, Arabs. But in Southern Rhodesia the majority of the fighters of 1896–1897 were Shona speakers.

Not only did these risings involve both Shona and Ndebele, they also involved almost everybody in the rebel areas. They were not only a matter of the soldier class fighting and the old ruling class leading. The 1896–1897 clash involved children and women and old men; the lower castes and the subject peoples as well as the Ndebele aristocracy. And where traditional leadership was not sufficient or efficient it was sometimes challenged. As Dr. Stokes says, "Here the Zambesian historian encounters a concerted movement of popular resistance unique in scope and intensity . . . what can be described as genuinely national revolutions in which for a time the traditional political leaders were set aside." [2]

1. L. H. Gann, *A History of Southern Rhodesia* (London, 1965).
2. Eric Stokes and R. Brown (eds.), *The Zambesian Past* (Manchester, 1966).

Part of the reason for the formidable character of the movements lies in the Ndebele and Shona past—so different from the history of most of the peoples who took part in the Maji-Maji rising, for example. The Ndebele system was remarkably strong and successful and now it showed that it was resilient in defeat. And we have already seen that the Shona survived the pressures of the nineteenth century much better than is usually thought and that they had a great deal of relevant history to call upon. It is easy to see that during the risings much use was made of an appeal to history. In Matabeleland, the two main leaders of the rising were Umlugulu, the chief priest of the Ndebele nation who had been entrusted by the dying Lobengula with the task of restoring the monarchy, and Lobengula's eldest son, Nyamanda. Many fighters in Matabeleland believed that Lobengula himself was not dead and would return from the north with an army. The military organization of the rising took the form of a revival of the old regimental system. In Mashonaland, there was an attempt at the end of 1896 to revive the authority of the Rozwi Mambo and the best claimant to the position was brought up out of a neutral area in order to lead a force of Rozwi who were gathered together from all over Mashonaland and eastern Matabeleland. This attempt failed with the arrest of the claimant by the whites but the prestige of the Rozwi was important in bringing many Shona people out into rebellion. The Rozwi were still believed to have the special protection of God and to be invulnerable. Military organization in Mashonaland was under the traditional leadership of the paramount chief and his sons.

Even the divisions inside the revolt had historical roots. In Matabeleland, the rebels were divided into two factions. One was grouped around Bulawayo; the other around Inyati. This reflected the two parties which had disputed the succession issue on Mzilikazi's death. One was led mainly by older *indunas;** the other by young men. This reflected the tensions of Lobengula's last years when the two young

---

* Chiefs.—Editor's Note.

men wanted to attack the whites and the older *indunas* supported the king's policy of peace. Among the Shona, some paramount chiefs kept out of the rising because old rivals joined it.

And yet as we have already said the risings were revolutionary. Something more than an appeal to history was needed to make Ndebele aristocrats and subject peoples and the Shona groups who had been raided by the Ndebele combine together; and something more than memories of the nineteenth century were needed to bring the Shona chiefs together on the very large scale that happened in 1896. People came together partly because white pressure compelled them to do so; but they came together also because the emergency threw up a revolutionary leadership appealing to unity and promising victory.

This leadership was given by men claiming religious authority. They were not "new" men. They were officers in one or other of two old Shona religious systems. These systems had roots deep in Shona history. The spirit mediums had been part of the whole Mutapa structure and had given support to the king; the Mwari cult was closely linked with the Rozwi empire. In one way, therefore, the religious leaders were appealing back to a golden past of unity. But there were other elements in their leadership. They claimed to lead not only the Shona but also the Ndebele. The influence of the Mwari cult had spread far and wide among the Ndebele, especially after 1893. Moreover, the main leaders in 1896 added new claims to spiritual authority over and above their place in the old religious systems, claims to possess new revelations, to be able to promise invulnerability to European weapons and to be able to guarantee success. The religious leaders, Mkwati in Matabeleland, Kagubi in Mashonaland, were allies of the *indunas* and the chiefs but they were prepared to challenge the authority of any *induna* or chief who thought the time had come to make a self-interested peace with the whites. Over and above their appeal to the Shona past, these leaders stood for total commitment, for the unity of black men against white men. These leaders were killed and their following broken up; in different ways both the whites and the Ndebele *indunas* regained authority. But it was important that the African peoples of Rhodesia had combined together under such leadership. Later on, other leaders who wanted to unite the African peoples and who wanted to commit them against the white men would be able to look back to the memory of the leaders of the 1896–1897 risings; this was one part of the history of Southern Rhodesia that could be used without creating tribal divisions.

We cannot describe the events of the risings here. There were many heroic episodes long remembered. The outbreak was a great blow to the whites and seriously threatened the continued authority of the British South Africa Company. But there was no real hope of success. The enthusiasm created by the religious leaders which made people prepared to face machine guns brought together the great numbers of the Africans against the small numbers of white settlers. If these had been the only whites concerned in the matter the Africans would have won; supplies were difficult, the settlers were not strong enough to move out of the towns, and life would soon have become impossible for them. But the whites in Rhodesia could call upon the help of the whites in English-speaking South Africa and upon the help of Britain. Reinforcements were rushed up by land and sea and more were prepared when the Ndebele were able to defend their hills and caves even against this larger number. The defeat of the risings cost a lot of money, quite a number of white lives, and large numbers of African lives. But the white thrust into Rhodesia was strong and its supporters were rich. The cost could be met.

As more white troops and supplies poured in and as the rebels were pushed back from the towns and the road systems and forced on to the defensive, the various leaders of the rebellion took stock of the situation. The religious leaders still wished the fight to go on to the end and they managed to carry most of the Shona chiefs and people with them. When the whites offered surrender terms to the Shona chiefs at the end of 1896 they were refused. Fighting went on in Mashonaland throughout most of 1897 and only ended with the arrest of the main religious leaders. In Matabeleland, however, the leaders of the Matopos faction, under Umlugulu, decided that they must treat for peace. They did not persuade everyone of this even in Matabeleland. Some of their younger followers sided with the Mwari priests to demand continued war; and in the north-east, Mkwati and his followers resisted to the last and went on fighting until they were driven out of Matabeleland and into Mashonaland at the end of 1896. But the greater part of the Ndebele aristocracy was now concentrated in the Matopos Hills under Umlugulu and the older *indunas* and they believed that the only way to save the Ndebele nation was to end the war. In this way the unity of the rebels, such as it was, came to an end.

On the white side Rhodes also wanted peace. The Company could not afford more money and more white lives because if the war went on it would either go bankrupt or lose its charter; the British commanders were asking for more and more men and supplies to win the war in 1897. So Rhodes sent messengers into the hills to contact the Ndebele and when contact had been made and he knew that there was a Ndebele peace party he went into the hills himself to meet them. These negotiations were unpopular with the whites because they wanted the Ndebele forced to surrender unconditionally. As it was, Rhodes promised a good many things. He promised that the administration would be reformed, he promised that the Ndebele would be allowed to come out of the hills and settle down on the land they had occupied before 1893, though he did not promise legal title to it. He promised that some of the rebel leaders would be given official posts and paid a salary as recognized *indunas* and that none of the senior *indunas* would be punished. Many of these promises were kept, though before long the Ndebele discovered that whites still owned the land to which they returned. But the terms were a small victory for the Ndebele and did result in some improvement by comparison with what had been going on in 1894 and 1895.

As for the Shona rebels they were hunted down throughout 1897, stronghold by stronghold. They were dynamited out of their caves and chased from one place to another. In the end most of them surrendered unconditionally, especially after the capture of the religious leaders. The Shona rebel chiefs were given no terms and promised nothing. Many of them were put on trial for murder and a number were hanged. Their place was taken by rival claimants who had shown "loyalty" to the Company. In this way the Ndebele *indunas* came out of the rising with a good deal of authority still left, but most Shona chiefs no longer appeared as leaders of their people in the old sense. In 1964, the old white leader Sir Godfrey Huggins, then Lord Malvern, spoke a belated epitaph on the Shona chiefs. The attempt by the Rhodesia Front to claim that the chiefs were the real leaders of the Shona, he said, "was a swindle . . . Many of the Shona chiefs are rather dodderers. Their real powers and influence were destroyed at the time of the rebellion—1896."

One last word is necessary on the rebellions in general, however. They did not win the really important victory which, in the context of the times, was not the evacuation of the whites but the end of Company rule. We can now see that if the British government had been forced to come into Southern Rhodesia in 1897 many things would have been different. But at least the risings showed that Africans could not be taken for granted, that they could hit back. In this way even the defeated Shona did win better treatment; they were still subjected to a system built in the interests of the whites but the open abuses and outrages of the past were brought to an end. And when new measures were planned which affected Africans, like an increase of tax, the British Resident Commissioner asked whether they would provoke another rising. Sometimes as a result of this question plans were dropped.

King of Benin's Ambush of British Officers in Nigeria, 1897

(*Excerpts from PAPERS RELATING TO THE MASSACRE OF BRITISH OFFICIALS NEAR BENIN AND CONSEQUENT PUNITIVE EXPEDITION* (*London, 1898. H.M.S.O.*))

No. 49.

Vice-Consul Gallwey to Foreign Office.—(*Received February* 15.)

Sir,   *Bonny, January* 16, 1897

I HAVE the honor to report, for Lord Salisbury's information, that, on arrival at Eberu in the Ibo country yesterday, I received news of the disaster that had happened in Benin. I proceeded on at once, reaching Bonny the following evening. I had been surveying the country between the New Calabar and Opobo Rivers; hence any delays that have occurred.

All particulars up to date have been given by cablegram. Benin not being a telegraph station, news takes a long time to reach Bonny and Brass. Launch communication has been started between Brass and Benin, but the round journey takes about 12 days or so. In addition to this, the water in the Niger is low.

I proceed today to Benin to learn full particulars from the two survivors, Captain Boisragon and Mr. Locke. I hope to return here about the 26th instant, when I will cable full details.

The following is an epitome of the object and movements of the ill-fated expedition:—

Mr. Phillips' opinion was that every pacific means toward approaching the King of Benin would not be complete until he, as Acting Consul-General, paid a visit to the King. Accordingly, on the 2nd instant, Mr. Phillips started from Sapele, having sent messages on many days beforehand of his intended pacific visit to the King. The officers, etc., accompanying Mr. Phillips were: Major Copland Crawford, D.S.O., Mr. Locke, Mr. Campbell, Captain Boisragon, Mr. Maling, Dr. Elliott, and two European agents, Messrs. Powis and Gordon. Also the Consul-General's chief Accra clerk, the Sapele storekeeper, about a dozen officers' servants, two interpreters, and about 220 carriers (Jakris and Krooboys).

Inclosure 2 in No. 50.

Statement made by Captain Boisragon and District Commissioner Locke, the Survivors of the Benin Expedition, to Assistant District Commissioner Lyons. [*Written January 10, 1897.*]

LOCKE and Boisragon tell me they were just getting to the village, where they were going to stop the night (village the fourth from Gwato); the Acting Consul-General was on in front, Crawford and the others following, when they heard shots fired in front; they tried to get their revolvers out of their boxes, but could not find the boxes, so they hurried up to the front, where Crawford (wounded) ran back, saying it was no good going on to the Acting Consul-General, as he was dead. They carried Crawford back a little way, when he was hit again two or three times. They got hit again and again. Maling was shot in the back, and died of wounds. The doctor (Elliott) hit in the back of the head dead. Powis (trader) rushed to the front; tried to stop the people, and was shot. When they had seen all was up, and they had seen poor Crawford die in his chair, they rushed into the bush and lay quiet. They saw the carriers lying dead. They worked their way, not daring to go near the bush paths, and in five days got near the waterside, where they found one of Dudu's boys, who brought them down, meeting me at Dudu's Creek. The only food they had was plantain, and their drink was the dew off the leaves of trees. They say there is no likelihood of any white man saved.

Mr. Lyons adds: "Locke and Boisragon were very exhausted and full of pellets, so I did not worry them to tell me too much last night. The carriers, out of 250 not 20 have come back, but I have hopes there may be still a few in the bush."

The people in the expedition were:

Phillips
Crawford
Boisragon
Maling
Locke }Europeans.
Campbell
Elliott
Powis
Jordan
Herbert Clarke, Interpreter and Native Political Agent.
Toway, Interpreter.
Baddoo, Chief Clerk, Consul-General's Office.
Baddoo, cook, Consul-General's Office.
Owoo, steward, " "
Officers' servants, 9, natives.
65 Krooboys, carriers.
150 Jakri carriers.

Mr. Lyons adds: "Mr. Flint, of the Royal Niger Company, is very kind, and helping us a lot." I have a similar assurance from District Commissioner Burrows.

(Signed)   R. MOOR, *Consul-General.*
"Theseus," at Sierra Leone, January 29, 1897.

No. 54.

Acting Commissioner Gallwey to Foreign Office.—(*Received February* 22.)

Sir,   *"Widgeon," at Benin, January* 21, 1897.

IN continuation of my dispatch of the 18th instant, I have the honor to report, for the Marquess of Salisbury's information, that I arrived in the Benin River on the 20th instant on board Her Majesty's ship "Widgeon."

2. I regret to state that, after interviewing the two surviving officers of the expedition, Captain Boisragon and Mr. Locke, and gaining all possible information from escaped carriers and messengers, and after holding a meeting of the leading Jakri Chiefs, no hope can be held out that any other officers have escaped.

Messrs. Boisragon and Locke are both wounded, not seriously; but wandering for five days and five nights in the forest seriously exaggerated the injuries received. Dr. d'Arcy Irvine has been most attentive in caring for these two officers.

3. In brief extract, the following is an account of what actually happened, taken from the statements of Messrs. Locke and Boisragon, and of several natives who accompanied the ill-fated expedition:—

The expedition left Sapele on the morning of the 2nd instant. It consisted of Messrs. Phillips, Copland, Crawford, Locke, Boisragon, Maling, Campbell, Elliot and Lyon, also of two European traders—Mr. Gordon, belonging to the African Association at Sapele, and Mr. Powis, belonging to the firm of Messrs. Miller Brothers at Old Calabar. These gentlemen accompanied the expedition on Mr. Phillips' invitation. There were over 200 carriers, 2 Government interpreters, the Consul-General's chief clerk and cook, 2 orderlies, 1 store-keeper (from Sapele), and 1 servant to each officer, with the exception of Mr. Powis, who it appears had 4 boys with him. Mr. Phillips also took the drum-and-fife band of the Niger Coast Protectorate Force with him, but sent it back from Gwato, after being begged by the Jakri natives not to take them.

The expedition anchored off Gilli-Gilli for the night. Mr. Phillips' messenger, whom he had sent to the King with a present a couple of days before, returned and reported that the King took the present, and expressed surprise at getting another present so soon.

The King further said that he had so much "custom" to make just now that he could not see the Acting Consul-General or any white man, but that in about a month's time he would send down and let the Acting Consul-General know when he was ready, and receive him and one big Jakri Chief only.

The messenger further stated, in private, that as he was leaving Benin city, the King of Benin gave orders for some of his soldiers to go to the different waterside towns. The messenger also told the Acting Consul-General quietly that the King had said to him, "If the white men are really coming, that he (the messenger) was to come on and let him know first of all."

This messenger is reported as being most intelligent, and was apparently an old friend of the King before the latter succeeded to the Throne, but this must be taken *cum grano salis*. The messenger, however, had a personal interview with the King, so the King's message was "first-hand."

Mr. Phillips then sent the messenger back to the King to say he was coming. A Jakri messenger next arrived, and said that all the Jakris (the Benin River tribe—distinct and un-connected with the Binis, except in trade matters) were frightened, and were leaving the waterside towns on the Benin city side of Gwato Creek, as the Bini soldiers were coming down from the city. Mr. Phillips then sent this man to the Headman or Chief of Gwato to tell that person that the expedition would arrive at Gwato next morning, and wanted accommodation for about 10 white men and 200 carriers. The next day the expedition reached Gwato—which is quite close to Gilli-Gilli—where they found all ready for them, the Chief having given up his own house to the white

men. Three King's messengers then came and said they were
sent to lead the expedition to the city.

Mr. Phillips explained that he had come as a friend to
the King, who had taken his presents, that he had no wish
nor intention of interfering with any of their customs, and
that he wished to proceed on his way the following morning,
as he had plenty of work to do elsewhere. Mr. Phillips then
introduced each officer in turn, with his rank, to the King's
messengers.

The messengers begged for a day's delay to give the King
time to prepare. This was refused. The messengers then
asked Mr. Phillips to give them a "token" to send to the
King, to show that the expedition was really coming. Mr.
Phillips sent a uniform cane belonging to Captain Boisragon.
The messengers departed for Benin city.

After this, everything appeared to go most smoothly, and
the Gwato people (subjects of the King) seemed very pleased
to see the white men. One Benin city Chief, named Mary
Boma, with several other people there, recognized with much
evident pleasure Major Crawford and Mr. Maling, who had
visited Gwato before.

The expedition went through the recognized custom of
"feet washing" before entering Gwato town. That evening
Mr. Phillips issued two or three orders, one of which was to
the effect that he would lead the column with the guide and
one interpreter, and another, that officers might carry revolvers if they so wished it, but that they were not to show them.
As a matter of fact, no officers carried revolvers on their
person.

The next morning (3rd instant) at 8 A.M., the expedition
started from Gwato, Mr. Lyon returning to Sapele to take
charge in Mr. Campbell's absence. Dr. d'Arcy Irvine had
already relieved Dr. Elliot temporarily at Sapele. At 11 A.M.
the expedition halted for breakfast. The natives seemed extremely pleased to see them. The road, although they could
only walk comfortably in single file, was in excellent order
(bearing from east-north-east to east). After breakfast the

expedition pushed on, and somewhere near 4 o'clock in the afternoon it came to a small defile.

All the white men were walking in front, and when the head of the column got round a corner, they suddenly heard a fusillade of guns. At first, the officers of the expedition thought this was meant for a salute, but soon discovered they had been treacherously led into an ambush, and that the carriers were being massacred. The white men then ran back with a view to getting their revolvers out of their boxes, but failed in their efforts. Mr. Phillips, however, did not turn back, he being well round the corner at the head of the column. Then all went forward to close round Mr. Phillips, but Major Crawford came back, saying, Mr. Phillips had just been shot dead. Mr. Phillips' orderly then came up and corroborated the statement. The remainder then fell back slowly along the route they had come. They were all unarmed, and the enemy were firing at them on both sides at very close quarters. Major Crawford was then badly hit, and Messrs. Locke, Maling, Boisragon and Elliot tried to assist him along, as he, Major Crawford, had lost the entire use of his legs through the wound received. Major Crawford was almost immediately hit again, this time fatally; then Mr. Maling fell dead, as did Dr. Elliot shortly afterwards. Mr. Campbell doing his best to rally the carriers, with Messrs. Powis and Gordon, were all shot dead. Messrs. Boisragon and Locke, then seeing that all their companions were killed —they both being wounded—crept into the bush, and after wandering for five days and nights they reached a waterside market, called Ikoru, about twenty miles above Gwato, and were taken down stream in a canoe by a friendly Ijo man who happened to be there. On getting some way down the creek below Gwato they met Mr. Lyon in the steam-launch "Primrose," who was on the look-out for fugitives. Mr. Lyon brought them to the African Association factory in the Benin River, where they now are. During all the time they were wandering in the forest they went without food and drink, except what they could get by sucking the dew off the

leaves. Dr. d'Arcy Irvine informed me that they could not
have lived another day without food.

Both these officers go home by first opportunity. Mr.
Locke has more than completed his year on the coast. They
are both progressing very favorably, and out of all danger.

4. All property fell into the hand of the enemy, and those
natives who were not shot or cut down were taken as prisoners to the city. I have this day issued an ultimatum to the
King, which will be sent by a trustworthy messenger, demanding that all persons and property in his hands shall be
given up at once. I have taken care to say nothing further,
but issued the ultimatum in chance of saving some lives and
recovering private property: whether the King complies or
not will make no difference as to making any alteration in
the punishment to be inflicted, which cannot be too severe.

5. I held a meeting of the leading Jakri Chiefs today,
and thanked them for the loyalty they had shown in assist-
ing the Government during the present crisis. I urged them
to continue doing so, saying that all losses in carriers, etc.,
would be paid for, and their services properly noticed.

I am arranging for carriers and water transport with the
Jakri Chiefs of Warri, Benin, and Sapele, so that when I
meet Admiral Rawson at Brass, on or about the 30th instant,
I can give him full information of carriers, etc., available;
and I can also give him my views as to the best points of
attack, etc., having a sketch, drawn up by Mr. District Commissioner Burrows, showing the three landing points of
Ologbo, Ikuru, and Gwato. Great vigilance is being shown
in the way of messengers and spies to report on the King's
movements and plans.

6. Before coming here I thought that probably it would
be wise to have the assistance of a column of West India
troops, but I am now of an opinion that the navy and Protectorate force are fully able to carry out the object of the
expedition.

The Bini is not a fighting man, and a great coward into
the bargain.

7. I take this opportunity of mentioning here the very

excellent work done by Messrs. Burrows and Lyon in this district during a most trying and anxious time. They have both acted with great energy and tact in most difficult circumstances. Mr. Burrows has done most useful work in surveying the water approaches to Ikuru and Ologbo. Before I arrived, and a few days after the facts of the expedition were known, he took a few men with him and burnt Ologbo. Since receiving your cable, no further forward action will be taken until Mr. Moor's arrival, and I have issued strict orders to that effect.

I also am much indebted to Mr. Assistant District Commissioner Murray at Bonny, who had great responsibility thrown on his shoulders during the few days between hearing the bad news and of my return from the interior. He showed himself to be an officer of judgment and great energy.

8. I might add that the station of Sapele and the Benin River factories are perfectly safe. The Benis, not being watermen, cannot leave their mainland, and, in any case, they are too great cowards to do so had they the chance, so there is no fear of any offensive movement on the King's part.

9. I would add that the destruction of Benin city, the removal and punishment of the King, the punishment of the fetish priests, the opening up of the country, etc., will prove a wonderful impetus to trade in this part of the Protectorate, and at the same time do away with a reign of terror and all its accompanying horrors.

10. I proceed to Sapele tomorrow, and then on to Brass and Bonny, where I hope to meet Admiral Rawson about the 30th instant. I shall have all detailed information, etc., ready for the Admiral and Mr. Moor on their arrival. I expect Mr. Moor to arrive at Forcados about the 7th February.

11. I do not think the King will offer much resistance as far as actual fighting goes. The people (there being no regular army) are probably only fighting under pressure, and on the first reverse I fancy nearly the whole country will flock in and claim protection. The people live under a heavy yoke

of oppression and starvation at times. They are badly armed
—chiefly long danes. Captain Boisragon and Mr. Locke say
that they saw no rifles on the day the expedition was attacked. If not already removed, the ivory at Benin city
should fully pay the cost of the expedition.

I am, etc.

(Signed)   H. L. GALLWEY.

Inclosure in No. 64.

Proclamation.

WHEREAS, by the orders of the King of Benin City and
his Councillors, a peaceful party of Government officers,
whilst proceeding to visit the King, unarmed and unescorted,
have been attacked by the soldiery of the King, and seven
Europeans and over 200 natives murdered:

Notice is hereby given that steps are about to be taken to
punish the King and his people, and that the following re-
wards will be paid to any person or persons who may capture
and hand over to Her Britannic Majesty's Government the
persons hereafter mentioned:—

	Puncheons.
King Duboar	50
Ojomo	10
Okrigi	5
Head fetish priest	10
Five fetish priests, of whose importance I shall satisfy myself	5 each.

Baganda Chiefs Negotiated Special
Conditions for British Occupation, 1900

D. A. LOW AND
R. CRANFORD PRATT *

Although the kingdom of Buganda has often been regarded as an excellent example of indirect rule in practice, the Uganda Agreement of 1900, which was the basis of the relationship between the protectorate and Buganda until 1955, was not itself the product of any philosophy of indirect rule. The appropriateness of European ways and institutions for Africans had yet to be questioned. The preservation of indigenous institutions was yet to be regarded as having high value in its own right. Johnston[1] and his subordinates still enjoyed unimpaired their Victorian assurance in the rightness and urgency of their mission.

In fact, the protectorate had little choice but to come to a settlement with the Baganda chiefs. Alone it did not have the force necessary to control the territory, let alone to administer it. Already the British had relied heavily on these chiefs in their efforts to consolidate their influence in Uganda. The alliance continued to be essential. Sir Harry Johnston, therefore, in negotiating the new Uganda Agreement, sought to stabilize the relation between the protec-

* From D. A. Low and R. Cranford Pratt, *Buganda and British Overrule* (London, 1962).

1. Sir Harry Johnston, appointed Special Commissioner, Consul-General, and Commander-in-Chief in Uganda in 1899.

torate and Buganda. He sought also to secure two further
fundamental concessions for the protectorate which the
earlier agreement had not provided—a greater measure
of control over land alienation and regular tax remittance
by the Baganda to the protectorate.

The decision in 1895 to build a railway from Mombasa
to Uganda made it essential to the Crown that it acquire
further power over land. The promotion of European settlement and European-managed plantations was regarded
as necessary if the railway was not to be a serious liability.
Although it was expected that such settlements would be
concentrated in what is now Kenya, sections of Uganda
were at that time regarded as suitable for plantation development. In any case, with the railway approaching, there
was the danger that unless there was greater control there
might be irresponsible alienation by individual chiefs to
[individual European] land speculators.

His second objective was to secure a stable, local revenue
for the protectorate. The troubled years since 1894 had
been costly. Sir Gerald Portal, sent in 1893 to advise on
whether a protectorate should be declared, had estimated
that an annual grant of £20,000 would be required. In
fact, by 1899–1900 the grant was £397,000. The home
government regarded as paramount that this dependency
on the British treasury should be cut sharply. It was argued
that in any area where a continuous administration was
established and law and order maintained it was legitimate
to impose regular taxes. Johnston hoped through a new
agreement to secure the collection of such taxes by Baganda chiefs.

They were not without their fears about the proposed
agreement. The first of these centered on the land sections.
Johnston's original intention was to secure for the Crown
control of all waste, forest, and uncultivated lands, to give
each leading chief an estate suitable to his position, and to
invest the remainder of the land in a board of trustees
whose responsibility it would be to safeguard the interest
of the people living on the land. Such was his ignorance of

the traditional land tenure system that he felt that this would stabilize and put into legal form the indigenous system.

The leading chiefs strongly criticized two specific aspects of his land proposals. They stressed that it was not enough merely to recognize their rights over cultivated land, arguing that, because of shifting cultivation, unused land should also be granted to the chiefs. Secondly, they feared that without individual land grants the lesser chiefs would be reduced to the status of peasants. Johnston's first proposal would give to these chiefs, as to everyone else, the right to the land they actually worked. It would not give them any tenants. In a society where influence was largely a product of the number of people under one's control, this would mean a serious, perhaps irreparable, blow to their position.

Secondly, the chiefs feared that the traditional native government was to be abandoned. This fear Johnston regarded as "peevish nonsense," a phrase which he insisted his translator should try to translate into Luganda. Johnston's impatience with this fear reflected again his lack of knowledge of the indigenous system. Suggestions that land alienation should become the concern of the protectorate, that *ssaza* chiefs should spend far more time in their *ssazas,* and that European officers should supervise their administration of certain matters were all reasonably interpreted as serious threats to the traditional political system.

The final agreement was produced to meet the immediate needs of the British and to placate the fears and suspicions of the Baganda. It is the interaction of these two factors that explain its various articles. The agreement clarified and defined the structure of the Buganda Government, recognizing the Kabaka as the native ruler and providing also for three "native officers of state . . . [who would] . . . transact most of the Kabaka's business" and an advisory council, the *lukiiko,* whose members were to be entirely appointed by the Kabaka, or his Regents.[2] It then proceeded, point by

2. Articles 10 and 16, the Uganda Agreement (1900).

point, to cover the main preoccupations of the protecting force at that time. Hut and Gun Taxes were instituted and were to be collected by the chiefs; it was agreed that the Kabaka henceforth would only exercise the right of conscription, or of levying native troops, under the advice of protectorate officials; the upkeep of public roads was required of the Buganda government and the protectorate government's control was secured over forest and mineral rights.[3]

The land settlement which was finally accepted differed significantly from Johnston's original proposals. As in the original proposals, there were to be official and private estates for the Kabaka, members of the royal family, Regents, and *ssaza* chiefs. However, instead of the remainder of the occupied land being put under a board of trustees and the unoccupied land becoming Crown land, the Agreement specified that "One thousand chiefs and private landowners will receive the estates of which they are already in possession and which are computed at an average of eight square miles per individual," [4] and the remainder, estimated to be 10,500 square miles, would become Crown land. With this settlement, Johnston acquired a wide measure of control over land alienation for the Crown and secured the loyal cooperation of the chiefs. To achieve these ends he did not hesitate to drop his plan for a board of trustees. Nor did he concern himself with the vast social implications of this entrenchment of the ruling oligarchy as a landowning aristocracy. The pragmatic and political nature of the settlement was underlined by a private agreement between Johnston and the three Regents that, once the agreement itself was signed, they would receive an extra forty-five square miles between them and Apollo Kaggwa would receive, in addition, a hundred head of cattle.[5]

British overrule was asserted on several important specific

3. Ibid., Article 13, p. 358.
4. Ibid., Article 15, p. 359.
5. These grants were a compensation for the abandonment of Buganda's claim to tribute from Busoga.

matters. Newly elected Kabakas and newly appointed ministers and chiefs required the approval of Her Majesty's Representative before assuming office. The dismissal of a chief could be requested if he failed in his tax-collecting duties. The Kabaka had to consult with Her Majesty's Representative and explicitly follow the advice offered before giving effect to *lukiiko* resolutions. No *lukiiko* member could be dismissed without the Governor's sanction. Most important of all were two articles which gave British overrule its widest definition. Article 20, *inter alia*, freed Her Majesty's Government from the agreement "should the Kabaka, chiefs or people of Uganda pursue a policy which is distinctly disloyal to the British Protectorate." [6] Article 6 promised recognition of the Kabaka "so long as the Kabaka, chiefs and people of Uganda shall conform to laws and regulations instituted for their governance by Her Majesty's Government and shall cooperate loyally with Her Majesty's Government in the organization and administration of the said Kingdom of Buganda." [7]

Wide as were these provisions of control, they were significantly narrower than the equivalent clauses of other treaties and agreements between the British and native rulers. Normally such treaties contained a clause requiring either that the native ruler must seek and follow the advice of Her Majesty's Representative, or, more frequently, that the ruler follow loyally and faithfully the advice of Her Majesty's Government. Nothing in this Agreement involved as extensive an assertion of British control.

---

6. Ibid., p. 362.
7. Ibid., p. 352.

Mende Rising Against British Tax Administration in Sierra Leone, 1898

SIR DAVID CHALMERS *

On August 31, 1896, a Proclamation was published setting forth that Her Majesty had assumed a protectorate over the territories adjacent to the Colony of Sierra Leone in which Her Majesty had acquired power and jurisdiction.

For purposes of administration, the hinterland was divided into five districts, intended to be of about equal size, avoiding severance as far as possible by the district boundary of the territories of paramount chiefs. These districts have been named as the Karene, Ronietta, Bandajuma, Panguma, and Koinadugu districts.

Sir Frederic Cardew, with praiseworthy zeal to become acquainted with the colony and hinterland by personal visitation, made various tours therein in 1894, 1895, and 1896. During these tours he traversed a large extent of country, and held meetings with some of the chiefs of places which he visited, and explained his intended policy. During the two first tours, his statements and explanations to the chiefs appear to have been confined to matters connected with slavery, and only in 1896 were the subjects more fully shadowed out which were afterwards embraced in the subsequent Protectorate Ordinance, including the intended taxation. Sir F. Cardew does not himself seem to have at-

* From Sir David Chalmers, *Report by Her Majesty's Commissioner and Correspondence on the Subject of the Insurrection in the Sierra Leone Protectorate 1898,* Vol. II (London, 1899).

tached importance to the consents of the chiefs, nor to have thought he obtained any active assents, although he states that apparently there were no dissentient voices.

Under direction of Sir Frederic Cardew, an explanation or epitome of the Ordinance was prepared and transmitted about October 1896, along with printed copies of the Ordinance, to several of the principal chiefs in the Mende country. Instructions were sent to district commissioners throughout the protectorate as to the several provisions of the Ordinance and the working of them, and they were directed to give as wide publicity as possible to the Ordinance, explaining its details as far as practicable to the native chiefs, and these instructions appear to have been well carried out. Further, a government messenger (Renner) was sent with copies of the Ordinance, and instructions to explain it to chiefs in the Timini countries. He visited Magbena and Mahera in Kwaia, Mabele in the Marampa country, Marforki, Port Lokko, Sanda Lokko, Karene, and Bullum. There were no expressions of approval at any of these places; at some places specific objections were made to the hut tax.

For some little time the scope of the Ordinance does not seem to have been fully realized, but it was not long after the promulgation when notes of disapproval began to be heard. Mr. Parkes, the Secretary for Native Affairs, an experienced observer, and who had wide opportunities of gauging generally the native feelings, stated that the Ordinance, when the provisions became generally known, was unfavorably received. The chief sent down messengers asking that the "law should not be put into force." They objected mainly to the hut tax, and "to their not having jurisdiction in all cases."

Many written petitions to Sir Frederic Cardew against the Ordinance also came in. Amongst the earliest which I have seen on record is one by Bai Simera, October 26, 1896— the single instance, as I have already stated, of a paramount chief who had in a measure previously committed himself to a sort of acquiescence. He stated his apprehensions that the slaves would become free by going before the district commissioners, that the chiefs' power of holding their courts would be taken away, that wives would leave them, "and, worst of all, in 1898 tax must be paid on every house from 5s. to 10s., which will bring down a heavy burden on us, when we consider our poor state in which we live." This plea of disability from poverty was much dwelt on afterward.

On October 20, 1896, the chiefs of Bumpe, in the Mende country, sent a petition saying they would not be able "to abide to the new instructions, such as the paying of land tax and house tax," stating their poverty as a reason. The same chiefs, with some others, followed this petition a year afterward by sending to the Governor a representative to explain all that they wished to say. "The most principal is the house tax . . . we are not opposing, but we are really poor, and not in a position of paying; therefore we humbly pray that his Excellency will pity our case in this respect."

Madam Yoko, Paramount Chief of the Lower Mende country, sent a letter to the Governor of the colony on November 3, 1896, expressing acceptance of the Protectorate Ordinance, but provisionally and tentatively—"as this being a new Ordinance which we are not accustomed with, we shall make a trial of it, for we do not know what it is like yet . . ." This communication is the only one I have seen in which the Ordinance has been commented upon by a native authority without deprecatory expressions. Madam Yoko has been, and still is, distinguished for her unqualified loyalty and support of the English government.

In Ronietta, Dr. Hood, Acting District Commissioner, sent in December 1897 a notice by letter to the principal chiefs of that district, to the effect that the hut tax would become payable on January 1, 1898, and calling upon them then to make payment. The account which Dr. Hood gave in his evidence before me was to the effect that Madam Yoko paid some hut tax, and Chief Smart, a subchief of Bai Kompah of Kwaia, also paid part of his tax, but against the order of his paramount chief, and that another chief was anxious to pay but was not permitted; that he then wrote to the Governor, and Captain Moore was sent up and relieved him of the office of District Commissioner.

Dr. Hood's official report to the Governor was more ample. He stated that there was a disposition on the part of the majority of the Chiefs in Ronietta district to make no effort to pay the hut tax, that the Mabanta and Bagru districts were in a very disturbed state, that the Timbi, Bumpe, and Ribbi were quiet, but had done nothing toward payment; that the subchiefs of Kwaia were more or less prepared to pay, but that the two principal chiefs were opposing; that the Mendies under Madam Yoko had paid a certain amount, which Dr. Hood thought had been paid by Madam Yoko herself to make the officials think an effort is being made by her people; and that the majority of her subchiefs were paying very little attention to her orders unless for his assistance, and "if only the paramount chiefs could be made to give the necessary orders to their respective subchiefs, a great effort would be made by the people to pay the tax." Upon receiving this report, Sir Frederic Cardew placed Captain Moore, an Inspector and the adjutant of the Frontier Police, in charge of Ronietta district, relegating Dr. Hood to his normal position of medical officer, and expressed his views on the situation in a minute communicated to Captain Moore.

Captain Moore took charge of Ronietta district on January 21. He tells us that he knew the reason he was appointed was that the tax would have to be collected by force, that there was resistance offered, and that the people were arming. His first act seems to have been to dispose of the case of Pa Nembana, as to which Dr. Hood had said he thought the Governor ought to be consulted.

Pa Nembana, who was next in rank to Bai Kompa in the Kwaia, was taken as a prisoner to Kwallu and put upon his trial on the information of Chief Smart. The charge was: *1*) intimidating Chief Charles Smart, in that he unlawfully conspired with other chiefs to prevent Chief Smart in paying his lawful dues, "the house tax," and using his influence with other chiefs to do the same; *2*) not obeying the orders of the Acting District Commissioner contained in a letter of December 31, 1898. The sentence awarded by Captain Moore, Acting District Commissioner, was *1*) deprivation of his chieftainship, an order the district commissioner had no jurisdiction to make; *2*) twelve months' imprisonment with hard labor, the hard labor being also outside of the district commissioner's jurisdiction; and *3*) thirty-six lashes. Fortunately the Governor remitted the lashes. It will be seen on looking at the evidence, that there is no evidence of conspiracy, nor of intimidation, what was said by Pa Nembana not being a threat, but a warning of danger. The second count in the charge expresses no offense; the duty of paying the hut tax is under the Protectorate Ordinance a civil liability (Section 43–49): no order or warning to pay could convert the non-payment into a crime. The district commissioner's letter is simply in the position of a tax-gatherer's notice.

Captain Moore's next act was to call a meeting of the chiefs. Some sixty or seventy paramount and subchiefs attended upon his invitation at Kwallu, the headquarters of Ronietta district, about January 24 or 25. Before they met, a statement was made to him by one of the chiefs, Foula Mansa of Yonni, that all the chiefs had taken an oath to resist the government in the collection of the hut tax. Captain Moore states that at the meeting he demanded from the chiefs a definite promise to pay the hut tax, otherwise he would arrest them, allowing them to answer on the second day, and that as on the second day they still demurred, he arrested ten or twelve of the paramount chiefs; and that on the next day after this the chiefs agreed to pay the tax, and did so, "after an interval of a month or so." It does not however appear that they were set at liberty upon giving the promise: they "were told that they would have to remain at Kwallu till they had paid a certain amount to show that they intended to agree to pay the tax." This was not stated by Captain Moore but by Captain Fairtlough, who took charge of the Ronietta district on March 17, and who says he found the chiefs, or several of them, at Kwallu when he went there.

. . .

I revert to the outbreak in the Mende country. I have already mentioned some of the proceedings adopted by the government authorities in Ronietta and Bandajuma districts to compel the assent of important chiefs to the hut tax.

When the chiefs were arrested and imprisoned after the meeting at Mafwe, they were released on an agreement, as they at least understood, to pay £5 for each of their considerable towns, instead of paying according to the number of the houses. Afterward, the houses were ordered to be counted, and additional tax was required in respect of the number of the houses. Upon this a great deal of ill-feeling appeared.

In March, a powerful chief, Momoh Jah, was arrested for not paying the tax by a sergeant and twenty frontier police. Previous attempts had been made for his arrest, when he was not found, but the police seized goats, sheep, and cattle at his town, as many as they could find, and carried them off, some of which, it is said, they appropriated to their own use—an example likely to provoke retaliation.

I cannot doubt, therefore, that the lawless outrages and severities of the frontier police, when they were thus let loose, so to speak, in collecting the hut tax, materially contributed to bring about that angry discontent which, pent up and smouldering for a time, at last broke out in massacre and plunder.

The outbreak commenced on the April 26. Within less than a week, the male British subjects in Bandajuma, Kwallu, and Sulymah districts, with few exceptions, were murdered. A number of women also were murdered, and after an order went forth from the leaders staying the killing of women, they were treated as captive slaves. All property belonging to British subjects was plundered, except at Bonthe and Yorke Island, which were saved by the arrival of the marines and troops. Two explanations have been given of the almost simultaneous outbreak over so wide an area: the one is that, at the last meeting of those who formed the plan of the rising, each of the principal chiefs took

with him an equal number of small stones, one of which was
to be thrown away every day commencing from the day of
the meeting, and that the day on which the last one was
thrown away, all of them were to set their forces in motion
in rebellion and kill all English-speaking people they could
lay hands on. Another statement is that, starting from
Bumpe as the center, a number of messengers bearing a
sort of fiery cross in the shape of a half-burned palm-leaf,
sped very rapidly to the different places where the rising was
to begin and delivered their message that the time had come.
Whichever was the method, it seems clear that there was
very definite pre-arrangement. Once started, the rebellious
mob grew rapidly; at every place they came to, they were
joined by their countrymen—those who were in sympathy
and those who were compelled to join by threats; those who
had paid their hut tax and those who had not paid. The
more resolute pressed on the less resolute to join in the war,
and the stronger natures had their way. The police station,
which was also the headquarters of the district commissioner
at Bandajuma, was attacked, as was also that at Kwallu.
The attacks, which seem to have had little system, were
repelled with very little casualty on the side of the defend-
ers.

The Mende rising, although really war, would be better
understood as to many of its practical aspects if considered
as a very aggravated riot. The riot once launched, various
motives would come into operation. There was doubtless
the all-pervading sense of the hostile treatment which had
been meted out toward themselves, but it is no ways necessary to suppose there was unity of aim among all who
took part in the riotous work. Plunder is always an object
with a Mende man when he engages in war, but there is
no reason to think it was here a chief motive. Where there
was plunder there might also be the desire to put possible
witnesses out of the way by killing them. Again, if a rioter
had been ill-treated or unjustly dealt with by a Sierra
Leone trader he might wreak his vengeance on whatever
Sierra Leone people he laid hands on. The attack on the

barracks at Bandajuma and Kwallu need have no more significance than the mad rush of a mob on a police barrack, which has occurred in our own country in less happy times than the present, when the mob was only guided by a temporary instinct for mischief or revenge. The diversity of individual aims may very fully account for differences in the statements of different persons as to motives, but the weight of the evidence very clearly points to the general and pervading motive to have been that the rioters, identifying all English-speaking people with the English government, and believing that in one way or other they had taken part with and aided the government in bringing the hut tax, with its concomitant grievances, upon them, were wrought up to the desire of taking vengeance upon them. A circumstance which there is much reason to believe was connected with the murder of missionaries, seems in accordance with this view, and to confirm it. Missionaries had been in the Mende country for more than thirty years, and the native inhabitants had always been most friendly with them, so much so that in previous risings the mission stations had always been considered safe places of refuge. The animosity, so contrary to precedent, shown in the recent raid, has been attributed to the fact that the missionaries at some of the Mende stations had preached sermons shortly before the outbreak in support of the hut tax, and advising the people to pay the tax. It is beyond doubt that such sermons were preached, nor does it seem improbable that the people considered the missionaries showed by these sermons that they identified themselves with the government, and had common purpose with the government in the enforcement of the hut tax. There is no evidence that the missionaries were disliked or feared as the introducers of a new religion or the enemies of old superstitions.

The disturbance in the Mende country was quelled by two military expeditions. The first of these, under Colonel Woodgate, left Freetown on May 9, and the second, under Colonel Cunningham, on May 31.

PART **II**

Methods of and
Adaptations to
Colonial Government

Modes of Adaptation

The manner in which African societies adapted to European colonial rule from the turn of the twentieth century onward depended in large part on the policy of administrative and political overrule employed by European powers. There were, in general, two types of policies of colonial administration established in African colonies. One, utilized by the French, Belgian, and Portuguese, is known as Direct Rule; the other, utilized by the British, is called Indirect Rule. The selections in Part II illustrate the administrative methods of these two types of colonial overrule; they also illustrate the wider sociological and political consequences of these differing methods of colonial administration.

The systems of Direct and Indirect Rule differed in their theoretical approach to colonial administration. The system of Direct Rule assumed that indigenous African authority groups and administrative institutions were incapable of providing the kind of control and political security required by modern colonial regimes. The overwhelming majority of African societies subjected to colonial rule at the turn of the twentieth century were preliterate societies. Their lack of written languages and a literate culture was merely an expression of their general stage of technological evolution, this being largely Neolithic and early-to-middle Iron Age. In view of these cultural characteristics typical of most

African societies south of the Sahara Desert, French colonial administrators concluded that little in the indigenous political institutions was adaptable to modern colonial government. Ergo, Direct Rule sought to replace African categories of government with administrative units fashioned by European official and operated largely by them.

On the other hand, the system of Indirect Rule, while sharing the view that the political systems of African Neolithic and Iron Age societies were not directly adaptable to the needs of modern colonial government, assumed that African authority groups should have an established role in colonial government. British colonial administrators like Lord Lugard, who established British authority in Nigeria in 1900, and Sir Donald Cameron, who also helped organize British rule in Nigeria as well as in Tanganyika, were somewhat doubtful of the African's capacity to adjust to modern or Western government and strongly questioned the cultural desirability of directly requiring such adjustment.[1] Moreover, for most purposes of day-to-day colonial administration in local African communities, it was believed desirable to have indigenous African rulers performing a wide range of governmental functions customary to African societies. It was also considered financially less burdensome to have such functions performed by indigenous rulers than by imported European officials; and since British colonial territories were required by the home government in London to pay their own way, this financial consideration was of no mean importance.

Thus, rather than fashion new administrative units as the basis of colonial administration in African territories, the policy of Indirect Rule accepted the prevailing indigenous administrative or authority units as the basis of local colonial administration. The African rulers or chiefs who ran the indigenous authority units were endowed with powers, rules, and regulations which enabled them to per-

---

1. See, e.g., Sir Frederick Lugard, *The Dual Mandate in British Tropical Africa* (Edinburgh, 1922).

form initially a limited and later a wider range of modern governmental functions. Those African chiefs so organized as units of local colonial administration were officially dubbed Native Authorities or Native Administrations.

It should be remarked that what was a fairly clear conceptual difference between Direct and Indirect Rule at the early period of colonial rule in Africa tended to be less so by the 1920's and 1930's. The policy of Direct Rule, as applied by the French, increasingly accepted many of the assumptions underlying Indirect Rule as applied by the British. This is apparent in the selection on French administration in West Africa in the 1930's by Robert Delavignette, former administrator in French Africa.

Even so, there remain many practical differences between Direct and Indirect Rule throughout the colonial era in Africa. For one thing, the policy of Direct Rule consistently required a higher ratio of colonial official to African population: there was, for example, one British administrator for every 100,000 Africans in Northern Nigeria in 1926 and one administrator for every 70,000 in Southern Nigeria (total population, 18,000,000 in 1920's); whereas in French West Africa (population, 12,000,000 in 1920's) only one territory, Upper Volta (population, 2,300,000 in 1920's), even approximated the ratio of administrator to African population in British Nigeria—the ratio being one French administrator to 48,745 Africans.[2] By the mid-1930's this situation changed little: aggregate figures show 1,315 British administrators in local administration in Nigeria, whose African population was 20,000,000, and 3,660 French administrators in French West Africa, whose African population was 15,000,-000, and 887 French administrators in French Equatorial Africa, whose African population was 3,200,000.[3] The situation in the Belgian Congo, as seen in the selection by

2. Raymond Leslie Buell, *The Native Problem in Africa,* Vol. I (New York, 1928), pp. 983–984.

3. Robert Delavignette, *Freedom and Authority in French West Africa* (London, 1950), p. 18.

Professor Crawford Young, was similar to that in French West Africa, though the ratio of Belgian administrator to African population was somewhat higher. The Christian church and capitalist firms also had a more direct role in colonial policy in the Congo than elsewhere in Africa. Inevitably, the higher ratio of colonial administrator to African population meant a more immediate, intensive, and probably more repressive form of colonial administration. Certainly policies relating to agriculture, taxation, labor recruitment, and mandatory public works were much more intensively pursued in French West Africa and the Belgian Congo than in most of British Africa. The selection from Geoffrey Gorer's important account of a trip through French West Africa in the 1930's illustrates this rather well.

Repressive policies in local colonial administration were not, however, limited to European officials. The selections from Professor Kofi Busia's study of Ashanti chiefs under British rule and my own study of colonial rule in Sierra Leone indicate how African chiefs under Indirect Rule exercised the modern authority given them in a rather heavy-handed and corrupt fashion. Chiefs were no less abusive in exercising the more limited modern authority granted them under Direct Rule in French Africa, though, as suggested in Professor Elliot Skinner's account of colonial policy in Upper Volta, they confronted more interference from local colonial officials—called *Commandant du Cercle* in French Africa and District Commissioner in British Africa.

One consequence of the position of African chiefs in the native administrations in British Africa was the rise of militant popular groups who sought to redress the harsh or repressive forms of local administration. This is illustrated in the selections on Ghana and Sierra Leone. By the end of World War II, this pattern of militant popular outbursts against repressive features of chiefs' role in colonial government had politicized important segments of the rural population, making them rather receptive to the more articulate anticolonial and nationalist politics of the well-educated new elites.

Another consequence of chiefs' role in colonial government was the use chiefs made of their position to acquire modern wealth and affluence. This is illustrated in detail in my selection on Sierra Leone, and remarked on in the selections relating to Ghana and Upper Volta. Chiefs also derived educational advantages for their offspring, with the result that at the end of World War II the sons, nephews, and other kin of chiefly families were disproportionately represented among the well-educated new elites in both British and French Africa. This in turn enabled chiefs to survive the radical political changes in postwar Africa consequent on the rise of nationalist movements for independence from colonialism. Though their former power under colonial administration was significantly curbed during the postwar period of decolonization, the nationalist leaders, especially in British Africa, often reserved a prominent place for chiefs in postwar local government. They fared less well in French Africa, due in part to the policy of Direct Rule which allowed chiefs less political sway than under Indirect Rule, but nowhere in postwar French Africa were traditional rulers totally eclipsed, save in the Republic of Guinea in the period following independence in 1959.

M.K.

Colonial Government through Direct Rule: The French Model

ROBERT DELAVIGNETTE *

When I was head of a subdivision on the Upper Volta, I went on tour in the first months of my stay, and landed unexpectedly in a distant village, little visited. The chief gave me a good reception. I came back there two years later, at the end of my tour, and had a still better reception. The chief, however, did not seem to me to be the same man. I had before me an old man, while it was a young man who had received me the first time, and I recognized him, standing behind the old man. I asked the two of them why the chieftainship of the village had passed from the one to the other without my being told of it. The old man said to me: "He whom you see behind me was in front of me," and he explained, "It is I who am the chief, today as the other time, and in front of this man, as behind him. But two years ago we did not know you, and he showed himself in my place." It is not unusual to fail to recognize the real chief right away, but it makes one stop and think. And I propose to analyze the machinery of our administration through the chiefs, bearing this incident in mind.

In all territorial administration, the native chiefs act as cogwheels between the colonial authority and the native peoples. In French West Africa, which is a federation of

* From Robert Delavignette, *Freedom and Authority in French West Africa* (London, 1940).

colonies, the supreme authority in each colony is vested in the governor. Within the colony, authority is exercised, in the name of the governor and under his control, by the commandants of districts (*cercles*); the *cercle* may be divided into subdivisions, but nevertheless it constitutes the administrative unit, and the commandant of a *cercle* represents the administrative authority. How does the government, which is centered in the *cercle*, establish relations with the native peoples? This is precisely the function of the *cercle*. It is the motor mechanism which directly engages with the native machinery, the canton, which in turn sets in motion a certain number of villages. Colony and *cercle* on the one hand, *cercle*, canton, and village on the other, these are the interlocking parts of the administrative machinery. Commandants of *cercles* and heads of subdivisions belong to the Colonial Administrative Service,[1] and to the Civil Service of the Federation of French West Africa. Chiefs of cantons and villages are the native chiefs properly so-called, and by abbreviation "the Chiefs."

In French West Africa, which is eight times the area of France and comprises a population of fifteen million, the territorial administration is like a power current passing from the 118 *cercles* to the 2,200 cantons and the 48,000 villages. The native policy that affects fifteen million men depends to a considerable degree on the character of the 118 *cercle* commandants and their collaborators and the 50,000 native chiefs.[2] Native policy is worth what they are worth. It is what their relations with each other and with the native peoples make it.

The importance of these relations must be thoroughly understood. The *cercle* is only a motor mechanism so long as it is a transformer of energy. The commandant of the *cercle* is not truly a commander except in so far as he can understand the chiefs and get a hearing from them. If his

---

1. In 1937 there were 385 Colonial Administrators in French West Africa, half of them posted to offices at headquarters in each colony.

2. See the chart on pp. 80–81.

Chieftainships in the Colonies of

	Provincial chiefs, or chiefs of a group of cantons or tribes	Canton chiefs, or chiefs of tribes
SENEGAL	2	135 (auxiliary chiefs, temporary chiefs, chiefs, deputy chiefs)
Circonscription of DAKAR and dependencies		1
MAURITANIA	3	50
GUINEA		262
SOUDAN	1 paramount chief, 8 provincial chiefs or chiefs of a group of tribes	719
NIGER	3	183
DAHOMEY	5 (known as *chefs supérieurs*)	161
IVORY COAST	10	516 canton chiefs, 62 tribal chiefs, 117 chiefs of groups of tribes
Totals	32	2,206

French West Africa

Village chiefs or assimilated to that status: (48,049)				
Ordinary	*Independent*	*Assimilated* (*Ward chiefs*)	*Dependent Divisions*	*Independent Divisions*
9,352				
41		51		

819 village chiefs, or chiefs of divisions or sub-divisions				
4,057	8	9 (mixed communes of Konakry and Kankan)		
10,907	132	15	622	40
6,585	5			
3,494		20		
11,892				
47,147	145	95	622	40

authority is to be effective he has to work through the chiefs, in daily contact with them. And this brings me back to what happened to me: authority is like a force running to waste if it contacts a false chief instead of finding the real one. And among the hundred-odd villages of the dozen cantons of my subdivision, I had at least once lost my authority.

What, then, are the characteristics of a real native chief?

As a rule, the chiefs are studied according to the classification used by the administration: first of all the village chief, then the canton chief, sometimes a chief of a province, more rarely still a great chief whom we call king or emperor. But this is merely an account of the hierarchy of authority among the chiefs, and not a definition of the chiefly power itself. But the power of a chief may be defined in relation to its quality rather than its extent; it may happen, for example, that an ordinary village head-man wields more power in his village than a chief of a province in his province. Instead of considering chiefs in relation to the hierarchy in which we place them, let us consider their authority as it is exercised in relation to their own territory. And let us remember that the real chief does exist, though he may be concealed.

Chiefs like the one I saw the first time in the village where I learned my lesson are, so to speak, more or less men of straw. They play the part which, in certain big department stores, is assigned to the employee who has to receive the complaints of short-tempered customers. At any demand from the administration—tax, labor service, recruiting, census, new crops to be tried—the fake chief is put forward. On him will fall the wrath of a hoodwinked administration.

Canton chiefs rarely have "straw chiefs." Obviously it is more difficult for them than for village chiefs to hide themselves and mislead the administration. But, more than this, it seems that after fifty years of colonization, the spiritual quality of native power has left the big chiefs to take refuge with the small ones, who have not been so much affected by European influence.

The canton is in most cases a former feudal province turned into an administrative district. *The village, on the other hand, is not an administrative creation. It is still a living entity.* And, in spite of appearances, it is the *village* chief who retains the ancient, intrinsically African authority.

It does not matter if the chief is old, infirm or blind; the essential thing is that he should be there. If necessary he can take a young and active man as his colleague. If he is illiterate and has some difficulty in dealing with natives educated in our schools, let him be given clerks and assistants. Only one thing counts, and it does not depend on education, age or health: that is the sacred character of his power. In the old Africa, the community which the chief represents lives in him and there can be no life without a supernatural element. Hence the force which binds the people to the chief; hence the ritual which permeates social unity and solidarity, which orders the form of greeting addressed by the people to the chief and gives a religious sanction to the authority of the humblest village chief, the chief of the cultivated and inhabited land.

What principles of action in colonial administration can be drawn from these facts? We must proceed, so to speak, from the "straw chief" to the chief of the land, who seems indeed to be the product of the land itself, and it is almost always in the village that he is to be found. Thus we are driven to make an important distinction between the village chief and the chief of a canton.

As the village chief derives from a primitive feudal Africa based on the holding of land, so the chief of a canton belongs to modern Africa, and is part of the mechanism of colonial administration.

The administration nominates all chiefs, whoever they may be and in all circumstances. The most frequent case is also the simplest; the government has only to follow native custom, which varies from hereditary succession to election, according to the locality.

Greater care is needed where there is no hereditary dynasty or well-established rule to take into account. There are two cases to be considered: either the chief will be drawn from the country, or from outside. Except in very rare cases the village chief will never come from outside. If the family which provided the village head has died out, it is still from within the area that the branch must be chosen which will bear the new chief. And if the whole village is awakening to a new life, it will be possible to arrange for an election on a broad basis including not only notables and heads of families, but also the young people and women.

It is, however, in the exercise of his functions rather than by the method of his appointment that the chief of a canton differs from a village chief and acts as an agent of the administration.

The primary function of a chief, whether he is chief of canton or village, is to be there, to be in residence. Nothing takes the place of the real presence. If the courtyard of a *cercle* commandant is always paved with chiefs waiting for him to receive them, we can be sure that the administration is not good. The commandant who keeps his chiefs at headquarters, far from their chiefdoms, injures their authority and his own. And indirectly he oppresses the villages. In fact, in order to put in an appearance at headquarters, the chiefs drain their territories, where they are represented by deputies who oppress the peasants. There is another method, which consists in requiring the canton chiefs to maintain representatives at headquarters. This procedure may be a bad one if these representatives are themselves a heavy charge, and if they encroach on the status of the chiefs.

In fact, we are confronted with opposing and mutually contradictory necessities: on the one hand we are well aware that it is essential to preserve the native character of the canton chief and to make use of the traditional feudal spirit which still survives in him; on the other hand the very fact of colonization forces us to shape him to our administrative outlook. Our major fault is lack of method in our dealings with him. We demand from him too many trivial tasks and we set too much store by the way in which he performs them. Instead of entrusting to him certain important tasks—a tax, a main road, a new crop—and judging his achievement on the spot in our tours, we make his authority a travesty by using him as an intermediary in small affairs—provisioning a camp, receiving a vaccinator, collecting witnesses for a petty court case, providing a supply of chickens. We think that because he is a native, we are carrying out a native policy with his assistance, while in fact by putting menial tasks on him we treat him as sub-European. And we tolerate a hypocritical maneuver: in theory, the canton chief executes administrative orders; in practice, he resorts to feudal methods to get them carried out. He turns the tax into feudal tribute, the labor service into a *corvée,* and cultivation into requisitioning.

Should the traditional authority of the canton chief be restored? We have already shown that this is a negative program. We could certainly reconstitute a décor of pomp and ceremony around them, but we should not be able to recreate the soul of their ancient authority. No, the tendency of the administration is all toward making these feudalists into officials. But then we must face the thing. They should be specialized officials and exercise a distinctive function. We have already involved them in implicit officialdom; they receive rebates on the tax, which is not always without danger for the taxpayers; they are paid a salary and it is small enough; on the Ivory Coast there are five hundred of them to share 1,500,000 francs, while the European administration of the *cercles* costs 7,430,000. They enjoy a status of a sort, in the sense that they do not come under the "Native Status Code," [3] and that they can-

---

3. This "Indigenat" is a disciplinary code, applied by administrative officials to all persons legally of native status, i.e., not French citizens, nor of any legally defined intermediate status.

not be arbitrarily deposed. They have a personal file in the records at the station and they are scrupulously given good and bad marks by their commandants. They are decorated, they are welcomed at receptions on national holidays, they are invited to visit exhibitions; they are sent as delegates to Dakar and even to Paris; they are brought together on councils where they collaborate with Europeans. And they are rightly treated as important persons; but what is needed is not to re-establish them, but to establish them. Not to re-establish them in a social structure that is dying, but to establish them in a modern Africa that is being born. And it is there that we should make officials of them. This need not mean making them robots or abstractions. To make officials of them is first to define their official duties, and then to establish not only their administrative status but their social personality. We must reconsider with them— and for them, as for ourselves—the problem of the function of the chief.

Colonial Government through Direct Rule: The Belgian Model

CRAWFORD YOUNG *

The Belgian colonial edifice at its height was a remarkably solid structure. A masterful summary of the precepts of the system has been put forward by Thomas Hodgkin, who suggests the term "Platonism" to epitomize Belgian colonial rule:

> Platonism is implicit in the sharp distinction, social and legal, between Belgian philosopher-kings and the mass of African producers; in the conception of education as primarily concerned with the transmission of certain unquestioned and unquestionable moral values, and intimately related to status and function; in the belief that the thought and behavior of the mass is plastic, and can be refashioned by a benevolent, wise, and highly trained elite; that the prime interest of the mass is in welfare and consumer goods—football and bicycles —not liberty; and in the conviction that it is possible, by expert administration, to arrest social and political .change.[1]

It is traditional to analyze the colonial power structure in the Belgian Congo in terms of a trinity composed of the administration, Church, and large enterprises. It is important to recognize that not only was this triple alliance a virtually

---

* From Crawford Young, *Politics in the Congo* (Princeton, 1965).

1. Thomas Hodgkin, *Nationalism in Colonial Africa* (London: Frederick Muller, 1956), p. 52.

seamless web but each component, in its area of activity, was without peer in tropical Africa in the magnitude of its impact.

On the administration side, Buell has observed that as early as the 1920's the density of administration in the Congo was unequaled in Africa, with the insignificant exceptions of Mauritania and Dahomey.[2] By the time of independence, there were 10,000 Belgian civil servants and officers in the administration, magistrature, and army.[3] No Congolese, rural or urban, could have failed to perceive that he was being administered. In the urban centers this is hardly surprising, but what differentiated the Belgian system from others in Africa was the extent of its occupation and organization of the countryside. Most familiar, and most unpopular, was the agricultural officer, of which there was at least one per territory, seconded by several African agricultural assistants and a network of *moniteurs* with rudimentary training to bring the administrative system in contact with virtually all the population. Legislation permitting sixty days per year (forty-five after 1955) of compulsory cultivation (or other public works) was generally applied until 1957 and was still legally authorized, although largely abandoned, in 1960.[4] The most active enforcement was in the cotton zones, which covered vast sections, mainly in the eastern half of the country, and in the rural hinterland adjacent to urban centers and mining camps to supply the African population with the staple elements in its diet. As early as 1937, it was estimated that 700,000 heads of family were covered by the compulsory system.[5] Between

2. Raymond Leslie Buell, *The Native Problem in Africa,* II (New York, 1928), p. 466.

3. J. Gérard-Libois, "L'assistance technique belge et la République du Congo," *Etudes Congolaises,* II, No. 3 (1962), 2.

4. Decree of December 5, 1933. This was reduced from sixty to forty-five days by the decree of December 29, 1955, and maintained after long debate and considerable opposition in the decree of May 10, 1957, reforming the *circonscriptions indigènes.*

5. Edmond Leplae, "Résultats obtenus au Congo Belge par les cultures obligatoires alimentaires et industrielles," *Zaïre,* I (February 1947), 137.

the European agricultural agents of the administration, and those in the employ of the cotton companies, the objective was to have one for each two thousand to three thousand planters.[6]

The administration made its presence felt in many other ways. The relatively dense network of secondary roads had to be maintained by the villages. Until recent years and the more general use of the automobile and truck, portage levees were a frequent element in village life. In many areas, villages had been required by the administration to relocate themselves alongside the roadways. In an earlier day, recruitment pressures for service in the mines, plantations, and army had been intense, although in the postwar years the problem had been to halt the rural exodus rather than to use administrative pressure in recruitment.

One cannot fail to be impressed by the scope of the evangelical effort in the Congo. In 1958, it was estimated that the Congo counted 5,371,785 Christians, 80 percent of whom were Roman Catholics. At the end of the colonial era, the Catholics maintained 669 mission posts, manned by nearly 6,000 European missionaries. These were aided by nearly five hundred African priests, with new ones being confirmed at the rate of 35–40 a year. The clergy was in turn seconded by 25,566 catechists, offering rudimentary religious instruction in the villages. In the teaching and charitable orders, there were an additional 386 Congolese brothers and 745 nuns.[7] Not only was each village in regular contact with the administration but there were few which did not receive at least occasional visits from a missionary. Further, in no other African state, with the minor exceptions of Basutoland and Burundi, was university education launched by the Church. A 1906 concordat was negotiated with the Vatican which set forth the salient prin-

---

6. A. Brixhe, *Le coton au Congo Belge,* 3rd ed. (Brussels, 1958), p. 51.

7. Chambre des Représentants, session de 1959–1960, *Rapport sur l'administration du Congo Belge pendant l'année 1958,* p. 165.

ciple which remained in force until 1960: the missionary effort was to be essentially Belgian.

The 1906 concordat then provided a framework through which a system of cooperation could be developed between missions and administration. The state not only subsidized the Catholic mission schools but paid for the maintenance of the missionaries. An important indirect material aid was in the legal provision authorizing a land grant of 200 hectares for each mission station established, which could be used not only to help sustain the mission station with provisions but for commercial exploitation. The result was that the missions possessed relatively substantial resources with which to carry out their task in the Congo.

The Belgian administration itself was far more committed to evangelization as an integral part of its objective than were the British or French, who were confronted with the responsibility of ruling large Muslim populations. Functionaries were reminded by the government: "Government servants are not working alone in the task of civilization. The religious orders are participating in at least equal measure . . . Civil servants, whatever their own religious views, are under a strict obligation to aid the Chrisian missionaries." [8]

In part these companies were a survival of the concessionary regime by which Leopold sought quickly to make effective the occupation of the country by the Free State or by its surrogates. (There was little continuity, however, between the Free State economy and that later built up. The former reposed essentially on wild rubber and ivory; these accounted for nearly all exports in the 1890's, and as late as 1908 accounted for 36.7 million francs of an export total of 43.4 million.[9]) The equatorial forest zone of the

---

8. *Recueil à l'usage des fonctionnaires et des agents du service territorial au Congo Belge,* 5th ed. (Brussels, 1930), pp. 57–58.

9. A. J. Wauters, *Histoire politique du Congo Belge* (Brussels: Pierre Van Fleteren, 1911), p. 164; Georges Hostelet, *L'oeuvre civilisatrice de la Belgique au Congo de 1885 à 1953* (Brussels: ARSOM, Sci. Mor. et Pol., T. XXXVII, fasc. 2, 1954), I, 467.

central basin became the site of the immense plantations of oil palm and rubber of companies of the Lever group and the *Société Générale* (*Compagnie de Kasai,* Busira-Lomami, etc.). Large-scale mining operations really only got underway on a large scale in the 1920's, but these, once started, operated on a labor-intensive basis which made their impact enormous. The mining operations were largely concentrated in the eastern half of the country; copper and allied metals were found in southern Katanga, tin in north Katanga and Maniema, diamonds in two major deposits at opposite ends of Kasai, and gold in the northeastern part of Orientale and south Kivu. Rare were the areas, such as the Kwango district, where there was not at least one major enterprise, either plantation or mining, which dominated the zone around it.

As with the missions, the colonial administration was expected to give full support to the companies in recruiting labor and seeing that food was produced for the labor camps. Investment was attracted to the Congo in part because the administration was prepared to go to unusual lengths both in making available the necessary land in the case of agricultural enterprises and in supporting recruiters with whatever administrative pressure was necessary. Government policy was set forth in a 1922 circular: "It is a mistake to believe . . . that once taxes are paid and other legal obligations met, the native may remain inactive. Under no circumstances may magistrates or officials express this opinion. In every case, I should consider this to be a lack of discipline violating the recommendations of the government and our most positive duties toward our black subjects."

Later that same year, Governor-General Maurice Lippens added that every government official should be "penetrated with the idea that his reason for existence is to favor and develop our occupation and that this duty consists of supporting every enterprise." [10]

---

10. Buell, *op. cit.,* II, 539. Lippens, it should be added, was

Another factor operating in this direction was the career structure of the colonial service. After twenty-three years of service, when many were still at the peak of their vigor, colonial civil servants were retired. The pension was not spectacular, and many sought further employment. Since the large companies frequently recruited such persons, it was inevitable that many functionaries would define their administrative role with some view of their own future prospects of obtaining responsible, well-remunerated employment in the private sector upon retirement. The liberal PSC Minister of Congo Affairs, Maurice Van Hemelrijck, was shocked on attaining office in December 1958 to discover how many of the top functionaries at the Ministry were drawing handsome salaries from colonial companies for sitting on boards of directors, with bonuses for "services rendered"; they were allegedly representing the interests of the state, which was part owner of many of the companies. That the private sector should seek to influence policy formulation on its own behalf was natural enough; what was unusual in the colonial situation of the Congo was the relative absence of "countervailing" influence putting forward a fundamentally different view of the public interest. The colonial trusts had easy access to policy-making organs at all levels both through membership in formal consultative institutions and informal channels.

Although the tripartite alliance tended to display a monolithic face to the external world and to the Congolese, it would be misleading to underestimate the continual dialogue that went on among them. Their interests were not in fact entirely the same: the administration was, in the final analysis, most concerned with an effective scheme for governing the country, the missions in evangelical work, and the companies in expanding their enterprises. A classic example of this occasional tension arose over the pace of

---

more inclined to act in the interests of the business community than most of his successors, who probably would not have worded the circular quite so strongly.

economic development in the 1920's. The competition for labor was reaching a point where widespread abuses were committed in forced recruitment, and large areas of the countryside were being literally stripped of their adult males. The Catholic missions and many individuals in the administration began to rebel at a policy which seemed to reach a point where there had to be a choice between limiting expansion by the companies or compromising permanently the essential tasks of missions and administration. The Apostolic Prefect of Ubangi district, in the north of Equateur province, declared, "The territory of Ubangi is emptied of every able-bodied man. The majority of the young men, the hope of the future, are taken from their district of origin and transplanted in the country from which they will return, if ever they do, corrupted and contaminated by every kind of subversive idea which they will spread upon returning here."

And one territorial administrator, in a Lever plantation recruiting area, wrote in September 1925, "The territorial administrators . . . are in a position to know that the exactions are becoming more numerous every day in every realm, and that they no longer leave to the populations respite or liberty . . . Perhaps one may pardon the functionary who gives way to sentiments of bitterness when he believes himself daily becoming more and more a veritable merchant of men, when his villages empty at his approach, as at the approach of a slave-trader." [11]

---

11. Ibid., II, 505, 542.

Colonial Government through Indirect Rule: The British Model

LORD MALCOLM HAILEY *

The use of traditional native authorities as agencies of local rule is now so widely extended that it must necessarily occupy the chief part of our attention. Their value depends largely on the care taken in ascertaining the real seat of indigenous native authority before making the grant of those statutory powers which mark the position of a native authority as part of the machinery of our administration. There are large areas in which the seat of indigenous authority has been easily ascertainable. It has been mainly in conditions of which southeastern Nigeria, or some of the pagan areas of its northern provinces present the most typical examples that difficulty has arisen and some mistakes have occurred in the past. As remarked above, however, the principle is everywhere now well recognized, and the investigations undertaken on the subject by the administrations have had the additional advantage of giving the local officers a greater interest and more extended knowledge of the social organization of the people.

But adherence to tradition, valuable as it is, is only a means of securing acceptability of the institutions on which we place our reliance, and acceptability is the essential quality which they must possess. That is a consideration

* From Lord Malcolm Hailey, *Native Administration and Political Development in British Tropical Africa* (London, 1943).

which applies not only to the initial recognition of native authorities, but to their subsequent adaptation to the more advanced requirements of modern rule. Treasuries, federal councils, or group courts are (as remarked above) novel to native custom. But that fact is of less practical importance than the degree to which they have proved acceptable to native opinion. The changes in the constitution of native authorities which may be needed in the interests of middle-class or educated opinion are not to be tested by the extent of their adherence to tradition, but by the extent to which they recognize the balance of forces which is being developed within the native authority jurisdictions.

Although in the early stages of administration there was a tendency to entrust power to a single chief or head-man, far less difficulty is now felt in using councils of various kinds as native authorities. These may have no permanent presidents, as in Warri and Ibibioland; or they may meet under the presidency of a chief, as in the reorganized chiefdoms of Sierra Leone, or the presidency may rotate among the chiefs controlling the component units. The organization of native authorities now follows an almost infinite variety of forms, and the only standard by which their relative value can be judged is the success with which they operate in practice.

It is at the same time essential that the forms in which they receive statutory recognition should reflect as closely as possible the real character of the organization, particularly in respect of the position of the native administration council. This has in the great majority of cases an essential part in the authority exercised by a chiefdom. There is in this matter a considerable variety of official practice. In Nyasaland, for instance, the practice is to gazette single chiefs as native authorities, but to pay regard to the councils which are invariably associated with them. In Northern Rhodesia, on the other hand, the gazetted native authorities are chiefs-in-council, but in some instances at any rate administrative officers have been accustomed to deal with the chief without taking his council into account. In Tanganyika there are cases in which chiefs have been gazetted alone, without mention of elders or other assistants; in other cases the gazette notice confers authority on the chief "and his elders." Our discussion on Nigeria calls attention to the importance which this point assumes in regard to the Yoruba states. It is of interest here to note the practice in Sierra Leone, where the legal definition of "tribal authorities" is made a reality by the practice of district commissioners in keeping lists of the council members and ensuring that they are properly summoned and consulted.

It is of great importance that administrative officers should in their personal contact with native authorities have regard to the traditional position occupied by the council or elders. It is no doubt a temptation, especially in matters involving some urgency, to follow the easy course of dealing with the chief alone. But apart from the offense which this may cause to native custom, it is not possible to secure a true view of native opinion on any proposed measure unless the council or the elders are brought freely into consultation. There is moreover the risk that the native authority may seek to avoid taking its proper share of responsibility on the ground that it is "working under government orders."

A further point of considerable importance arises in connection with the composition of the native authority councils. At various places in this report, attention is drawn to the necessity for securing that a place should be found in the councils for the educated and other more progressive elements in the community. It has, again, been pointed out that there are areas in which it is necessary that important elements of stranger natives should be represented on the council of any native authority to which they are subject. In the majority of cases, the composition of the native authority councils is now determined by native custom and usage. But men who at an earlier stage had sufficient position in their own society to voice its views or to exercise influence over the personal actions of the chief are not necessarily the most suitable in the conditions with which the native authorities now have to deal. It is, for instance, common for age to be the main qualification of the elders, and experience shows how serious a disqualification this may impose where advice is required on new situations. There is, again, a danger that the elder may be out of touch with the younger men, of whom increasing numbers have some education, and many of whom have experience gained in wage earning in industrial areas and in other European enterprises.

In some areas, as for instance in the Yoruba states, some measure of association of newer elements in the work of the councils is in process of being secured by the pressure applied by political associations. The Nigerian government has itself given countenance to the association of the Youth Movement in the activities of the native councils in such places as Ijebu-Ode. It has again arranged that the Sabon Garis of the north should have their own representative boards with an approach to the Emir. The Uganda government has welcomed a resolution by the Lukiko of Buganda to summon to its meetings an unofficial representative from each county. The law which regulates the constitution of tribal authorities in Sierra Leone seems explicitly designed to render it possible for district authorities to influence the composition of the tribal councils. Again, in eastern Uganda, the government appears to exercise a direct initiative in the formation of representative councils.

For the most part, however, it did not in 1940 appear to be the policy of the administrations to attempt any formal intervention in the manner in which the traditional councils were composed. Intervention in the interests of the educated or similar elements may of course have its own dangers. An educated or trading section which can obtain a controlling position in a native council may in time constitute an oligarchy which will not be less harmful to the interests of the general community than the dominance of a chiefly family or of conservative elders. It would be equally unfortunate if the direct intervention of government were to result in the creation of artificial bodies which

commanded no support in the social organization. But if
this is an argument for the exercise of caution, it is not a
reason for neglecting the matter until an insistent demand
for representation expresses itself. The Kenya government
has given an example, in the institution of its system of
native councils, of methods by which a channel can be
provided for the expression of different types of African
opinion. It may be added here that in certain of the de-
pendencies there is already some movement to secure the
expression of the women's point of view in the native authority councils. It is noteworthy that the women in Anlo
have complained that the native authorities' measures to
augment local revenues take the form of levies upon activities carried out mainly by women. The Native Advisory
Council at Kitwe has suggested the inclusion of a woman
member, and it is of interest to note that the Kikuyu Provincial Association has women delegates at its conferences.

Official opinion frequently expresses the conviction that
the existing structure of one type or another of traditional
native authority is adequate to provide machinery for the
expression of any popular discontent. That, however, is
not sufficient. It is necessary to distinguish between the provision of machinery for the expression of discontent and
the provision of opportunities for the positive association
of the population in the work of local government. Modern
conditions make it necessary to put in force many measures
which, unless they have the active cooperation of the people, are liable to be represented as oppressive. The progress
of the type of development and welfare work which is now
an increasing preoccupation of the colonial governments
will be seriously hampered unless we can obtain positive
cooperation of this nature. This must, if possible, be secured to the point at which it is possible for the government to entrust to local authorities the responsibility for
measures which may possibly incur a certain amount of
unpopularity. It would not serve the cause of African development if the administration, from a desire to strengthen
the position of the native authorities, allowed them to dis-

tribute the benefits attendant on an expansion of the social or economic services, while itself accepting any odium which may attach to the measures which this may involve.

It will be appreciated that the experience so far gained of the exercise of executive functions by traditional native authorities is, so far as the majority is concerned, confined to the conduct of the somewhat rudimentary functions which it has so far been possible to entrust to them. It has not been difficult to secure their cooperation in these activities, but they have for the most part shown little ability to comprehend the financial background which lies behind them. Many have been slow to realize the importance or to understand the procedure of preparing estimates or maintaining accounts. That is not a difficulty which now occurs in the more highly organized units, such as Buganda or the larger Emirates or the Yoruba states of Nigeria. But in the generality of native authorities, there are only a very limited number who can prepare their own budgets, even with substantial help from the district staff, while in the great majority of cases this task falls entirely on the administrative officers. There is, however, in such cases a preliminary discussion with the native authorities concerned, and this is said to have considerable value. There is evidence that some officers have taken great pains to explain these processes to the native authorities.

A device frequently employed is that of the finance committee. This may consist of those councillors who are literate and money-minded, or it may be composed partly or wholly of men who, not being themselves full members of the native authority, are associated with it for this purpose. The Ngwa clan council has an estimates committee which is able to prepare the native authority budget, and the Southern Auka authorities have finance committees consisting of about seven members. Several of the Kenya local native councils have finance subcommittees to assist the district commissioner in the preparation of the estimates. The Buganda finance committee contains two unofficial members. Recent legislation in the Gold Coast colony pro-

vides for the creation of finance boards in each native state
as a first step in the reform of the indigenous authorities of
that area.

The greater part of the revenues of the native authority
treasuries is derived from direct taxation in one form or
another, or from judicial fees. But there are also receipts
of some importance from local services, such as lorry park
fees, market fees, ferry tolls, and the like. In a number of
instances, however, the services with which these receipts
are connected are not handed over to the native authorities. It is important to impress on them the relationship
between rights and duties. It seems advisable therefore
that when minor revenues are handed over to the native
authorities, responsibility for the services connected with
them should be at the same time entrusted to them.

The difficulty occasioned by the lack of financial com-
petency of many native authorities is not limited to the
preparation of budgets. It is necessary for district officers
to control closely the course of expenditure. In the majority
of cases, their countersignature is required on every check
drawn. In some of the less efficient treasuries, the accounts
have to be maintained in the district office. The method of
auditing these accounts has occupied much attention and
is still under discussion in some territories. In Northern
Nigeria and in Buganda, this duty is carried out by the
Colonial Audit Department. In parts of Nigeria a firm of
chartered accountants is employed for the purpose. Tanganyika and Sierra Leone have entrusted the duty to the
administrative officers who advise and control the native
authorities.

Taxation and Labor Practices
in French West Africa in 1930's

GEOFFREY GORER *

"The idea of colonization becomes increasingly more repugnant to me. To collect taxes, that is the chief preoccupation. Pacification, medical aid, have only one aim: to
tame the people so that they will be docile and pay their
taxes. What is the object of tours, sometimes accompanied
by bloodshed? To bring in the taxes. What is the object of
ethnographical studies? To learn how to govern more
subtly so that the taxes shall come in better. I think of the
Negroes of the A.O.F. who paid with their lungs and their
blood in the 1914–1918 war to give to the least 'nigger'
among them the right to vote for M. Diagne; of the Negroes
of the A.E.F. who are the prey of the big concessionary
companies and the railway builders . . ." So writes Mi-
chel Leiris in the diary which he kept while working for the
Griaule ethnographical expedition.[1] It is, at least as far as
concerns French West Africa, a judgment which it is difficult to quarrel with. (Except that the Negroes did not even
get the right to vote for M. Diagne by the sacrifice of their
lungs and blood; they had had that for several years before.
The victims of the 1914–1918 war were simply blood sacrifices on the altars of the white fetishes Gloire and Patrie;

---

* From Geoffrey Gorer, *Africa Dances: A Book About West
African Negroes* (London, 1935).
  1. *L'Afrique Fantôme,* p. 169.

they didn't get any more out of the transaction than sacrificial animals usually do.)

All Negroes, with the exception of a few towndwellers, are subject to taxation in two forms—"capitation" or head-tax, and "prestation," which is defined by Larousse as "a local tax used for the upkeep of roads in the neighborhood, payable either in money or work." As far as I know this latter is assessed everywhere except in the towns at twenty francs a head; but except as a favor Negroes are not allowed to pay in money; they have to work off the tax under conditions which I shall describe in the next section.

The amount and incidence of the head-tax varies with each district. In the most favored it is only levied on all males over the age of fifteen; in the majority on all people over that age; in the most unfortunate on all people. The amount varies between six and fifty francs a year. It is usually the smallest sums which are the hardest to pay, for the taxes are assessed more or less according to the richness of the country; if they are under fifteen francs a head it is a pretty safe bet that there is no work to be found in the district and no produce which can be sold.

The district administrator is instructed from Dakar of the amount of taxes he has to collect—a sum usually calculated on the last census figures; the administrator is made responsible for seeing that the stipulated amount is brought in. He in turn assigns to the *chefs de canton* the sum for which each is responsible in his district, and they in their turn tell each village chief how much his village must contribute. The village chief is personally responsible for the taxes of the entire village; if he is unable to get enough out of the villagers he has to make up the sum himself; if the village does not pay to the full the administration takes a hand, and the village chief is the first to suffer. The village chiefs will consequently go to almost any lengths to collect the required sum, and it is on them that the chief onus is thrown.

If the money can be earned, either by selling produce or labor, the tax is not unduly hard. Moreover the census figures—which were, I think, last taken in 1931—then probably bear a reasonable relation to the population. But the districts which fulfil these conditions are almost exclusively situated within a hundred miles or so of the coast—that is to say the forest region of the Ivory Coast, with its numerous and flourishing coffee plantations, the banana area of New Guinea, and at any rate until the slump in Senegal and lower Dahomey, with groundnuts and palms respectively. But between this prolific band and the Sahara to the north there is a large area of savannah, save on the banks of the Niger indifferently watered, which can produce little beyond the food needed to support a scanty population. It is this very extensive region on which the taxation falls hardest. There is no money to be earned locally; except for rice or cotton in a few small areas there is no exportable product; however moderate the tax, it is almost impossible for the natives to acquire any money unless they go south to seek work. A considerable number do this, and all do not return, which is one of the numerous reasons why the census figure is in most districts far higher than the present population—in Bodi in North Dahomey, for instance, the 1926 census figures on which the tax is collected give the population as three thousand: according to a native estimate it is now six hundred, a statement which the number of abandoned huts confirmed—and consequently the tax which is demanded of the village works out at far more per head than the official figure. To pay the sum required is almost an impossibility; and there are numerous cases of unscrupulous administrators and/or *chefs de canton* demanding the tax two or three times in the year. There is no redress against this, except a personal appeal to the governor; and that is made very difficult.

When a village fails to pay its taxes the administration steps in brutally and ruthlessly. When punitive measures are taken, as they frequently are, the administrator himself is never present, and therefore has a complete alibi; he sends his Negro soldiers—naturally always of a different race to the people they are sent out against, most usually

Bambara—with instructions to collect the money. It is axiomatic that no one treats servants so badly as a servant set in authority; no one could be more heartlessly brutal to the Negroes than the uniformed Negroes who act for the administrators. This employment of Negroes for the dirty work serves a double aim; it keeps lively the interracial hatred which is so essential for colonies where the subject races are more numerous than the colonizers, and it enables the administration to deny forthright the more inhuman practices in which they tacitly acquiesce, or should the facts be irrefutable, to lay the blame on the excessive zeal of their subordinates.

I heard on my journey a very great number of stories nauseatingly horrible, but obviously unproved. I shall only tell of those incidents which I know to be true, either from personal experience or from abundant evidence. I am not indicating the district exactly for fear of getting my informants into trouble. None of the cases are exceptional.

A village in the southern Sudan was unable to pay the taxes; the native guards were sent, took all the women and children of the village, put them into a compound in the center, burned the huts, and told the men they could have their families back when the taxes were paid.

In North Dahomey two men who had not paid their taxes fully (they were twenty-five francs short of the hundred at the proper date) were flogged with the *chacoute* (a heavy leather whip) in front of the assembled village until they fainted, were taken to prison without medical attention where they had to work for fifty days, and were then sent back with the remainder of the tax still owing. I spoke to one of the men in question and saw his back covered with suppurating sores.

In a village in the northern Ivory Coast, the chief's son had been taken as hostage until the tax was paid. The chief had not seen his son for nearly two years. Incidentally this practice of hostage-taking is very common; and I cannot remember how many times I have been offered young girls and boys to enjoy or keep as servants for the price of the head-tax.

The following letter was received by the servant of a doctor from his father: "Envoie vite 30 francs pour impôt. Ils nous avons pris tout le bétail et tout le mil et nous crevons de faim." (Send thirty francs for taxes at once. They have taken all our animals and millet and we are starving.) In a village in the Upper Volta, people were collecting winged ants; they explained that they had nothing to eat, for the whole of their livestock and grain had been taken for taxes.

In the whole of the western Ivory Coast flogging with the *chacoute*—legally nonexistent—and imprisonment follow unpunctuality in taxpaying.

On the way to Abengourou in the Ivory Coast, though not in that *cercle*, I was stopped by a native guard who mistook my car for the administrator's. The guard was slightly wounded in the head and had with him the most miserable man I have ever seen. He was naked with his genitals much swollen, his belly puffed and bruised, his eyes closed and bloody, and blood pouring from his nearly toothless mouth. His hands were tied, but he could barely stand, much less run away. The guard explained that the man was behindhand with his taxes; he had therefore gone to fetch him to work on the road, and the man had refused on the ground that if he left his plantation at such a critical moment he would never be able to pay taxes. He had tried to resist, slightly wounding the guard, who thereupon "lui avait foutu dans la gueule." He was obviously very pleased with himself and waited anxiously for my commendation. I told him that he deserved the legion of honor.

"Forced labor" and "prison labor" were a few years ago the two most popular anti-Bolshevik warcries; with Russia's increasing respectability they have now become rather old-fashioned; but they are very adequate descriptions of how nine-tenths of the public work in the French West African

colonies are performed. Fifty centimes—one penny at the
normal rate of exchange—is considered the proper rate of
remuneration for a ten-hour working day; and the "prestation" or work tax, fines, and arrears of taxes are worked
off at that rate. Consequently every adult male Negro—
in some districts also women and children—does at least
forty days' work for the state, chiefly road making, and if
it happens that he has to make roads when he should be
cultivating his fields, that is just too bad. The more con-
scientious administrators try to avoid this contingency,
but the fields have to be worked during the rainy season,
which is also the time when the roads need the most attention.

Except in the districts where there are railways, the roads
in French West Africa are reasonably plentiful and good.
They have been built and kept in repair by unpaid laborers
working without any tools except the short-handled hatchet
which is the Negro's sole agricultural instrument. The roads
are made of earth and in the southern part of the colony the
soil is laterite, which makes a particularly good and hard
surface. The best roads are slightly raised above the surrounding country, on account of the rains; the earth to
make them up is scooped out of the neighboring land
with these hatchets into wicker baskets which are then
carried on to the road and dumped. The surface is smoothed
by having mud poured on to it which is beaten by women
standing in serried lines holding pieces of wood and beating the earth to the time given out by the forewoman. They
keep this up for ten hours, continually stooping, many of
them pregnant or with babies strapped to their backs. Unfortunately a photograph I took of these "tapeuses," as they
are jovially called, at work, was not successful.

Except in the case of a couple of bridges being built by
private contractors, I did not see any instruments of any
sort being used in public works in French West Africa.
Albert Londres has already described the building of the
Congo-Océan railway, where each sleeper literally represents a Negro life, and where the only instruments he found

were one hammer and one pickaxe, for making tunnels,[2] and I have no reason to believe that conditions are better in French West Africa. Negroes cost far less than shovels, not to mention cranes. I did not see any railway building, but the Thiess-Niger line is so bad that part of it will have to be relaid shortly; still, after the strike of 1925 the government may take a few more precautions.

In the forest regions of the Ivory Coast there is a great deal of work to be done with woodcutting and plantations and a very sparse population; consequently workers have to be recruited elsewhere, and particularly among the Mossi of the Upper Volta (now part of the Ivory Coast) who were by far the most populous tribe of the savannah; this is done both by public and private enterprise. On several occasions the administration have settled large groups of the Mossi in the Ivory Coast—sixty thousand have been moved to the neighborhood of Yammossoukro, in the middle of the forest, this year; but the Negroes support the changed climatic and dietary conditions so badly—not to mention hard work on inadequate pay—that something like half die in the first year. Private woodcutters and planters can also get permission to go and recruit the men they need; the local administrator merely tells the chiefs that so many men are required and are to be delivered at such a place and date. The men cannot refuse to go.

When men are working away from their village, they are meant to be fed and housed. What is more they sometimes are, though in more than one case that I have seen the Society for the Prevention of Cruelty to Animals would have prosecuted me if I had given a dog the same quantity and quality of food and shelter.

---

2. *Terre d'Ebène,* p. 234.

Colonial Administration and Social Change in Ghana, 1900–1920's

K. A. BUSIA *

Ashanti has been administered on the system of indirect rule which is "the system by which the tutelary power recognizes existing African societies and assists them to adapt themselves to the functions of local government." [1] Dr. Lucy Mair has defined indirect rule more comprehensively as "the progressive adaptation of native institutions to modern conditions." [2]

In Ashanti a characteristic of the system has been the support which government has given to the chiefs.

Soon after the British had taken over the administration of Ashanti there was a rising, in 1900, occasioned by Governor Hodgson's demand for the Ashanti Golden Stool. After the rising the candidates who were known to have been loyal to government were elected as chiefs even though they had no title in native law and custom to the offices. Confident of government support and scornful of the traditional checks on the chief, these men ruled badly, and in many places there was a move to get rid of them so that

* From K. A. Busia, *Positions of the Chief in the Modern Political System of Ashanti* (London, 1951).

1. Hailey, *African Survey,* p. 413.
2. L. P. Mair, *Native Policies in Africa* (1936), p. 56.

they might be replaced by men elected from the authentic lineages.

The movement to destool the government-sponsored chiefs started at Agona, where in 1905 the people refused to serve their chief, Kwame Boakye; but government backed the chief, and ordered the people of Agona to continue their allegiance to him. The rebellion subsided for a few months, but burst out again in September 1906. The Acting Chief Commissioner investigated the matter, upheld the chief, and punished the ringleaders of the malcontents. Rebellions occurred in the same year at Ejisu, Akropong, Ahinkuro, and Nsuatre, where chiefs had been similarly appointed. In each case the government backed the chief and kept him on the stool.

A constitutional case occurred at Juaben in 1907 in which the government followed the same policy. The Chief of Juaben, Yaw Sapong, had died in November 1906. His younger brother succeeded him in 1908. The queen-mother of Juaben and members of the royal lineage opposed the election, and they were supported in this by some of the elders. The Chief Commissioner who investigated the matter not only retained the chief on the stool, but deposed the queen-mother, Amma Sewaa, detained her in Kumasi, and inflicted fines on the elders who opposed the chief's election.[3] The constitutional custom which governed the election of chiefs did not now depend solely on the will of the people, but also on the will of government.

The commoners in Ashanti did have a recognized way in which they expressed their wishes in political matters, and that their opinions were considered. They kept careful watch on the way the chief and his council exercised their authority. The struggle between the commoners and the traditional authority took a new turn under British rule. As the examples given above have shown, the commoners had now to reckon with the new government as well. As

---

3. *Colonial Reports: Ashanti,* 1908.

early as 1909, the Chief Commissioner stated the official
policy regarding constitutional disputes.

The Ashanti organization so powerful in olden days still
maintains many elements of cohesion, but with the spread of
Western Civilization and more liberal ideas, the inevitable
conflict between youth and authority has already commenced.
In so radical and, so to speak, brusque a change of conduct,
custom, and condition as has been experienced by this country
of late years, it is, perhaps, but natural that the younger members of the community should wish to throw off an irksome
and restraining, albeit legitimate authority.

It is the duty of the Administration to check this tendency
when it oversteps the bounds of prudence and reason, or the
country would experience a convulsive collapse of a tribal
system which, when purged of certain repugnant features, has
proved worthy of admiration and support, and one which has
been of the utmost assistance in carrying out a succession of
constant and rapid reforms.[4]

In the Report for 1910 the Acting Chief Commissioner
had this to say: "Referring to the contest between youth and
authority mentioned in the concluding observations of the
1909 Report, the Administration continued throughout
the year to watch and guide the inevitable change, maintaining the rightful authority of the chiefs, but discouraging
retrogression and superstition." [5]

The report of a destoolment case which occurred at
Bekwai in 1920 confirms the view that in these political disputes the commoners were exercising a recognized constitutional right. The Commissioner who investigated the
dispute reported:

In the case of Bekwai, for instance, the "youngmen," that
is to say the lower classes, those who were not elders, complained that they were not consulted in the choice of the head-
chief, that they did not regard him as a credit to the Stool,
that people did not respect him in Bekwai itself, or when he
visited the villages, and to a man they refused to serve him.

---

4. *Colonial Reports: Ashanti*, 1909.
5. Ibid., 1910.

The Elders remarked that "One cannot be a chief without subjects. If we support the Head-chief we shall be alone. The whole of the youngmen refuse to serve the Head-chief and we support them." [6]

There was no dispute about the legitimacy of the youngmen's action in accordance with native custom.

The policy of supporting the chief has been consistently followed, and many examples could be given.

In 1915 the commoners of Kumawu rebelled against the chief. One of the reasons for this was that the chief had kept for himself money which had been collected for the War Fund. This was found to be true on investigation, but government retained the chief on the stool. He was made to refund all the money he had collected and pay a personal contribution to the War Fund. The Chief Commissioner who settled this matter reported: "The youngmen of this division have become rich through their cocoa farms, and are of a rather turbulent nature." [7] The following year the commoners again rebelled against their chief, and this time he was destooled. The Chief Commissioner, recording the destoolment in the Annual Report for 1916, explained: "Kwame Afram, Omanhene of Kumawu, was destooled. He had become tyrannical and harsh in his conduct towards his subjects, and the only solution of the difficulty was destoolment."

In 1915, the Chief Commissioner had reported: "The growing importance of the youngmen class through better education and increased wealth is a factor that has to be taken into serious consideration." The warning was justified. In 1918, there were political disputes between the youngmen and the chiefs at Ejisu, Juaben, Bompata, Obogu, as well as in other divisions. There was a common element in these disputes: the youngmen petitioned for the reduction of the "oath fees" charged by the chiefs and elders at the hearing of cases which came before them. Government

---

6. Ibid., 1920.
7. Ibid., 1915.

agreed that the fees should be reduced, but no destoolments were permitted.

During 1920, there were widespread political disputes and dissensions all over Ashanti. Many chiefs were involved, amongst them the headchiefs of Bekwai, Offinsu, Kumawu, Agogo, Agona, and Wenchi. In the case of Offinsu and Kumawu, the chiefs were mobbed and wounded. Government recognized the destoolment of the chiefs of Bekwai, Offinsu, and Kumawu, but punished the rioters. The other chiefs were retained on their stools.

Since the British administration, government support for the chiefs has been a new and important factor in the constitutional development of Ashanti. On the one side, the commoners have been struggling to keep the chiefs in check so that they may have regard to the popular will in the government of their tribes; on the other, the government has protected the chiefs from excessive restraint by the people. Such constitutional changes as have been made have therefore resulted not solely from the sensitivity of the political organization to the popular will, but also from government control and policy. This has been an underlying factor in constitutional disputes down to the present day. The efforts to restrain chiefs have resulted in frequent political disputes and destoolments.

The consistency of government policy is illustrated by the following extract from the first address delivered by the present Governor, Sir Alan Burns, to the Legislative Council of the Gold Coast at its session in 1942:

As a newcomer to this country I have been struck—and struck with dismay—by the large number of interminable stool disputes which disturb the peaceful life of the community. From enquiries I have made, I learn that within the last ten years, no less than twenty-two paramount chiefs have been destooled, in addition to twenty-two others who have abdicated in that period—in most cases in order to forestall destoolment; that seven stools of paramount chiefs are now vacant, and that in many states no paramount chief has succeeded in maintaining his place on the stool for more than a very short time. In the case of subordinate chiefs, I understand the position is as bad or worse, and since my arrival in the colony, rioting has occurred in small villages over stool disputes.

Now I want to make it quite clear that such disorders will not be permitted and will be put down with a strong hand. It is intolerable that the peaceful life of the community should be disturbed by irresponsible minorities or by a few irreconcilables who will agree to no reasonable solution of any problem however trifling.[8]

An important contributory factor in the disputes so strongly commented upon by the governor was clearly put by the Chief Commissioner of Ashanti in the Annual Report on Ashanti for 1920:

> Generally, native affairs in Ashanti have reached a stage of transition. A new generation which has grown up under the British administration is coming to the fore. *Prima facie* also, native institutions which suited the environment of the old order are hardly likely to be adapted as they stand to the radically changed and changing conditions of the present. A strong central government superimposed upon the tribal administration must affect adversely the power and prestige of the chiefs, and allegiance is apt to be transferred from the chiefs to government. This accounts to some extent for the paramountcy cases, chiefs desiring to serve government direct rather than through a paramount chief.[9]

The existence of the British administration implies the reduced status and prestige of the chiefs. This is a most significant fact.

In 1906 the Chief Commissioner reported of the Southern Province:

> The Ashantis of the Southern District have given no trouble during the year. They have marked the year 1906 by their

---

8. Gold Coast Colony Legislative Council Debates, 1942. The Governor's figures refer to the whole colony, but the picture is true of Ashanti.

9. In 1920 the Chief Commissioner, Mr. Harper, heard three cases in which subordinate chiefs desired to withdraw their allegiance from their headchiefs and serve Government direct. These are the "paramountcy" cases referred to.

excellent behavior, absolute obedience, and a desire to help and cooperate with government. I think they have further begun to recognize that government is the chief guardian of their interests, judging by the way they have sought advice on every matter, however small, that concerned them, and they have displayed a trusting and friendly spirit towards the commissioner of their district that is most pleasing to record.

This, the index of the success of the administration, is the index of the decreasing authority of the chief over his subjects. When they regard the District Commissioner as the chief guardian of their interests, they take to him complaints which they would otherwise have taken to the chief. Under the British administration the chief has become a subordinate authority. This is constantly in evidence in his relations with the District Commissioner, the police, the military, and other officials of the central government.

British Colonialism and Transformation of Traditional Elites: Case of Sierra Leone

MARTIN KILSON *

A much neglected feature of the study of colonial change in Africa has been the transformation of the traditional elite. As a group they claimed a disproportionate share in modern social change, owing largely to their role in local colonial administration. Their position enabled them to retain traditional authority while simultaneously pursuing wealth and power in the modern sector of colonial society. Among the sources of new wealth available to chiefs were *1*) direct money payments by governments, *2*) tax extortion, *3*) salary payments by Native Administrations, and *4*) the commercialization of chiefs' customary economic rights.

Direct money payments to chiefs began with the foundation of the Protectorate in 1896 and continued in various forms until the 1930's. The most important payment was the 5 percent rebate from collection of the hut tax. The rebate on tax collection was common throughout sub-Saharan Africa, and in French territories it continued alongside regularized salary payments well into the post-World War II period.[1] Other direct payments to chiefs in Sierra

* From Martin Kilson, *Political Change in a West African State* (Cambridge, Mass., 1966).
1. V. Thompson and R. Adloff, *The Emerging States of French*

Leone included treaty stipends, annual gifts, and entertainment allowances.[2] Though these payments were never large in absolute terms, they were significant relative to the incomes available to other groups in rural areas.

As the chiefs strengthened their position in the Native Administrations after the late 1930's, additional incomes became available through illicit use of tax authority. Though it is difficult to provide precise figures on the sums accruing to chiefs through tax corruption, there is some evidence on this issue. For instance, in the report of inquiry into the tax riots in 1955–1956 it was revealed that chiefs had been accustomed to providing for themselves modern houses, automobiles, and sundry other modern conveniences through tax corruption.[3] One paramount chief, who was a member of the Sierra Leone Legislature, had levied an unauthorized tax upon his subjects in order to finance a modern house costing £5,000; at the same time he owned three other modern houses also believed to have been financed by illicit taxes. Another paramount chief owned a four-story concrete house which cost somewhere between £10,000 and £15,000.[4] The man in question, Paramount Chief Bai Farima Tass II, who was in the Legislative Council, claimed before the commission of inquiry that this house cost only £4,000; but this was flatly rejected by the commissioner: "Having seen the house I do not believe it cost only £4,000

Equatorial Africa (Stanford: Stanford University Press, 1960), pp. 74–75.

2. _Sierra Leone Financial Report for the Year 1930_ (Freetown, 1931), p. 24.

3. Sir Herbert Cox, _Sierra Leone Report of Commission of Inquiry into Disturbances in the Provinces, November 1955–March 1956_ (London, 1956), esp. pp. 151–160. Such behavior was widespread in West and East Africa. Lloyd noted in 1956 that among the Yoruba "some of the more popular _obas_ have made a town levy to contribute towards the cost of their car." P. C. Lloyd, "The Changing Role of the Yoruba Traditional Rulers," in _Proceedings of the Third Annual Conference of the West African Institute of Social and Economic Research_ (Ibadan, 1956), p. 61.

4. Interview with District Commissioner, Kambia District, April 1960.

if all the labor and materials were paid for at current rates. It must have cost much more than that sum . . . If the sum of £4,000 mentioned by him is correct, then it only reinforces my opinion that forced labor was used to keep the cost down to a minimum." [5] Another instance revealed by the inquiry was that of Paramount Chief Bai Bairoh II, who forced his subjects to contribute £300 in unauthorized levies to purchase an automobile for his personal use.

Another source of modern wealth available to chiefs in Sierra Leone was the regularized salary payment from Native Administration revenues. Table 1 shows that within

Table 1
*Average Salaries of Paramount Chiefs
by District, 1947*

Districts	Salary (£)	Districts	Salary (£)
Bo	180	Kenema	212
Bombali	164	Koinadugu	104
Bonthe	197	Kono	176
Kailahun	197	Moyamba	226
Kambia	147	Pujehun	180
Karene	101	Tonkolili	109

Source: *Annual Report on the Sierra Leone Protectorate, 1947*, p. 8.

a decade of the establishment of Native Administrations, the average salary of paramount chiefs ranged from £101 in Karene District to £226 in Moyamba District. Although by the immediate postwar period illegal or quasilegal sources of income may have contributed more to chiefs' total income than their salaries, during the 1950's the latter increased significantly and became an important component of total income. Table 2 shows that between 1949 and

5. This and the following examples are taken from *Reports of the Commissioners of Enquiry into the Conduct of Certain Chiefs* (Freetown, 1957), pp. 51, 67.

Table 2
Salary Payments to Paramount Chiefs, 1949–1956

Year	Salary payments (£)	Year	Salary payments (£)
1949	23,070	1953	49,448
1950	29,942	1954	53,770
1951	34,456	1955	61,114
1952	42,681	1956	63,664

Source: *Report on the Administration of the Provinces, 1956* (Freetown, 1959), p. 22.

1956 the total salary payments to chiefs more than doubled and these payments were supplemented by a central government grant that totaled £141,998 during 1957–1960.[6] As regards the more recent salaries of some chiefs, their range may be gauged from the salaries of paramount chiefs in Tonkolili District as shown in Table 3.

Table 3
Salaries of Paramount Chiefs in Selected Chiefdoms, Tonkolili District, 1960

Chiefdom	Salary (£)	Chiefdom	Salary (£)
Yoni	579	Kholifa-Mabang	360
Bonkolenken	600	Sambaia	700
Kholifa	822		

Source: *Tonkolili Chiefdom Estimates, 1960* (District Commissioner's Office, Tonkolili).

It may be noted by way of comparison that even larger salaries were claimed by traditional rulers elsewhere in Africa. Some of the highest chiefly salaries anywhere in Africa were found in Nigeria. The Emir of Kano Native Authority, for example, received a £7,700 salary in 1960; the Emir of Kazaure Native Authority received £1,320;

---

6. *Sierra Leone Government Estimates of Expenditure and Revenue, 1959–1960* (Freetown, 1959), p. 43.

the Emir of Argungu Native Authority received £1,430; and many Yoruba *obas* claimed salaries of £2,000 in 1956.[7] In East Africa, traditional rulers received somewhat smaller salaries on the average, but relative to the incomes available to most of the population these salaries were comparable to those of West African traditional rulers. For instance, in 1953 the Sukuma Chiefs in Tanganyika received salaries ranging from £100 to £500; the Bunyoro County Chiefs in Uganda received salaries from £400 to £500; and Ganda County Chiefs in Uganda received salaries from £270 to £600.[8]

It is seldom recognized that much of colonial socioeconomic change was mediated by traditional relationships. Such traditional economic relations as chiefs' customary rights to tribute and labor were carried forward as social and economic modernization proceeded. During the early period of colonial rule in Africa, such customary rights were not merely left undisturbed by colonial government but were often embodied in colonial laws.

The maintenance of these customary rights under colonial modernization necessarily gave chiefs an initial advantage over other segments of the population. Under the money or exchange economy, chiefs' customary rights to tribute and labor were readily convertible from a status of wealth in kind to modern forms of wealth—money and capital. Thus, having accommodated to colonial rule, it was of no surprise that traditional rulers were among the first groups in local African society to participate in the market economy through cash-crop production and marketing. Three years after the promulgation of the Protectorate and a year after

7. *Native Administration Estimates, 1959–1960, Kano Province* (Kaduna, 1960), pp. 60, 117; *Native Administration Estimates, 1959–1960, Sokoto Province* (Kaduna, 1960), p. 6; Lloyd, "The Changing Role of the Yoruba Traditional Rulers," pp. 60–61.

8. A. I. Richards, *East African Chiefs* (London, 1960), pp. 64–65, 92–93, 244; John Beattie, *Bunyoro: An African Kingdom* (New York, 1961), p. 43.

the Hut Tax War, the Colonial Secretary informed the British government in London that Sierra Leonean chiefs were accommodating to indirect rule and were especially "taking to trade and beginning to understand that there are other chattels besides a multiplicity of slaves and wives which conduce to material wealth and prosperity . . ." [9]

Chiefs employed several methods in converting their customary rights into modern economic gain. First, they marketed the sizable stores of agricultural products secured as tribute from peasants; second, they expanded their own cash-crop output with the aid of free labor; third, they utilized traditional authority to establish and protect markets for themselves; and fourth, they manipulated their role in the traditional land-tenure system to expand their own cash-crop holdings and especially to claim rents or royalties from expatriate mining firms in return for mining concessions backed by the colonial government. Unfortunately, there is not sufficient evidence to document fully the scale of the chiefs' penetration of the money economy by these methods. Undoubtedly, however, this penetration was considerable. The reports of the inquiry into the 1955–1956 peasant disturbances show one paramount chief, for example, who claimed £375 per annum from the sale of surplus rice. Another claimed £400 from the sale of similar products; one established a mineral water factory and transport firm in addition to the sale of surplus products; and another chief, whose total chiefdom income was nearly £4,000, gained £1,666 per annum from rent paid by an expatriate iron-mining concern. [10] When set against the income of thirty shillings per head or £4.10s. per adult male claimed by the average farmer, these chiefly emoluments certainly placed chiefs in a very high income bracket. [11]

9. *Sierra Leone Report for 1899*, Cmd. 354 (London, 1900), p. 45.

10. *Reports of the Commissioners of Enquiry into the Conduct of Certain Chiefs*, pp. 38–39, 51, 68; Cox, *Sierra Leone Report of Commission of Inquiry into Disturbances in the Provinces*, pp. 153, 160, 161 n. 2.

11. J. T. Jack, *Economic Survey of Sierra Leone*, p. 6.

Some chiefs' incomes equaled and even surpassed those of the more modernized African income groups such as merchants, businessmen, lawyers, and doctors.

The participation of chiefs in the colonial economic system has made it exceedingly difficult to categorize them simply as a "traditional elite." In reality they are both traditional and modern authorities. This situation has both weakened and strengthened their authority and power, depending upon the particular combination of modern circumstances confronted by chiefs at any given point in time.

As regards their authority, chiefs had superficially the best of both worlds: they freely invoked either traditional or modern justifications as circumstances required. In reality, however, this double standard was not easy to uphold unless the peasant masses remained unqualifiedly attached to traditional authority. The fact of the matter was that the same forces of change that made chiefs what may be called a traditiomodern elite equally influenced the peasantry and undercut or questioned allegiance to traditional authority. As we have shown, some peasants considered the chiefs' role in the modern economy an unfair competitive advantage and refused, often in violent ways, to accept it.

As regards their power—i.e., the physical means enabling chiefs to command or influence people—there is little doubt that traditional rulers have become essentially modern. Most if not all of their traditional sources of power (e.g., slavery, war making, economic preemption) were either destroyed or regulated by the colonial state. What remained of these (e.g., customary rights of tribute, labor, land rights) was so closely articulated to the colonial processes of social and economic change that they can scarcely be called "traditional."

The political implications of this situation are, I think, crucial for understanding the role of traditional rulers in African political change. The traditional rulers may be expected to support that political arrangement which will enable them *1*) to maximize modern sources of their power and *2*) simultaneously maintain as much as possible of traditional authority. Under colonial rule this political arrangement prevailed in its purest form: *ergo,* the accommodation by chiefs to the colonial system. Similarly, in the period of nationalist political change one can expect to find the traditional rulers shifting, especially as the central political power shifts, slowly but definitely away from accommodation to colonial rule toward a shrewd selection of political alliances among competing nationalist groups. Again, this shift will be governed by the chiefs' calculation of which nationalist group will best enable them to maximize modern sources of power and simultaneously retain much of their traditional authority.

Another factor that enabled traditional rulers to pursue the political strategy sketched here is that, though traditional values were shaken by social change, their hold on the rural masses did not dwindle completely. Despite the important occasions of peasant rebellion against certain uses of traditional authority in the context of modernization, the masses displayed the ambivalence toward chiefs and traditional authority that we have already noted. Thus there is still a real sense in which chiefs continue as the sole legitimate representatives of traditional values (especially as they relate to personal or group allegiances to authority) in the eyes of most people. In the context of modern political change this was a fact of considerable significance. The nationalistic new elite, in its attempt to secure mass political support beyond the urban centers of its own origin, normally accommodated its political organization, methods, and policies to the strategic position held by chiefs in local society. Such was particularly the case for the Sierra Leone People's Party, the dominant party in the rise of postwar nationalism in Sierra Leone.

French Colonialism and Transformation
of Traditional Elites: Case of Upper Volta

ELLIOTT P. SKINNER *

In an effort to undermine the power of the Mossi chiefs, change the traditional Mossi administration, and incorporate the Mossi territories into the colonial complex, the French attempted to weaken the structure of the Mossi political organization. They tried at first to apply their policy of *assimilation,* which was characterized by direct rule and by "giving the colonies institutions analogous to those of metropolitan France, [which] little by little removes the distances that separate the diverse parts of French territory and finally realizes their intimate union through the application of common legislation." [1]

The French attitude toward the Mossi political organization and its chiefs is clearly defined in the instructions Commander Destenave gave to Captain Scal for the administration of a territory that had not yet been brought completely under French control. Destenave writes:

> We have no interest in strengthening the power that is regarded as central, nor in increasing the power of the various Nabas; on the contrary, we must look for points of stress which will permit us to divide the country, and thus preclude any coalitions against us . . . In so doing, the authority of

* From Elliott P. Skinner, *The Mossi of Upper Volta* (Stanford, 1964).

1. Arnaud and Meray, pp. 1–32. See also Roberts, I, 89–102.

the Mogho Naba itself will be weakened, because we can easily acknowledge the independence of these great [princes] and free them from his influence. This is an excellent measure from a political standpoint; for we must not lose sight of the fact that we have no interest in strengthening the power of the central authority. On the contrary, we must encourage as much as possible the tendency of the great chiefs (vassals) to break the last bonds that still attach them to Ouagadougou. This is the course which has been followed by the Resident Officer. It has produced excellent results, and the requested taxes have come in regularly. In future, we should seize every opportunity to weaken the authority of these vassals by declaring the independence of the villages under their command. Just recently, the chiefs of Coundiri and Tema were removed from under the command of the Yako chief, and are now under the direct command of the Resident.[2]

At first the Mossi resisted all changes in their political organization and all demands for foodstuffs, information about their territories, and laborers.[3] In desperation, the French sought help from those very chiefs whose power they wished to curb, especially from the Mogho Naba of Ouagadougou, whom they regarded as the supreme ruler of the Mossi. However, they met with the same resistance:

> The king of the Mossi, Kouka Naba [Mogho Naba Sighiri], is lavish with vows of devotion and fidelity, but these vows are never translated into action. It is impossible to obtain from him any pertinent information about the country—he tries to give the impression that he knows nothing about it—or any information about Boukary Koutou [then in exile, but still a threat to the French], of whom he pretends to have no news.[4]

One cannot tell whether the Mogho Naba knew about Boukary Koutou's activities, but it is highly unlikely that he could have given the French much information about the country even if he had wished to do so. No Mogho Naba ever possessed this kind of information. The Dimdamba and the Kombemba paid allegiance and tribute to their superior

---

2. IFAN.
3. Archives, Doc. 15G-190 (1877–78).
4. Ibid.

ruler, but did not furnish him with specific data on their principalities and districts.

The death of Mogho Naba Sighiri in 1905 enabled the French officials to secure the election of a Mogho Naba they could control and to change the Mossi political organization. Sighiri's principal heir was his sixteen-year-old son, Saidou Congo, who in the opinion of the Mossi electoral college "could not keep the country" because of his youth. The French, keenly aware that they could more easily control a young ruler, insisted that Saidou be given the name, and he became Mogho Naba Kom. Two years later, in 1907, the French began to reorganize the kingdom of Ouagadougou and the surrounding territories. They suppressed certain districts and principalities, enlarged some, and unified others by granting them control over the smaller political entities that lay near or within their boundaries. These changes were often made without regard for the traditional hierarchies, and many district chiefs found themselves controlling other district chiefs, while Dimdamba were reduced to the level of district chiefs.

The French also reorganized the provincial administration, replacing the five ministers with persons more favorably disposed toward their rule. The Larhalle Naba was replaced in 1908 after he had mysteriously left the capital for Koudougou. The Kamsaogho Naba was deposed by the Mogho Naba, and was replaced by a nominee of the French. As in the case of the district chiefs, the French shifted the territorial responsibilities of these ministers "without taking into consideration the hierarchy prevailing among [them]. The intention of the administration apparently was to reward certain young and capable ministers to the detriment of those who were old." [5] One commentator concludes: "In view of the youth of the reigning king, Naba Kom, and also owing to certain difficulties, the administration was compelled to grant more authority to the five great ministers

---

5. *Bull. d'information et de Renseignements Coloniaux* (hereinafter cited as *Rens. Coloniaux*), XLVIII (Aug. 25, 1938), 307.

and to make them true provincial chiefs with whom it could deal and who would govern their territories directly." [6]

Some of the demoted chiefs and their followers opposed these changes. In 1910, they refused to pay taxes and fought the police. However, they were forced to accept the changes when the police burned their villages, seized their goods and animals to pay the taxes, and deposed unco-operative chiefs. These harsh measures so shocked the Mossi that they remained docile from that time onward, and thereafter the French were able to rule a country with one European administrator for every 60,000 Mossi.[7]

The implementation of full colonial rule among the Mossi was to have a profound effect on their traditional political organization and on the relationship between the people and their chiefs. One of the principal contributing factors was the demand of the French administration that Mossi country not only share in the over-all development of French West Africa, but pay for its own administration as well. The resources of Mossi country were largely limited to agricultural production and stock raising, however, and revenue from these activities was slight. The full weight of administrative expenses thus fell on the Mossi people. Apparently, the first taxation was of a collective nature, for according to the official government report for June 1899, "No regular tax has been levied, but taxes have been collected from the Mogho Naba and the other chiefs." [8]

Decrees of July and November, 1903, authorized "native chiefs to collect taxes, and granted them a commission on the tax yield to arouse their interest in the regular payment of taxes." [9] Accustomed as they were to giving taxes (gifts) to their rulers with the knowledge that subordinate chiefs

---

6. Ibid.

7. De Beauminy, "Une Féodalité," p. 24. During this period and for many years afterward, the neighboring acephalous Lobi and Gurunsi groups refused to pay taxes (*L'Afrique Française* [Feb.-Mar. 1910], pp. 77, 341).

8. Mahaut, pp. 20–27.

9. Mahaut, p. 31.

would extract a share before sending the remainder up the hierarchy, the Mossi were not averse to paying taxes through their traditional rulers to the "new chiefs," the French administration. However, when taxes grew to excessive proportions and chiefs continued to get a percentage, the people accused their rulers of cheating them. The reasons for the Mossi complaints about taxation are described by Tauxier, himself an administrator:

> This tax, light at first, has grown rapidly over the last few years. In 1906 it was 311,000 francs for the territory of Ouagadougou, which had a population of 861,000 inhabitants. In 1907, the tax was raised to 360,000 francs; in 1909, to 555,000 francs; and in 1910, to 656,000 francs. Furthermore, from 1908 onward this tax was exacted with such rigor and on such short notice that it was exactly as though the amount had been tripled. Under the circumstances, the Mossi were compelled to resort to trade in order to obtain the French money they did not have, since the local currency is the cowry and the French administration does not wish to receive it . . . To meet this difficult situation the Mossi now organize small caravans in the villages, and send the young men to Wanke to sell cattle, sheep, goats, asses, horses, and bolts of cotton. They bring back with them either French money or kola nuts.[10]

If a man refused to pay his taxes, the Mossi chief was permitted to sequester his goods and sell them. If the man had neither the taxes nor the goods, the chief had to send him and his wife (or wives) to the administrative post to be punished. Sometimes, a man and his wife would be made to look at the sun from sunrise to sunset while intoning the prayer *Ouennam co mam ligidi* ("God, give me money"). Other times, a man would be made to run around the administrative post with his wife on his back; if he had several wives, he had to take each one in turn. Then his wife or wives had to carry him around.

A further source of difficulty for the Mossi chiefs, and one which became more serious as time went by, was that

---

10. Tauxier, *Le Noir du Soudan*, p. 538.

they were charged by the administration to recruit men for both labor and military service. Initially, the chiefs had to supply men to transport grain for the French-organized agricultural societies from one region to another; later, they were commanded to supply labor for private and public works.

The manner in which the Mossi chiefs administered their territories before the First World War was conditioned by the colonial administrators even when it was not directly controlled by them. The Mogho Naba had gradually lost most of his power, and he had no authority to act without the specific authorization of the French. He retained most of his ceremonial activities, especially since they were considered interesting "feudal" anachronisms to be shown to visiting officials and travelers. He also retained the power to appoint district chiefs, but the French often vetoed men they disliked and suggested that other candidates be elected. He also lost all control over his provincial administrators. The administrative chain now extended from the *cercle* commanders, through the provincial ministers and district chiefs, down to the village chiefs. Many provincial ministers, out of loyalty to the traditional system, occasionally briefed the Mogho Naba on the policies the French had ordered them to carry out, and told him about the state of affairs in the districts. This was completely unofficial if not illegal, but it made little difference to the French.

At the end of World War I, the French administration tried to establish a new policy toward the Mossi chiefs, but new economic programs that were implemented at the same time rendered these plans ineffective and further undermined the old institutions. A new Governor-General of French West Africa, Joost Van Vollenhoven, strongly influenced by one of his predecessors, Merleau-Ponty, and by the policy of *association* between France and her colonies (a policy based on the idea that colonial policy should be determined by the geographic and ethnic characteristics and the level of social development of the regions involved), advocated respect for the chiefs and for strong traditional political systems. Van Vollenhoven stipulated that the chiefs should not be harried by administrators, subjected to corporal punishment, or legally prosecuted without the sanction of higher officials (*cercle* commanders and lieutenant-governors). They should be granted higher salaries and help for agricultural labor, and should be shown techniques for improving their material well-being. They should also be decorated more often with the Legion of Honor, in order to heighten their prestige and to demonstrate "French generosity." Their relatives should be educated, given prestige and remuneration, and permitted to retain some status.[11]

Although the Mossi chiefs had little autonomy in the administration of their subjects, and had to look to the administration for guidance in nearly everything they did, they were not completely powerless. They were the representatives of the colonial administration on the local level, and as such they could control their subjects through the differential allocation of prestations. Those Mossi who had maintained the traditional respect for the chiefs could look forward to less arduous tasks for the administration and to the avoidance of forced labor or army recruitment. Those who by their actions or attitude indicated that they had lost respect for the chiefs were penalized accordingly. Chiefs were also able to retain some control over their subjects because they were still the centers of social, economic, and political relations within their territories. They still received homage and presents from their more loyal or traditionalistic subjects, and with these goods and services they could bind other persons to themselves. Clever chiefs were able to manipulate the colonial administration and use it to enhance their traditional position so successfully that the administration and the missionaries had to take these men into account whenever they wished to establish contact with the population.

---

11. *L'Afrique Française,* XIX (1909, 348–49; see also Van Vollenhoven, pp. 187 ff.

PART III

Emergence of the Masses

Patterns of Mass Transformation

The masses or popular strata, the overwhelming majority, in African societies in the colonial era may be classified along a number of indices, including education, income, occupation, rural-urban habitation, style of life, culture preference (i.e., traditional or modern), and so on. During most of the colonial period, those Africans described as masses or popular strata ranked low in such stratification indices as education, income, occupation (i.e., were in manual and menial jobs requiring little or no education), resided in rural areas (or if in towns or cities were slum-dwellers), and displayed traditional cultural preferences in regard to interpersonal relations, marriage patterns, food, clothing, recreation, and religion.[1]

Yet there was differentiation within the popular strata: the majority ranked at the bottom of the stratification indices, claiming no Western education, peripheral occupation in the modern cash economy (entering it as petty trader or small-scale cash-crop farmer in order to gain income for a few consumer goods or to pay taxes to native authorities, etc.), and no sustained contact with Christian missions: a few, however, ranked high in the stratification indices, compared to the vast majority among

1. See Paul Bohannan, *Africa and Africans* (New York, 1964).

the masses, possessing several years of Western schooling and thus semiliteracy, quasi-regular employment (characterized by high job mobility or turnover, which often meant high geographical mobility between town and country), diverse contact with Christian churches (as between Protestant sects, Protestant and Catholic churches, and African variants of Christian churches), and a variegated, though qualitatively low, cultural mobility (as between traditional and modern culture). Though these more advantaged segments among the popular strata hardly compared to the new elites in modern attributes (who usually claimed secondary-school and college education, stable and well-paid occupation in the liberal professions, administration, and business, and stable relations with the Christian church), they stood out among the majority of the masses, among whom their basic and most affective interpersonal relations persisted, unlike the new elites.

It was, then, the special position of this more advantaged segment of the masses (who may be called a subsidiary modern elite) which afforded it a crucial role in the organizational transformation of the masses under colonial rule. The selections in Part III illustrate the social and political activities or movements through which the masses were transformed (i.e., turned in a modern or quasi-modern direction) under colonial rule and in which the subsidiary modern elites were prominent.

In some instances the form of popular transformation was not very articulate in terms of modern ideas or organization. This was clearly so in regard to peasant riots and disturbances, as illustrated in my own selection on the comparative features of peasant risings in colonial Africa. These outbursts were normally limited to ad hoc issues like tax abuses by chiefs, pelf among the staff of Native Administrations, and oppressive labor exactions by chiefs and colonial officials. The outbursts seldom resulted in a more sustained form of political or social organization: indeed, once frustration and grievance were vented through riot, the peasants returned to normal relationships with the offending chiefs. This was so because peasants were at the bottom of the modern stratification ladder, claiming no education, only peripheral contact with the modern colonial economy, and displaying largely traditional interpersonal relations.

Yet there was an element of the modern implied in peasant risings: the issues sparking riots emanated from the modern governmental functions of chiefs within local administration such as taxation, labor for modern public works, etc., and there is ample evidence that the more articulate individuals among rioting peasants understood this modern dimension of peasants' relations with colonial society. Furthermore, the persons who provided some measure of leadership in peasant risings were often members of the group we have called a subsidary modern elite: they were semiliterate and, though residing in rural areas, had more contact than other rural-dwellers with occupations in the cash economy (e.g., as small traders, miners, laborers on cocoa or cotton plantations, catechists in Christian mission, messengers, etc.). Consequently, to the degree some peasant risings were organized, members of the subsidiary modern elite in rural areas were responsible, though the organization assumed mainly traditional forms.[2]

The selections in Part III from H. Debrunner on anti-witchcraft cults in colonial Ghana, from Professor Weinstein on a revivalist cult in Gabon, and from Professor Rotberg on an African separatist church in Northern Rhodesia (now Zambia) all involve movements which have syncretistic organizational features, blending modern and traditional forms and values. Invariably, semiliterate persons among the popular strata head these forms of religious organizational transformation of the masses in colonial Africa. The quality of popular institutional change they effect is seldom substantial, though not insignificant. The leaders of anti-witchcraft cults in Ghana in the 1930's and

---

2. This issue is treated in some detail in Martin Kilson, *Chiefs, Peasants and Politicians: Grassroots Politics in Ghana 1900–1960's* (Forthcoming).

1940's occasionally built a church edifice, gave a quasi-modern organizational form to a small group of semiliterate aides, and sometimes initiated auxiliary modern functions like a primary school, a health dispensary, and a welfare agency. Their followers, especially those whose frustrations and pains have origins in contact with the modern sector of colonial society, often derived from neotraditional religious organizations a sense of sufficiency and security in dealing with modern change.[3] In the postwar period of decolonization and nationalist parties, many of these followers proved adept enough in modern activities to become local organizers of nationalist political parties. Indeed, few African nationalist parties, in their early stages, missed the opportunity to build popular support through neotraditional religious organizations like the Lenshina Movement in Zambia.[4]

The selection from Dame Margery Perham on the market women's riot in a town in eastern Nigeria in 1929 illustrates still another form of popular transformation. Riots were not restricted to rural peasants in the colonial era; but rather occurred in marketing and mining towns and in the capital cities. These riots involved mainly wage-workers, market women, and lower-level clerks.[5] Dame Perham's account of the market women's riot at Aba puts into relief most of the issues underlying riots and disturbances among these towndwelling segments of the masses in colonial Africa. Unlike most peasant riots, the riots of towndwellers were more modern in organization—based on a functionally specific structure like a trade union, a market association, or some other voluntary association—were focused directly and functionally on some colonial or

3. Cf. F. W. Welbourne and B. Ogot, *A Place to Feel at Home* (London, 1967).

4. The Convention People's Party in Ghana made use of such organizations. See, e.g., Dennis Austin, *Politics in Ghana 1946–1960* (London, 1964).

5. For an example of a riot among workers, see Martin Kilson, *Political Change in a West African State* (Cambridge, Mass., 1966).

modern institution (e.g., industry, government departments, an official, a licensing procedure, prices, wages, etc.) and, in consequence, had reasonably well articulated goals.

The selection by Professor Epstein on the politics in a colonial mining town in Zambia reveals the complex and sophisticated interplay of forces that underlay popular transformation among towndwellers. Different segments within the masses interact more sharply around modern change in towns than in rural areas. Invariably, modern conditions govern the forms of popular transformation in towns and cities of colonial and postcolonial Africa, and traditional groups like the town-based chiefs or elders in Zambia's mining towns can retain influence only insofar as they master modern conditions. This is certainly true in the long run, though in the short run the ascriptive authority accruing to traditional groups like chiefs and ritual leaders, combined with the tendency of popular elements to fall back atavistically on primordial norms and relations (e.g., tribal ties) in times of conflict or crisis, afford traditional groups a special leverage in modern African politics.

M.K.

Modern Anti-Witchcraft Movements in Ghana, 1900–1940's

H. DEBRUNNER *

The movement began after the middle of the last century, almost simultaneously with the intensification of government interference with native customs. The first anti-witchcraft activity on any considerable scale that I could trace in old records, was that of an "anti-witch exorcist" called in by an association of Ga, Efutu, and Agona towns, *ca.* 1855. This was done on the advice of the priests of the traditional tutelar spirits. This witch-hunter's success at Agona-Swedru, and his failure at Obutu owing to the influence of Christianity, have been well described by Rev. Bohner.[1]

His ordeal for tracking down witches consisted of applying a black powder which was supposed to make the witches sneeze, but be harmless to the innocent ones. Bohner maintains that he was an impostor, and used black pepper when he wanted to find somebody guilty on the secret advice of the local pagan priests. The witches he hunted out being in the main unpopular rich men.

A second impostor, a woman, worked with a tobacco-ordeal at Dodowa in 1889. She made a strong concoction from American tobacco to be taken in rum. This draught was said to kill the witches and to purify the others "from

* From H. Debrunner, *Witchcraft in Ghana* (Accra, 1956).
1. Bohner, *Im Lande des Fetisch,* pp. 214–218.

all evil thoughts dwelling in the heart of man—especially those thoughts suggesting poisoning to the mind." [2]

These were the relatively insignificant predecessors of far greater movements which set in after 1900. British government control became more strict, and spread over Ashanti bringing durable peace, and at the same time came educational, economic, religious, and moral revolution in full. Since that time, the countertide and reaction of the anti-witchcraft shrines has never ceased completely. It comes in waves—sometimes strong—sometimes weak. The names of the shrines often changed, but basically they remained the same phenomenon.

The more important of these shrines are the following (I try to give the historical sequence): Aberewa, Hwe me so, Anhwere (usually called Kwasi Badu's medicine), Kune (or Brakune), Kupo (or Senyakupo), Tongo, Kankamea, Tigare. Then the Wenchi group of Kwasi Kukuro and Diamono, Kwaku Firi and Mframa. The list could be augmented by the names of many smaller ones.

Some of these shrines have been suppressed in the past by the government while others still linger on, though they have long lost their original force. Some are at present declining rapidly; others still have some influence.

Roughly speaking, there have been three main crests in the waves of anti-witchcraft shrines: before 1912, between 1924 and the economic crisis, and in and after World War II. At each of these times the influx of foreign ideas was particularly strong and the country had something of an economic boom.

Most of the new shrines dealing in witchcraft are offshoots of those in northern Ghana. The further people had to travel in order to get to them the more highly were they esteemed. Barakune and Kankamea came from the Dagati. Tongo is at home in the Tong hills near Zuarungu, Kupo at Senyon near Bole (hence Senyakupo), Aberewa comes from the region of Boundoukou,[3] Tigare from Ypala near

---

2. Steiner, *In: Globus*, 1894, pp. 297 ff.
3. Tauxier, *Le noir de Boundoukou*, p. 407.

Wa, Asasi from the Ivory Coast, etc. In their original homes some of these shrines were of the ordinary protective type, without specializing in witchcraft. But since they were the shrines of far-off vigorous tribes not yet under the mental stress and conflicts arising from the culture contact in the south, they attracted the attention of the southerners who came here to get help from their troubles.

Captain Rattray has described how people from the south came up to the shrine of the Ton-nab or Tongo (often with private cars!) with their petitions for children and profit, for protection against witches and rivals, and for prevention from getting into debt.[4]

The shrine of Kankamea is at Birifu in the northwestern corner of Ghana. It is in the charge of the influential Birifu chief, who showed me most of it himself. He has an extraordinarily big compound with a comfortable apartment at the top of it, and a private car. The arrangement of the actual shrine of Kankamea is much the same as that at Kwapera near Kumasi. The Birifu Na told me that he has two hundred various shrines in his compound. He said that his father had obtained Kankamea, his most important shrine, from a Namdam man who had got it at Zinguna in the neighboring French colony. (The set-up of the shrine is that of a Lobi temple.) The name "Kunkumbea" he explained as "I cannot live with evil men." Kankamea is principally a witch-hunter, and gives promotion to people and fertility to women. Annually, when the great rains begin, there is a big festival at Birifu which is attended by many devotees from the south. Other shrines kept at Birifu are Lompo (who protects farms, by making the thieves suffer from rheumatic pains in the neck), Nwene (a rain fetish connected with lightning, since lightning is only supposed to affect evil persons), Kodwoku (the children's doctor who kills persons daring to attack children under his protection), Wio (a hunting shrine), Bamba, and many

---

4. Rattray, *Tribes of Ashanti Hinterland*, Oxford, 1932, Vol. II, pp. 361–5.

others. The house of the Birifu Na looks like a medieval fortress and is situated on a lovely scarp. The Birifu Na also plays a certain role in politics, and acted for some time as a recognized government dispenser. He attended the coronation of Queen Elizabeth in London.

Not everyone was able to visit northern Ghana, and therefore the tendency arose to set up shrines of these tutelar spirits in the south as well, in order to have "a child" of Tongo or Kupo in one's own town for constant consultation. Individuals and even whole towns began to "pull out something" from these shrines in the north, and to set them up in their homes.

A student wrote about his home town A. in Kwahu, where gold dust had been found in the remote past. The town had been founded by an old man, and its "river" was revered as the town's tutelar spirit, who helped the inhabitants to obtain gold. Black hens were sacrificed at the obosom's shrine and festivals held for him. People "became as rich and prosperous as the car-king Henry Ford." The readily accessible gold soon began to diminish however, and the astonished people realized that their gold industry was declining. As they attributed it to witchcraft, the chief went to buy a fetish from northern Ghana to assist their local tutelar spirit to drive away or ruin the witches. Not long afterward, an additional shrine was procured, because there is a saying that unity is strength. So in this Kwahu town, it was the economic difficulty over gold which created the need for an anti-witchcraft shrine.

In another instance it was cocoa and disease. I once visited a place, A., in the Ahafo district in western Ashanti. It lies right in the bush fifteen miles from the nearest lorry road, but civilization has already penetrated. There are cocoa farms, and concrete houses roofed with iron sheets, even though each bag of cement had to be head loaded the whole fifteen miles at a cost of ten shillings per bag. There is even a little Roman Catholic school there. This tiny place has three shrines: one for the tutelar spirit brought by the founder of the town, the second for Tano, the famous tutelar spirit of the Ashanti nation, and the third an anti-witch-craft shrine, brought from the Dagati about ten years ago. It was no small matter to set up this new shrine. It cost the elders a considerable amount of money, and two months to acquire. But the chief told me that he was badly in need of the shrine, since cocoa had brought strangers, unrest, and diseases into town; many young men and children had died, so they had just had to fetch a new tutelar spirit to help the old ones to look after the town.

We now come to the question of whether the new anti-witchcraft shrines have really provided a satisfactory answer to the new needs. They have most certainly enjoyed a con-siderable measure of success. People from all classes have been attracted by them, thousands have joined their cults, neurotics have found relief there, and many have even be-come mentally readapted to the spiritual strains of contem-porary society.

Mr. William Ofori Atta (in an article in the *Ashanti Pioneer*, Friday, June 13, 1947, quoted by Mr. Akesson) describing the good sides of the Tigare cult said:

> With the present rate of progress of true missionary activity and of the spread of education (especially scientific educa-tion), and with the present ineffectualness of the old sanctions of our society and the low standards of ability to detect crime and criminals, there is not the least doubt that Tigare has done good to the Gold Coast. As a result of the last war, both civilians and soldiers made certain contacts which tended to demoralize most of them. The present condition of em-ployment in a society of rapidly rising prices, and especially among classes of people who received tolerable incomes in legitimate and illegitimate markets during the war, has en-hanced the tendency towards demoralization. We have, how-ever, been saved greatly by the fear of evil visitation, which the members of the Tigare cult believe will inevitably follow the breach of the code of the morals of Tigare. This fear has been one of the most effective deterrents with the class of demoralized people above.

Bwiti Revival Movement
in Gabon in 1930's

BRIAN WEINSTEIN *

At the same time that movements to restore something from the past were important, some people looked to new systems through religion and the state, in the running of which they were allowed but a very small part. The two religious movements were *Bwiti* and the Great Revival.

Something called *Bwiti* had originally been practiced among the Mitsogo and Bapindji people in the southern part of the country. Slaves who had been brought to the coast danced the *Bwiti*, so that the noninitiated, including Fang who had been sent to the south as traders for French-owned companies, saw it.[1] The Fang changed *Bwiti* to fit their own needs, and it is now a syncretistic religion which combines some aspects of traditional Fang religion with Roman Catholicism. It is considered a way to come to terms with the older religion and the power of newer European religions.

Members of the church believe they are protected from witchcraft and that they have values to live by; ancestors are regarded as once again efficacious forces on earth which will strike down anyone in the religion who might practice witchcraft. A non-Fang Gabonese claimed *Bwiti* gave great

* From Brian Weinstein, *Gabon: Nation-building on the Ogooué* (Cambridge, 1966).

1. In villages near Lambaréné, where Fang live near Mitsogo, they dance the Mitsogo *Bwiti* together.

power to its adherents. He claimed when he wrote about the alleged *Bwiti* bible that it would be the beginning of the assertion of the black race: "Three Magi Kings came to the cradle of the white Christ: a yellow man, a white man, a black man. The Yellow has spoken and is silent, the White is speaking now, the Black has not yet said anything. Is he mute? I should like these pages to be the first words of his response." [2]

A syncretist religion, *Bwiti* was considered by missionaries as a threat to the integrity of the Western religion from which it had drawn many of its elements. Even the clothes of the members clearly recall the robes of priests. The missionaries noted its appearance in Woleu-Ntem in 1945 and wrote what they did about it: "*Bwiti* is spreading more and more in this region—of Asucbere; it has won over Nkein, then Aderayo, and finally Elelem . . . I have had their hut at Aderayo destroyed, also that of Nkein, but once I leave they build it again and even more beautifully than before." [3]

The administration sent troops to raid and destroy the chapels because people reported that *Bwiti* adherents were engaging in ritual murder and cannibalism. Chapels were sought out deep in the forest and burned to the ground. In recent years the administration, French and Gabonese, has more or less permitted the practice of the religion, although some of the Fang leaders in Woleu-Ntem and all missionaries preach against it. People in Libreville related that at one time the Bwitists marched to the Roman Catholic church to take part in a Mass or to conduct their own service there; they reportedly claimed that it was their church just as much as it was that of the Roman Catholics. As a way for the Fang to reorganize, *Bwiti* has been a failure because of pressures from the Whites and Blacks who were nonad-

2. Prince Birinda, *La Bible secrète des Noirs selon le Bouity* (Paris: Omnium Littéraire, 1952), p. 125.

3. "Tournées," Catholic Mission of Oyen, entry April 13–23, 1945.

herents and because it was not really efficacious; only about 8 per cent of the Fang belong today.[4]

To seek a new order and to protect themselves against witchcraft, the Fang turned to a Christian religious movement introduced by a European. This was the Great Revival which started about 1935, after it had already become an important movement in Europe and America.

Pastor Vernaud who, like many French-speaking Protestant missionaries, is Swiss, began his work in Gabon in 1930. During a vacation in Europe in 1934 he was, according to his own testimony, "possessed with the Holy Ghost." [5] In 1935, he returned to Gabon and preached the Revival, about possession by the Holy Spirit; his prayers were answered and the Revival took place among the Fang and among the non-Fang south of the Ogooué as well. It spread fantastically, particularly in Woleu-Ntem; people rushed to the Protestant and Roman Catholic churches; people said they had a thirst: "I had thirst, thirst for prayer, thirst for—God." At Lastoursville in the south there had been no mission because an early missionary had been mistreated by the Badouma. These same Badouma in 1936 begged the Roman Catholics to set up a church and to send a priest. The missionary who went to them, Father Hee, reported that prayers were said everywhere, chapels were built before he asked for them to be built, people brought him their "fetishes": "We don't need them." Along the river, the priest collected 2,141 people who said they wanted to become Christians. "In one grandiose ceremony we baptised 504 people together." [6]

----

4. J. W. Fernandez, *Redistributive Aculturation and Ritual Reintegration in Fang Culture* (Ph.D. Thesis, Northwestern University, 1963.)

5. Pastor Vernaud was kind enough to tell me the history of the Revival during an interview in Paris; the details of it are also found in a brochure written by him, "Le Plein Evangile au Gabon" (Peseux, 1957).

6. R. P. Hee, "Les Adouma du Gabon" in *Les Missions Catholiques,* No. 3.299 and No. 3.300, n.d.

Although Hee did not appear to understand the Revival, Protestant pastors knew very well what was going on, for there had been revivals in Europe and there was a church, the Pentecostal Church, which preached possession by the Holy Ghost. A pastor who was in Woleu-Ntem at the time told me the following: Easter 1936 in one mission of Woleu-Ntem there were 5,000 Fang who had come for the service; most stood outside the church as there was not enough room. A loudspeaker was set up. During the morning service the pastor saw about eighty people faint or go into a trance, and everyone visibly trembled: *"L'Esprit va venir."*

The Fang brought this pastor all their *bieri* which had not been taken from them previously; they were not asked to do so but said that they needed them no longer. They were saved, protected, they were possessed by the Holy Ghost. Possession by the Holy Ghost was regarded as protection against witchcraft and was regarded as a source of power. People asked the pastor: "Can a black receive the power of the Holy Ghost as well as a white?" During another Sunday service he requested an African pastor to preach and he, the missionary, sat in the rear of the church near the door. The door was open, the sun beat down outside; suddenly, the pastor reported, a crab crawled into the church. The European pastor saw it and placed it outside. Later, a woman was seized with the Spirit and went into a trance; she rose from her place, stumbled out of the church, fell to the ground. Relatives followed to help her; when they lifted her up they saw the crab on which she had apparently fallen. They shouted, people ran from the church: *"Evus, evus, evus!!* She has been saved!" They believed, the pastor says, that once she was possessed with the Holy Ghost, *evus* was expelled from her body and took the form of a crab. They believed that they would be protected from witchcraft by the Holy Spirit. After that, people came to the church regularly. They confessed that they had in the past stolen things, that they had cheated, and they sought absolution through and protection of the spirit. More recently the pastor of one Pentecostal church reported that a Fang who had just joined the church claimed that in so doing he had been relieved of an *evus* that was causing a pain in his chest.

In the course of my sojourn in Gabon, I sought out people who had been affected by the Revival, particularly the Africans who said they had received the Spirit. (There were Europeans who had received it as well.) In a Fang village, I talked with an African who took part in the Revival; he said that it was the custom during that time to pray during the day, any day. "We had the thirst." He was a student in a small trade school and one morning everyone wanted to pray, "We had the thirst." They all prayed, and suddenly everyone was seized by the Holy Ghost, including the white teacher who knelt with his students: "Hallelujah." They sang "Hallelujah" and they prayed together, "We had the thirst."

"I felt freed, I was freed. We felt light and we flew. Hallelujah. I was reborn. I confessed my sins; I had been evil and sinful, but no more. We prayed. We had the thirst."

People were also cured miraculously. Even those who did not belong to the movement say they saw miraculous cures; this is one of the things that disturbed the Protestant church. Church officials did not want what was going on to continue; it was a mass movement that was getting out of any kind of control in a colony, and supernatural things like miracles were happening. The administration was also concerned, for they saw a relationship between this movement and kimbanguism in the Congo—a movement which was anticolonialist as well as religious. At the end of 1936, church headquarters in Paris sent two of its high officials to preach against the Revival; they told the eager people crowded into Protestant churches that it was all a fake, that they were confused, that there was no miracle, that the Holy Ghost could not seize them and could not protect them. That was the end.

The pastor who started it all has continued his work, however, and has formed a Pentecostal Church in Gabon; it is most active among the Fang, although it is very small. The headquarters is at Medouneu in Woleu-Ntem; there are branch churches elsewhere: one among the Omyènè south of Lambaréné, one in Libreville with a Fang pastor, one at Booué among the Fang, also with a Fang pastor, and one near Makokou. The latter has an Omyènè pastor.

Neither syncretistic religion nor a Christian Pentecostal movement, as combinations of the old and the new or as rejection of the old for something new, was successful, although each of these attempts still has its adherents. Those who were part of these movements but who are so no longer say they feel a certain sadness that they failed.

The Lenshina Movement
in Northern Rhodesia,
1950's–1960's

ROBERT ROTBERG *

The Lumpa Church (from the Bemba for "above" or "highest") owes its creation to Alice Lenshina Mulenga and her disciples. It is among the strongest and most active churches in Northern Rhodesia, with responsible, contributing members, a devoted clergy, and a self-regenerating sense of martyrdom. Its congregations have drawn Africans in large numbers from the ranks of orthodox mission churches, and the new church has come to pose a substantial threat to the continuation of certain mission stations.

The Lenshina movement includes, conservatively, about 85 percent of those Africans who live in the leader's home district, and large numbers of Bemba, Nyanja, and Tumbuka-speaking persons in surrounding districts. The movement's strength lies predominantly among Bemba in rural areas between the Luangwa and Luapula rivers, and in urban Copperbelt centers and Broken Hill. It may also be powerful east of the Luangwa River in the Lundazi district of Northern Rhodesia as well as in central Nyasaland. There are also congregations in Lusaka and Livingstone, in Salisbury and Bulawayo in Southern Rhodesia, and on the Rand in Johannesburg. Estimates can only be rough, but it is

* From Robert Rotberg, "The Lenshina Movement of Northern Rhodesia," *Human Relations in British Central Africa* (Manchester, 1961).

likely that 65,000 Africans offer allegiance to the Lumpa Church.[1]

The center of the Lenshina movement is the Chinsali district of Northern Rhodesia. It may be described as a remote rural area five hundred road miles from the territorial capital at Lusaka.

The Chinsali district is populated almost exclusively by Bemba. They owe traditional allegiance to Senior Chief Nkula, assisted by government administrators who reside at Chinsali boma. Chief Nkula has had very little success in curbing the Lenshina movement, a rival center of power in his own precincts.

With the growth of the Lumpa Church at Lenshina's village of Kasomo, this pattern of traditional missionary activity changed. The increasing importance of Kasomo, twelve miles by road from Lubwa and six miles from Chinsali boma, has corresponded to a downgrading in the importance of Lubwa and Ilondola. The two missions had approximately 12,000 members or catechumens before 1955, when the Lenshina movement began to develop into the Lumpa Church.

Few other religious organizations in southern Africa have matched the Lenshina movement in the speed of their growth, in the fervor of their members, or in their members' demonstrated loyalty to a religious idea. Most mission bodies must themselves build mud and wattle out-churches if they are to have worship centers in the rural areas. In contrast, Lenshina's followers build attractive churches of thatch and mud wherever a local organization exists. They are quick to defend the honor of their congregation, and to persecute those who believe otherwise. They are faithful in church attendance and generous in their contribution to the church's coffers. In short, Africans who formerly were indifferent members of other churches have become de-

---

1. Lenshina claims 100,000 followers, but this is overgenerous. Her church makes little distinction between baptized and nonbaptized members when estimating membership. No proper records are kept.

voted followers of Lenshina. Such a profound spiritual metamorphosis in a remote locality could have transpired only as a result of a startling experience. Although the Lumpa Church has moral rules and a prescribed form and content to its ritual and dogma, the core of the church, and its vitality, comes from the essential oneness of Alice Lenshina, her faith, and her vision. The central experience, so essential to any religious movement, is Lenshina's belief in her own death, rebirth, and personal confrontation with God. Her teleological and spiritual awakening dates from this experience.

Among a people with traditional reverence for persons possessed of spirits, the events recounted by Lenshina in September 1953 must have come as a clear and definite call. The Bemba responded with alacrity after 1954 to Lenshina's purported vision of the Almighty, and to the prophetic word transmitted from above. They responded the more when they learned that Lenshina had received from the Almighty that which many had believed was the exclusive province of white men and their missionaries. Despite the earnest teaching of many missionaries, it is evident that few Bemba in Chinsali district had been convinced that Christ's death had been for Africans as well as for whites. After news of the vision spread throughout the Chinsali district, they came to believe that Africans could also possess that knowledge and body of religious and material experience which had heretofore appeared to be exclusively the province of whites. The cult of Lenshina developed only gradually into a full-fledged movement. Reports of her experience spread beyond Chinsali district to the Copperbelt and other sections of Northern Rhodesia. Slowly the wonder of her rebirth and her vision was communicated, presumably by word of mouth, to Africans throughout Central Africa. They came from all over Northern Rhodesia to see her and to hear about her own transformation. During the first two years after her vision, at least, Lenshina had believers more than followers. Those who believed were not, strictly speaking, a movement, and the cult of Lenshina posed little threat to orthodox missions or to the administration. Originally Lenshina was not labeled a heretic, and she herself did little to magnify her own role or to capitalize on her unique experience.

The leaders of the Lenshina movement have made considerable financial gain from their positions in the new church. Although it is difficult to believe that Lenshina herself planned her spiritual awakening in order to obtain material reward, she has clearly taken pleasure in her improved standard of living and in her new-found sense of power and adulation. Baptisms or special projects always call forth collections in the many Lumpa churches. Pennies, shillings, and goods in kind are asked of the faithful, and they may also be expected to contribute their labor to church projects. The local preacher always retains some of the proceeds of any collection. He ships the bulk of the proceeds to Petros Mulenga, who acts as the church's treasurer. Whatever his motive, Petros has certainly capitalized on his wife's religious vision to amass wealth and to build a financially strong church.

The Lenshina movement has developed into a fanatically puritanical one. Since 1955, Lenshina's teachings and energies have been devoted primarily to the eradication of witchcraft. She has made an outstanding success of gathering charms and objects used by witches, or by others to protect themselves from witches. To her, sorcery has been the scourge of her people, and she received a ready response when she preached a holy war against witches. Witchcraft, says Lenshina, is bad because "it kills a person made by God." Witches "take the position of a lion who catches human beings." [2] During the formative years of the church (1955–1958) adherents joined the Lumpa Church after surrendering objects of divination, making a profession of faith, and being received for baptism. Today one can see piles of these objects—looking quite harmless—in Kasomo village.[3]

2. Lenshina, personal information, August 22, 1959.
3. Most of the objects are amulets, pipes, beads, and hoes.

Lenshina herself has also set the tone of the movement's other simple dogma. Polygyny is inimical because "when a man has two wives the wives quarrel because of jealousy." Polygyny also "encourages women to get medicine and witchcraft to kill other wives, which is bad in the eyes of God." Adultery results in analogous problems and furthermore is prohibited, she says, by the Bible. The daughter of a second wife in a polygynous marriage might well feel strongly about these matters, and it is equally of little surprise that Lenshina's appeal is generally greater among the less educated rural women than among urban-dwelling men.

The use of beer, or the brewing of beer, is discouraged. Lenshina herself is adamantly against the consumption of alcohol, and against drinking by any of her followers, but in practice she has been no more successful on this score than have other temperance leaders in Northern Rhodesia.

The process whereby Lenshina has gained adherents— whereby the movement has made "conversions"—is similar in nature to that of most separatist sects and also to those Protestant groups which are roughly fundamentalist and evangelical. Regeneration of the soul, an assertion of new-found faith (so often epitomized by being "born again"), and profession of rigid and unswerving loyalty are typical of such groups. To the Lumpa Church, conversion logically implies "leaving all temptation behind." [4] Salvation is by faith, and faith in turn brings about good works and the pure life. For illustrative purposes three case studies of typical members of the Lumpa Church are given below. The individuals involved joined the church after some important change in their own lives. The case studies are reported almost verbatim; the word "sister" is used allegorically.[5]

Mr. A. was 35 years old and lived 45 miles from Kasomo. He was a regular visitor at Lenshina's court. He is an ir-

4. Lenshina, personal information, August 23, 1959.
5. Mr. Katilungu recorded these conversations, and others, at Kasomo during August 1959.

regularly employed carpenter and has recently been made a priest or deacon in the Lumpa Church. He is also a former Roman Catholic. His report was straightforward and simple: "I joined the Lumpa Church because one night [in 1955] I was sleeping and dreamed [*sic*] my mother [was] telling me that my sister had been given power by God to spread His Gospel. When I woke up the following day I received a letter from home, informing me that my mother was dead. I then hurriedly came back home [from Broken Hill] to look things over. I then joined the church."

Mr. B., a former Jehovah Witness, lived six miles from Kasomo but worked regularly as a tailor in a Copperbelt town. He is now a deacon in the Lumpa Church. He returned home to see Lenshina in 1957 after another dream sequence: "I saw my mother in a dream instructing me to join my sister's church. I paid no attention to this." Later. "I dreamed that my mother was urging me to join the church that God has given to Africa through an African woman." He returned to his village in 1957 and then journeyed to see Lenshina. After meeting her he was convinced she had had a real experience; the tailor promptly was received into the church.

Mr. C. was an adherent of the Church of Scotland. He served in the Rhodesian army during and after World War II. One day he went to ask his white officer for permission to go to church on Sunday. The officer told him he "was a fool" to worship a European God. When, some years later, he learned of the Lumpa Church, he promptly journeyed from his home in northeast Rhodesia to visit Lenshina. He was quickly baptized by one of Lenshina's priests.

The Lenshina movement has made itself a secular force important enough to be of concern to the territorial government. Religious ties have wielded disparate tribesmen into a cohesive and determined body of believers. Their unity of action extends, because of the prevalent racial antipathies in Rhodesia, beyond the purely religious realm to those concerns which affect Africans alone. Usually this results in conflict between the administration (white) and the church (black).

Lenshina insists the movement is not anti-white, as such, but it has clearly grown increasingly xenophobic. Many of Lenshina's priests are known to have strong nationalist sympathies, and it is evident to most observers that much of Lenshina's appeal is derived from the exclusively African nature of her church. The administration fears the Lumpa Church will become tightly allied with African nationalist movements, and that her large and devoted following will be difficult to control in time of stress. It is conceivable, of course, that Lenshina and her followers realize that their own involvement with nationalist movements could well damn the church to the point where it would be banned by the government. This could conceivably harm them financially, and so the Lumpa Church may always remain sympathetic to the mainstream of African nationalism without doing more than giving moral encouragement to the cause. In time of crisis or revolt, however, it is sure to lead its forces against whites thereby to follow today's prevailing tide in Africa.

The Lumpa Church has actively defied the territorial government on two occasions. Both disputes occurred after a series of petty incidents led to a showdown in which neither side could afford, for its own pride, to retreat. Both incidents illustrate the church's distrust of whites.

In May 1959 troubles again erupted between the government and Lenshina. For several years the Bemba hierarchy of chiefs had been concerned about Lenshina's increasing authority and her own, and her followers', increasing disregard for the chiefs' traditional authority. The Chinsali district commissioner agreed to cooperate with the chiefs in dealing with Lenshina's truculence. In particular, the village of Kasomo had existed for many months beyond the pale of any recognized African or territorial authority. It was evidently a region run exclusively by the Lenshina organization. It also harbored Africans there illegally from

other districts.[6] Chief Nkula elected to send his *kapasus*
to Kasomo to evict those illegally in residence; the *kapasus*
met with a lack of cooperation and threats of physical violence from the residents of Kasomo. After a series of incidents messengers were sent from the *boma* to enforce the
law in Kasomo. These men were denied peaceful access to
the village by Lenshina's followers. The district commissioner warned Lenshina to remove the immigrants from her
village; force would be used if necessary. A pitched battle
did take place when his warnings were ignored: spears and
stones wielded by the tribesmen were pitted against guns.
After blood was shed the illegal residents were removed and
order restored to the village.[7]

---

6. Interpretations of customary law forbid any African to move
from the area of one chief to the area of another chief without the
permission of both.

7. The illegal residents have since returned in large numbers.

African Peasant Risings
in Comparative Perspective,
1930's–1960's

MARTIN KILSON *

Perhaps the most important consequence of chiefs' abuse of local tax administration was the emergence of a characteristically modern group conflict in local African society. This conflict was characterized by a form of rural "radicalism," which in some instances constituted a virtual peasant revolt against traditional rulers and authority.

In Sierra Leone, this rural radicalism was evident in the 1930's, and it was particularly strong in the immediate post-war years (1946–1951) and has sometimes flared up since then. On one occasion (October 1950) it took the form of a violent riot which involved some 5,000 peasants and hinterland towndwellers in Kailahun district. Commenting on this riot in his annual report to the governor, the chief commissioner observed that "the extent and violence of the rioting, which spread from Kailahun to outlying towns and villages . . . with casualties and considerable damage to property, made it necessary to summon police help from Freetown." [1] In late 1955 and early 1956, a recurrence of

* From Martin Kilson, *Political Change in a West African State* (Cambridge, Mass., 1966).
1. H. Childs, *Reports on the Sierra Leone Protectorate for the Years 1949 and 1950* (Freetown, 1952), p. 5—cited hereafter as *Protectorate Report* by year.

rural radicalism approximated a peasant revolt properly so-called; the commission of inquiry described it as a "mass disobedience to authority." The disturbances, known commonly as tax riots, involved "many tens of thousands" of peasants and hinterland towndwellers and entailed widespread property destruction (especially chiefs' property— e.g., cattle, surplus crops, modern homes), with damages estimated at £750,000.[2]

Rural radicalism has occurred elsewhere in Africa, and it is such a potential source of instability in postcolonial African states that it warrants much more attention from social scientists than it has received. All we can do here, however, is to note its extent and character. In remarking upon the impact of social change on the relationship of Yoruba *obas* in western Nigeria to their people, Peter Lloyd observed that "great strains have been produced which have resulted in local conflicts . . . The excitement, occasionally leading to rioting, which breaks out over chieftaincy disputes or tax collection, is a similar manifestation of strain."[3] Other instances are worth mentioning here. The peasant disturbances in Chad in 1957–1958 have been described as "symptomatic of a revolt, widespread in northern and eastern Tchad, on the part of the peasantry against the exactions of their customary chiefs."[4] Of the riots in Uganda in 1945 and 1949, J. E. Goldthorpe remarked that "chiefs and wealthy Africans were the main objects of mass disapproval"; and peasant rioters in Tiv areas of northern Nigeria in October 1960 destroyed much property.[5]

2. Cox, *Sierra Leone Report of Commission of Inquiry into Disturbances in the Provinces*, esp. pp. 13–17.

3. Lloyd, "The Changing Role of the Yoruba Traditional Rulers," p. 57. Proceedings of the Third Annual Conference, West African Institute of Social and Economic Research (Ibadan, 1956).

4. Thompson and Adloff, *The Emerging States of French Equatorial Africa*, pp. 76–78, 455.

5. J. E. Goldthorpe, "Social Class and Education in East Africa," in *Transactions of the Third World Congress of Sociology* (London, 1955), pp. 115–122; David Williams, "The Tiv Are in Turmoil," *Daily Times* (Lagos), October 20, 1960, p. 5.

As regards the political meaning of this rural radical-ism, it is perhaps best described, following Max Gluckman's distinction between revolution and rebellion, as peasant *rebellion*.[6] The previously mentioned peasant riots seldom entailed demands for the destruction of the existing system of traditional authority (which Gluckman would call a revolution) but instead were aimed at ameliorating aspects of its use (what Gluckman would call a rebellion). Such a distinction assists us in grasping the rather peculiar ambiv-alence of many Africans (literate and illiterate, rural and urban-dwelling) toward traditional rulers. Lucy Mair has underlined this ambivalence in the case of West Africa as follows: ". . . In the eyes of the same persons the chiefs may be symbols of reaction, symbols of group unity, and symbols of pride in national history. That is why there has been no move to eliminate them from the political system altogether." [7]

Sociologically, this ambivalence toward traditional au-thority is related to the fragmented process of African social change. This means, among other things, that there is a tendency for some facets of a social and cultural sys-tem to change in a modern direction while other facets re-main intact or simply lag. Values (and attitudes toward traditional rulers fall within the realm of values) would appear to be one facet of culture least likely to change rapidly or in the first instance, as compared to such things as the mode of economy, dress, food, and the like. This is so because values more than other aspects of culture are, as it were, highly integrated into the total culture. They be-come fixed at the level of thought and in individual per-sonalities and tend to take on a momentum of their own, separate from the peculiar historical circumstances within which they originated.

Politically, the ambivalence toward traditional authority

6. Cf. Max Gluckman, *Custom and Conflict in Africa* (London, 1955).

7. L. P. Mair, "African Chiefs Today: The Lugard Memorial Lecture for 1958," *Africa* (July 1958), pp. 200–201.

has significant implications for the mode of change. It is likely to be one of the crucial factors in local African society that make for a stable, nonrevolutionary pattern of political development. Peter Lloyd has observed this process among the Yoruba and formulated his view of it as follows: "The hostility against many *obas* is against their persons and not their office; in fact, many crises peter out because no means can be found for punishing the individual without degrading the throne." [8]

For this process to succeed as a key stabilizing element in postcolonial African states, however, presupposes that traditional rulers (and other elite groups linked to them) will not use their position as an excuse for reaction and corruption. In northern Nigeria, for instance, an ambivalent respect toward traditional authority on the part of both educated and uneducated commoners has prevailed and has unquestionably facilitated a nonrevolutionary political change. But the situation whereby the traditional elite uses its power to recruit its own educated kin into higher educational institutions and government posts, to the relative neglect of commoner or pagan children (even though the latter's "performances at the local N.A. elementary school have regularly surpassed those of the Hausa boys") is likely to prove a source of serious conflict and instability.[9]

Apart from the foregoing, there are additional consequences of the role of traditional rulers in colonial change. In Sierra Leone, chiefs' involvement in cash-crop production and marketing created a competitive relationship between chiefs and the peasantry that had no precedent in tradition. The relationship was essentially modern or Western in nature. It stemmed from the money economy and related institutions established by colonial rule. It depended upon colonial legal and political support. Since there was no basis in the indigenous scheme of things for legitimizing this eco-

---

8. Lloyd, "The Changing Role of the Yoruba Traditional Rulers," p. 64.
9. Smith, *The Economy of Hausa Communities of Zaria,* p. 92.

nomic role of chiefs, the peasantry could not be expected to
relate to it in traditional terms.

As it happened, the peasantry viewed the chiefs' role in
the cash economy in modern competitive terms. It was seen
as an unfair competitive advantage. As early as 1903, a
Sierra Leone government report to the Colonial Office
recognized this situation: ". . . The chiefs cannot understand . . . that their young men prefer leaving their villages for work on the railway and in Freetown; but, considering that they got a good wage for their labor, from
9d. to 1s. a day, *they naturally prefer it to unpaid labor in
their villages under their chiefs.*" [10] Similarly, a correspondence to the *Sierra Leone Weekly News* in 1930 related the
economic relationships between chiefs and peasants in the
following terms:

> . . . The protectorate youths are forced to come to the colony
> proper because of the almost inhuman oppression that seems
> to be going on. The natives are forced to make the chiefs'
> farms, to do all public buildings for the chiefs, all govern-
> ment buildings, and the monies for all work done are paid
> to the chiefs; and if they refuse to turn up or are late, they
> are fined heavily; and they have to provide their food whilst
> doing these public works. Over and above that, they are
> fined heavily at Court even beyond their means, and if they
> can manage a little time to make a small farm, the chief's
> portion is also demanded. If you produce a good quantity of
> rice in your farm, the chief is sure to know it, and some
> charge is brought against you to take all that rice away . . .
> Further, if you show any attitude of resistance or unwilling-

---

10. *Sierra Leone Report for 1903,* Cmd. 2238 (London, 1904),
p. 28. (Italics added.) The new mobility in rural society was widespread in colonial Africa. Professor Wrigley noted it in Uganda at
an early period: ". . . In the 1890's, it had been noted that the
independence of the peasantry had been much enhanced by the
opportunity to gain an income otherwise than by the service of the
chiefs . . . Though habits of deference died hard, the Ganda
masses were incomparably freer under the new dispensation than
under the old . . ." C. C. Wrigley, "Buganda: An Outline Economic History," *Economic History Review* (August 1957), p. 77.

ness to conform to the chiefs' dictates, you are either recom-
mended for imprisonment or for deportation.[11]

Although the average peasant's attitude toward the chiefs'
advantage in the market economy was essentially economic
in origin, it eventually became part of a wider outlook which
would prove a basis for political action. A district commissioner's report for the year 1921, for instance, already mentioned that the "collection of tribute is the most fertile source
of abuse and complaint." [12] The transmutation of specific
economic grievances into a broader social and political
consciousness, however, had to await the penetration of
local African society by the middle-class nationalism of
the post-World War II period.

---

11. *Sierra Leone Weekly News,* November 22, 1930, p. 8.
12. Annual Report on the Southern Province for the year 1921
(Freetown, 1922), pp. 7–9.

The Aba Market Women's Riot in Nigeria, 1929

MARGERY PERHAM *

At the end of 1929, just when the government was congratulating itself upon the success with which the difficult task of introducing direct taxation into these provinces had been accomplished, rioting of a serious and unusual kind broke out in Calabar and Owerri. In Owerri province, in the heart of the Ibo country, where a particularly dense population inhabits the palm forest, there is a place called Oloko.¹ Here a warrant chief, Okugo, under instructions from the district officer, was making a reassessment of the taxable wealth of the people. In this he attempted to count the women, children, and domestic animals. A rumor at once spread among the women that the recently introduced taxation of men was to be extended to them. All through this densely inhabited forest country, at intervals of a few miles, are markets where many thousands, mostly women, collect to do petty trading, sell palm-oil to the small middle-

---

* From Margery Perham, *Native Administration in Nigeria* (London, 1937).

1. The following account, insofar as it has not been derived from information supplied directly to the writer, is based upon the Reports of the two Commissions of Enquiry, *Sessional Papers of the Nigerian Legislative Council,* Nos. 12 and 28 of 1930 (which will be referred to as No. 12 and No. 28) to the *Minutes of Evidence* issued with the latter, *Gazette Extraordinary,* February 7, 1930.

men, and gossip with each other. The rumor thus ran all through the locality in a few days, spreading anger and dismay which were all the more intense because at this moment the price of palm-produce was falling, and new customs duties had put up the cost of several imported articles of daily use. They were seriously perturbed. "We depend upon our husbands, we cannot buy food or clothes ourselves and how shall we get money to pay tax?"[2] They decided to combine. "We women," as one of them stated afterwards in her evidence, "therefore held a large meeting at which we decided to wait until we heard definitely from one person that women were to be taxed, in which case we would make trouble, as we did not mind to be killed for doing so. We went to the houses of all the chiefs and each admitted counting his people."[3]

Okugo, continuing reluctantly to carry out his orders, sent a messenger to count some of his people. This man entered a compound and told one of the married women, Nwanyeruwa, who was pressing oil, to count her goats and sheep. She replied angrily, "Was your mother counted?" at which they closed, seizing each other by the throat.[4] A meeting of women was called and Nwanyeruwa's excited story was told as confirmation of the rumor. A palm-leaf, which, it appears, is at once a symbol of trouble and a call for help, was sent round to all the women of the neighborhood. From the whole countryside women poured into Oloko and proceeded according to custom to "sit" upon the man who had tried to assess Nwanyeruwa. All night they danced round his house singing a song quickly invented to meet the situation. Growing hourly more excited, they went on to Okugo's compound where his own people tried to defend him with sticks and bird arrows. The crowd mobbed

2. *Sessional Paper of the Nigerian Legislative Council*, No. 12 of 1930 (Lagos, 1930).

3. *Sessional Paper of the Nigerian Legislative Council*, No. 28 of 1930 (Lagos, 1930).

4. *Minutes of Evidence* in *Gazette Extraordinary*, 7 February 1930 (Lagos, 1930).

him, damaged his house, demanded his cap of office, and charged him with assault before the district officer at Bende. The latter arrested him and brought him into the station. "The women," said this officer, "numbering over ten thousand, were shouting and yelling round the office in a frenzy. They demanded his cap of office, which I threw to them and it met the same fate as a fox's carcass thrown to a pack of hounds. The station between the office and the prison . . . resembled Epsom Downs on Derby Day." The women continued to camp in thousands round the District Office until Okugo was tried and sentenced to two years' imprisonment for assault. But this was not the end. The women, for a reason which we shall consider later, refused, in spite of all the assurances of chiefs and administrative officers, to believe that women, "the trees which bear fruit," were not to be taxed, and this even after a deputation of fifty had taken train to provincial headquarters at Port Harcourt to question the Resident.[5] From Oloko women went out in all directions, beyond the boundaries of the province and even into the neighboring Ibibio country, spreading the rumor, and from a wide area subscriptions began to come in to Nwanyeruwa who had become a figure of womanhood rising up against oppression.[6]

The trouble spread in the second week of December to Aba, an important trading center on the railway. Here there converged some ten thousand women, scantily clothed, girdled with green leaves, carrying sticks.[7] Singing angry songs against the chiefs and the court messengers, the women proceeded to attack and loot the European trading stores and Barclay's Bank, and to break into the prison and release the prisoners. The mobs were to some extent checked by the police supported by a hastily raised force of European traders and Africans, among whom the Boy Scouts worked hard on the side of law and order. After two

5. No. 28, p. 18, para. 50.
6. Ibid., p. 35, paras. 96–97.
7. Ibid., p. 43, para. 121.

days of rioting, troops arrived and dispersed the crowds without any serious casualties.[8] More or less successful attacks followed elsewhere upon "factories" and other buildings at railway stations and trading centers, but the women were far more interested in destroying the native courts and mobbing the warrant chiefs than in looting. It is impossible to follow the details of such diffused disorder, but one or two incidents are worth picking out.

During the second week of December, the movement spread from the Ibo divisions of Owerri and Aba to the Ibibio peoples of Calabar. At much the same time as the elaborate form of reassessment, which the women connected with female taxation, was being undertaken in Oloko, the Resident of Calabar had issued instructions for a similar kind of enumeration in his province. This was zealously enacted in one district by a cadet in the administrative service. In some villages, the people cleared into the bush at his approach, taking their small stock and chickens with them; here, however, he counted the houses, there being generally one to each woman, and the tethering pegs for the goats and sheep. These animals, we may notice, were often the personal possessions of the women. In the neighboring district the chiefs protested vigorously against these house-to-house visitations, though they professed themselves ready to parade all the men of each village in the central square.[9] Another cadet, in Opobo district, to the south, met with determined opposition from the chiefs as well as from the people who were already in touch with the women at Owerri. The women followed him about wailing and cursing; palm branches, doubtless reinforced with magic, were tied across paths and doorways, while on one occasion it was grimly pointed out to him that he was actually standing on a grave where a white man like himself was buried. Finally, he was assaulted and his tax

8. Ibid., pp. 43–51.
9. Ibid., pp. 20–23.

register taken.[10] At the neighboring center of Ukam, he and two senior colleagues were powerless to check the women, on this occasion accompanied by men, who opened the lock-up, destroyed the Native Court, and cut the telegraph wires.[11] At Utu-Etim-Ekpo appeared crowds of women scantily dressed in sackcloth, their faces smeared with charcoal, sticks wreathed with young palms in their hands, while their heads were bound with young ferns. It is interesting to note that no Europeans understood the exact significance of these last symbols though nearly all the native witnesses assumed that they meant war. They burned the Native Court and sacked and looted the "factory" (European store) and clerks' houses. They declared that the district officer was born of a woman, and as they were women they were going to see him. Police and troops were sent, and as, on two occasions, the woman ran toward them with frenzied shouts, fire was opened with a Lewis gun as well as with rifles, and eighteen women were killed and nineteen wounded.[12]

The following day an even more serious collision occurred at Opobo. Mobs of women passed shouting and singing about the town, "What is the smell? Death is the smell." They beat upon the iron-trading stores with their sticks and threatened the traders. To one, Mr. Butler a merchant, they shouted derisively, "All right, Bottle, no fear morning time five o'clock we go come for you," and the next day, "We'll get our Christmas clothes out of you today." [13] In order to calm their excited fears, the district officer agreed to meet the seven leaders at the district office the following day. Palm-leaves were sent around to all the neighboring clans, and when the time came not seven but several hundred arrived at the office, armed with stout cudgels and dressed only in loin-cloths and palm-leaves. In front of the

10. Ibid., pp. 24–26.
11. Ibid., pp. 26–27.
12. Ibid., pp. 66–68.
13. Ibid., pp. 75–77.

district office was a light bamboo fence, beyond that the road and, almost immediately beyond that, the river. The district officer, with a military officer and a platoon of troops, parleyed with the women from inside the fence. The leaders asked him to make notes of the discussion and then asked to see his notes.

All this time the meeting was becoming rowdier. More and more women were streaming up, until the numbers were estimated as being about fifteen hundred. When the copies were handed out, various other demands were made, such as that they must be put into envelopes, that they must have two-shilling stamps attached. They made threatening and obscene gestures toward the troops, called them sons of pigs, and said they knew the soldiers would not fire at them. At last they struck at the district officer with their sticks. The lieutenant caught the blows, made signs to the district officer as to whether he should fire (for it was impossible to make himself heard in the uproar) and, just as the fence began to give way before the rush of women, shot the leader through the head with his revolver. Two volleys were then fired on the crowd which broke and fled, leaving thirty-two dead and dying, and thirty-one wounded.[14]

This shooting was on December 17. Trouble continued sporadically in various parts of the disturbed area, but by the twentieth the situation was completely in hand, and the rest of the month was taken up with pacification by means of patrols, and punishments under the Collective Punishments Ordinance. The disturbed area covered about six thousand square miles and contained about two million people. Attacks were made upon Native Courts in sixteen Native Administration centers, and most of them were broken up or burned.

It is an encouraging feature of this unhappy incident that the responsible authorities in Nigeria, as in England, should have been so ready to face the fact that it resulted largely from defects in their government. Here the Aba riots point

_____

14. No. 28, pp. 73–85; also Annexure 2, pp. 1–28.

a moral that is applicable far beyond Nigeria. The difficulties in this region were exceptionally great. But beneath the peculiar local symptoms lies a pathological condition common to the whole of Negro Africa. It is produced by the sudden strain thrown upon primitive communities by the strong, all-embracing pressure of European influence. There are examples in various parts of the world of primitive peoples unexpectedly rebelling after years of apparent acquiescence in European rule, and their conscious purposes often draw strength from what is at bottom an unconscious cultural protest. The reaction may not be expressed in this form. Some tribes endure the stress of change so quietly that their rulers do not observe their difficulties. One relief for the desire for reassertion is found in the formation of secret societies or of quasi-Christian bodies independent of white control, whose proceedings express at once European influence and an anti-European attitude. The Watch Tower movement in Southern Africa, with its apocalyptic hopes of the fall of Christendom, "Satan's organization," clearly belongs to this category.[15]

---

15. *Report upon the Disturbances in the Copper-belt, Northern Rhodesia*, 1935, Cmd. 5009, p. 43.

Strikes and the Mine Workers' Union
in Northern Rhodesia, 1930's–1950's

A. L. EPSTEIN *

There was an indirect reference to the possible formation of African trade unions in the evidence of District Commissioner Ndola (Mr. Keith), given before the Commission of Inquiry of 1935. Keith pointed out that under the Employment of Natives Ordinance, which governed the relations between employers and African employees, the Africans could not strike legally—they were liable to criminal prosecution if they broke their contracts by not going to work. He said that all that the Africans had lacked in the strike was some organization by which they could elect their own representatives to put the objects of the strike before the mine or government. Sooner or later the Africans would have to have some means of representing their grievances, and of striking legitimately if they wished to do so. He thought that some such sort of organization should be introduced, and given legal recognition.[1] The Commission of Inquiry referred to the possibility of further industrial unrest on the Copperbelt, but did not take up the question of African trade unions; and it was not until after the disturbances of 1940 that the suggestion of forming trade unions seems to have been put forward seriously.

---

* From A. L. Epstein, *Politics in an Urban African Community* (Manchester, 1958).
    1. *Evidence,* i, p. 158.

The African strike of 1940 followed immediately upon a strike of European miners. The Africans were aware that the European strike had been undertaken in order to secure a general increase in wages to meet the rise in the cost of living for all Europeans employed on the mines. Therefore, according to the Forster Commission, the Africans took the view that if by strike action those objects could be attained by the Europeans, a strike must be the appropriate and, indeed, necessary means to obtain similar benefits for themselves.

The strike[2] itself had begun quite peaceably, and the actual disturbances only broke out at Nkana on the sixth day when a crowd of 3,000 strikers tried to prevent a queue of 150 men, who had remained at work, from drawing their pay at the mine compound office. Police and troops tried to push the crowd back, and tear-gas bombs were used, though without effect. The crowd, infuriated, made an attack on the compound office, where many of the Europeans had sought shelter. It was driven off by rifle fire. Looting in the compound occurred on quite a large scale. According to my own informants, one group of people attacked a tearoom. They took meal, nuts, sugar, and other foodstuffs, and threw these outside where people picked them up as they could. Others attacked the houses of domestic servants, clerks, and policeboys. Everything that was to hand was seized and burned. Petrol, paraffin, and benzine were all thrown on the houses of these persons, and personal belongings such as suitcases, bicycles, and

2. For an account of one meeting of African miners which preceded the strike see R.J.B. Moore, 1948, *These African Miners,* Livingston, pp. 78–80. One source of grievance, to which the Forster Commission does not appear to have referred, but which is mentioned by Moore and which was repeated to me by my own informants, was the question of tax. The rate of tax for Africans was 15s. p.a. on the line of rail in 1940. Rural areas paid a lower tax graded by distance from the line of rail. Since basic starting rates for surface and underground workers were 12s. 6d. and 22s. 6d. respectively for a ticket of 30 shifts, this meant in effect that many Africans were paying an annual tax roughly equivalent to their monthly wage.

"even chickens," were all burnt. Policeboys could not appear in the compound, and they were all sheltered behind wire fences to protect them from the people. Europeans, too, came in for some attention from the rioters, and stones were thrown at passing cars. Apart from the widespread damage, the riot had resulted in the death of seventeen Africans, while more than sixty were injured in the firing.

The Report of the Forster Commission drew attention to a wide variety of grievances on the part of Africans, in addition to those relating to their rates of pay, although it noted that these had not been raised previously with the mine managements. Indeed, one of the most serious problems to which the Report referred was the lack of an adequate channel of communication for presenting these grievances. This was particularly the case at Nkana, where no system of tribal elders, such as operated at Mufulira or Luanshya, had been introduced. But the Commission considered that the Africans were not yet sufficiently advanced to take a responsible role in organizing themselves in trade unions, and suggested the development of the system of tribal representatives as an interim measure.

The tribal elders, where they already existed, were now reorganized, and reappeared as tribal representatives. The significance of this change was that the tribal representatives were to work in closer contact with the government labor officers, who were charged with the task of educating the tribal representatives to "become intelligently familiar with all matters relating to native labor," and to teach them to present to management or the government "any case the native workers may have for the adjustment of labor conditions in a reasonable manner." [3] Later, Boss Boys' Committees and Clerks' Associations appeared for a short time. Then in 1946 it was decided to supplement the work of the tribal representatives by the introduction of works committees. The works committee at each mine was made up of African representatives from each of the mine departments.

---

3. Government Circular Minute No. 6-MIN/C of 1942.

The works committees represented another interim measure, for while they could discuss such matters as the distribution of working-hours, the provision of canteens, safety measures, and other day-to-day problems, they did not usually negotiate on wages or conditions of service. This was the position when, in 1947, under the policy enunciated by the British Labour Party for the postwar period, Mr. W. Comrie was sent to northern Rhodesia by the Colonial Office to help organize the African trade union movement. So, at length, the first branch of the African Mine Workers' Union came into being at Nkana in February 1948.

From Nkana the movement extended. Committee members of the Nkana branch toured the Copperbelt, seeking to make African converts to trade unionism. Their task was no light one. Sometimes they were unable to get the permission of compound managers to hold meetings within the compound, sometimes the meetings themselves were poorly attended. Recalling this period in its history, an article in *The African Miner,* the official bulletin of the Union, speaks glowingly of those men, "the first inspired, who did not mind where and how they slept, nor what and how they ate, wherever they went." Within a short time unions had been formed at all mines on the Copperbelt, and at Broken Hill where zinc and vanadium are mined. In March 1949, these unions amalgamated to form the present African Mine Workers' Union.

Shortly afterward, the union submitted to the Chamber of Mines claims for increases in wages for all African employees of the copper-mining companies on the Copperbelt. The companies insisted that first there should be an agreed method of procedure for dealing with points raised by the union. After some negotiation, the agreement was signed which now regulates the relations between the union and the mining companies. Further meetings took place on the wages issue in accordance with the terms of the agreement. Following lengthy but unsuccessful negotiations between the parties themselves, agreement was finally reached at

formal conciliation meetings under a conciliator appointed
by the Governor-in-Council. The union obtained wage increases, although these were substantially lower than its
claims.

During 1950, there was a major industrial dispute, following on the union's demand for a profit-sharing scheme
for the Africans identical in kind to that enjoyed by the
European employees, and for a general wage revision. Negotiations extended into 1951, and agreement was ultimately reached after the union had taken a strike ballot.
Then in March a strike was called at Nchanga on the
grounds of the alleged wrongful dismissal of a member of
the union. The union claimed that the member was dis-
charged not for inefficiency in his duties, but simply because he happened to be treasurer of the local branch and
that the management was seeking merely to test the power
of the union. A number of meetings followed, at which the
Labour Department was represented, but no agreement
was reached. The union gave notice that if the member was
not reinstated it would call a strike. At this point the company sought to persuade the tribal representatives to use
their influence to induce the people to go to work. The
strike continued for fourteen days, but in the end failed to
achieve its object.

The strike itself passed off peacefully and without incident and, although it failed to reinstate the dismissed member, it did serve to draw the attention of the union to the
position of the tribal representatives as a rival source of
authority and influence. Accordingly, at the next Annual
Conference of the Supreme Council of the Union held at
Broken Hill in 1952, a resolution was passed demanding
the abolition of the system of tribal representatives.

But while the discussion was still in progress in the
union, a more important issue developed. Following the
Annual Conference, the union presented demands for a
general increase of 2s. 8d. per shift. During the negotiations
which followed the mining companies made a number of
counteroffers which included improvement in the wages of

certain categories of African mine workers, a shift differential payment for afternoon and night shifts, increased payment for Sunday work, and certain other proposals concerning cost-of-living allowances. When these counteroffers were rejected by the union, the companies stressed that they would be willing to withdraw their counteroffers and allow the dispute to be settled by arbitration. The union declined to agree to arbitration, and, after a secret ballot of its members gave a strong mandate, the union called a strike on October 20, 1952. On this occasion the strike covered the whole of the Copperbelt, and lasted three weeks, during which production was totally halted. Throughout the whole of this period order was maintained, and there were no disturbances or incidents.

In mid-November, the union asked that the dispute be settled by arbitration on condition that the tribunal consisted of an arbitrator chosen from the United Kingdom, and two assessors of whom one should be nominated by each party. This was agreed to by the companies. The union claimed before the Arbitration Tribunal that the African workers were suffering from a deepseated feeling of frustration. While it was true, the union agreed, that the companies provided scales of remuneration which enabled a certain number of their African employees to maintain a standard of living that afforded some margin above the barest neccessities of life, this did not help the vast majority —74 percent of the total—who were in the three lowest grades. The counteroffers of the employers were described as an illusory gesture, and the union argued that it was necessary to get away completely from the existing levels: therein lay the justification of the claim for a flat-rate increase of 2s. 8d. per shift. This claim was based largely on the lowness of the cash wage,[4] particularly for the un-

4. It should be noted however that the cash wage did not make up the total cash earnings. There was also a cost-of-living allowance and a Christmas bonus, together with other bonuses of varying amounts for which a proportion of the workers could qualify. The real wage was much higher, since it included housing, hospital

skilled workers in Groups 1, 2, and 3. The starting rate at
that time for Group 1 (surface) was 45s. per ticket of
thirty working days, and the worker could reach a maximum
of 67s. 6d. per ticket in just over five years of continuous
service, if he did not in the meantime gain promotion to a
higher group. Group 1 indeed was of particular importance,
for it composed more than 50 percent of the total African
labor force.

In presenting their case before the Forster Commission of
1940 the Africans had evidently relied upon the Bemba
proverb, *ululombe nkwale ku mwaiche ukubalilapo ku
ikanga,* "if you wish to beg a partridge from a child you
must first ask for a guinea-fowl." It is not unlikely that a
similar principle was invoked on this occasion. At all events,
the union claimed a victory, and the measure of its popular
support among the workers was immediately manifested
in the abolition of the tribal representatives.

The prestige which tribal representatives enjoyed related
only to certain situations of African social life on the mine;
it did not apply over the total field of social relations in
which the Africans were involved. In particular, it did not
apply in those situations where Africans were involved as
workers rather than as tribesmen. Tribal values were ir-
relevant here, because such situations as a dispute over
wages involved a different set of relations, and a different
set of interests. The ties which linked Africans in these
situations cut across those very divisions in which the system
of tribal representation was rooted. The difficulties of the
tribal representatives thus stemmed in part from a confusion
about their social role; but these difficulties were also ex-
acerbated by the intercalary position of the tribal representatives within the authority structure of the mine. It was
the contradictions implicit in their position itself which
underlay the charges repeatedly leveled against them that
they were working in league with the Europeans, and

---

facilities, welfare, and other services provided by the mining companies.

brought them into immediate conflict with the newly-founded African union.

Although there were some tribal representatives who served on union branch committees, the relationship of the two bodies from the beginning was mainly one of opposition. Shortly after the formation of the union, it was reported that there had been differences of opinion between the union executive and the tribal representatives about the division of their respective spheres of work.[5] These squabbles continued, and, after the events of the strike at Nchanga referred to above, the union decided to press for the abolition of tribal representation. At length the Chamber of Mines was persuaded to allow a ballot to be held under government supervision to ascertain the wishes of their African employees on the question of tribal representation in the African Mine Townships. The Chamber of Mines insisted on a vote of 40 percent in favor, before it would accept

Table 1
Summary of Voting on Tribal Representation on the Copperbelt—March 1953

	Percent
Votes cast of the total labor force (35,000)	84.8
Votes cast for retention based on total votes cast	3.1
Votes cast against retention based on total votes cast	96.9
Votes cast for retention based on the total mine strength	2.6
Votes cast against retention based on the total mine strength	82.2

the abolition of the system. It is evident from Table 1 that the result was in fact a landslide.

----

5. *Annual Report on African Affairs (Western Provinces) 1950*, Lusaka: Government Printer.

Elite-Mass Nexus:
Formation of National
Institutions

Patterns of Elite-Mass
Institutional Ties

Apart from the influence of Western values and ide-
ologies which, modified by African minds and experiences,
enable African societies to evolve new norms to govern the
interaction of groups in a modernizing context,[1] it is the
new institutions, linking groups or social strata, which give
African societies their more durable modern characteristics.
The selections in Part IV illustrate the types of institutions
that have emerged to mediate relations between different
groups or strata in modern African societies. These selections also address the qualitative aspects of modern social
and political institutions in African societies. In all societies, old and new, there is unequal access to power and
influence, and this fact is characteristic of modern social
and poltical institutions in Africa.

As is already apparent from the selections in Part III,
voluntary associations are common among the early African-
controlled institutions which emerged in modern colonial
Africa. These associations took on many forms: educational,
religious (that is, Christian), economic, welfare or mutual
aid, and political. Some were rather specific or limited in
function, serving solely religious or educational purposes.
Most, however, were multi-purpose associations, serving

1. This subject is dealt with in Volume Two of *The Africa
Reader*.

several functions at the same time. The selection from Professor Baeta's study of *Prophetism in Ghana* illustrates the variety of tasks performed by an association initially founded as a religious body. Founded in the late 1930's, the Ghanaian Apostolic Revelation Society had become by the 1950's a veritable social system, or sub-system, with its own schools and teachers, farms, corn mills, health dispensaries, tailor shops, printing works, builders, and the like. In this way some fifty thousand persons, motivated by an Africanized Christian stimulus, were given a disciplined relationship with a variety of modern roles and tasks.

In the period from the early 1900's through World War II, the organizers and leaders of the primary forms of voluntary associations (separatist Christian bodies, farmers' cooperatives, trade unions, and a variety of mutual-aid bodies) were men of only modest Western education. They seldom claimed more than middle-school education, gained largely at schools provided by Christian missions. In regard to occupation, the leaders of voluntary associations in the period before World War II were often, if not invariably, employed as clerks in European firms, native administrations or some other branch of colonial administration, and Christian missions. These clerks experienced a special form of mobility within colonial society, as between town and rural areas, and interacted with European officials and technicians, learning the rudiments and style of modern organization and leadership. Clerks were also in close touch with diverse elements among the African masses. In their positions in European retail firms, for example, clerks had contact with carpenters, tailors, and other artisans who purchased tools and wares from European firms. Clerks who worked as crop graders and buyers for European cash-crop purchasing firms like Cadbury Ltd. and the Swiss Trading Company interacted with African cash-crop farmers. And clerks who worked in native administrations or in field branches of central government departments like Public Works and Agriculture interacted with a variety of Africans in the lower strata who came into contact with colonial government.

Thus, the special forms of mobility available to clerks in colonial Africa equipped them with both the skills and motivation necessary for assuming leadership roles. Voluntary associations of the primary sort were logical institutions for former clerks to organize in their quest for leadership, as can be seen in the selections from Professor Rotberg on so-called native associations and welfare associations in Central Africa, and from Professor Ralph Austen on cash-crop farmers' associations in Tanzania. Moreover, the experience of clerks in the formation and development of primary voluntary associations placed them in a position to assume leading roles in the more complex political institutions that emerged after World War II, especially nationalist organizations and political parties.

Nearly all nationalist organizations and parties in postwar Africa built upon earlier voluntary associations, and the leading role of clerks in these associations guaranteed them a special place in postwar party politics. The leaders of African parties, normally men of higher education and employed in professions such as law and medicine, required organizers who could muster support among the masses, and inasmuch as clerks who headed voluntary associations were experienced in working among the masses, they were given important roles in party organization. Some former leaders of voluntary associations were even awarded posts in the legislatures and cabinets established during the period of decolonization in the 1950's. Insofar as a high proportion of leaders of voluntary associations were clerks, the data in Table 1 provide some indication of the representation of these leaders among legislators in African states during the period of decolonization.[2]

2. It should be noted that the high proportion of clerks among the legislators in the Congo, many of whom, like Patrice Lumumba, headed voluntary associations, was due to the Belgian colonial policy of not educating Congolese to assume roles much higher than

Table 1
Proportion of Clerks in Selected Legislatures

Year	Country	Number of Legislators	Percentage of Clerks
1956	Ghana	104	22
1959	Eastern Nigeria	84	19[a]
1956	Western Nigeria	80	2[b]
1952	Ivory Coast	27	33
1946–52	Senegal	50	24
1947–52	Mali	28	40
1948–52	Upper Volta	40	42
1947–52	Niger	20	40
1947–52	Guinea	24[c]	28
1961	former Belgian Congo	23[d]	80
1961	Kenya	33[e]	7
1961	Tanzania	48[f]	20
1961	Sierra Leone	52	10

a This refers to dominant party only, the NCNC. Opposition parties had 18 percent legislators who were clerks.

b This refers to dominant party only, the Action Group.

c Data not available for eight legislators.

d Figure for members of Cabinet only.

e Figure for African members only; twenty other Asian and European members.

f There were fifty-one Africans in Tanzanian legislature in 1961.

The majority of leaders of African parties is drawn, however, from the highly educated groups. While it was only after World War II that the well-educated members of the African new elites could form political parties which were allowed to control the central government, parties which acted as pressure groups and avenues for election to local government bodies existed before the war. One of the first leaders of such a party was the late Blaise Diagne, whose career as a leading colonial politician in Senegal and French West Africa is the subject of the selection from Professor G. Wesley Johnson. Blaise Diagne had a canny comprehension of power and its use and during his lifetime he amassed in French West Africa immense power, as well as

clerks. Thus, at independence clerks were among the best educated groups in the Congo. See Crawford Young, *Politics in the Congo* (Princeton, 1965).

the wealth and affluence associated with men of power.

The acquisition and uses of political power and influence in modern Africa is also the subject of the selections by Professor Kilson on the Sierra Leone People's Party and Professor Post on the major Nigerian parties. The leaders of Nigerian parties have been most adept at converting political power into large-scale wealth, especially industrial capital. There is, in fact, a built-in need on the part of African elites to use politics as a means to acquire wealth, and especially capital, insofar as the basis of new African elites in finance and business activities is rather limited. Data on the occupations of African elites who hold political office show that prior to gaining office they are employed mainly in government service, teaching, and the liberal professions like law, medicine, and dentistry. (See Table 2.)

Table 2
Category of Skills of Ivory Coast Office-Holders in 1957, 1959, 1960 [a]

Type of Skill	Percentage in 1957 (N = 54)	Percentage in 1959 (N = 84)	Percentage in 1960 (N = 83)
Clerical	22	19	16
Educational	24	24	24
Health-Medical	11	14	18
Technical	6	8	12
Legal	9	8	7
Agriculture and Commerce	19	19	16
Managerial	9	8	7

a "Office-holders" means members of National Assembly and of the Cabinet. From Aristide R. Zolberg, *One-Party Government in the Ivory Coast* (Princeton, 1964), p. 275.

No doubt this situation, combined with the tribal diversity of politicians and interest groups in African societies, imposes much stress and strain on modern African political institutions. The rise of authoritarian one-party regimes in the early 1960's and the subsequent emergence of military regimes in some fifteen African states have their origins in the special form of stress and strain African polities have encountered. The need of African one-party regimes to keep in touch with the rural masses, after having disenfranchised them, has been a further source of conflict and cleavage. African one-party regimes have differed in their approach to this problem, and the selections from Professor Brokenshea and Professor Bienen illustrate the methods of two regimes.

The future of African political institutions as viable means of mediating the relations of the elites and masses is hardly sanguine. For most of the post-independence period, African regimes concentrated more on mediating disputes within the elites over the division of the spoils of office than on rationalizing elite-mass relationships. This obsession of African elites with their own political needs has proved detrimental to the viability of African political systems, and only greater attention by the elites to the needs of popular forces will give these systems greater stability and efficacy.   M.K.

Voluntary Associations
in Central Africa, 1920's–1930's

ROBERT ROTBERG *

The white people cannot fool the black man all the time, they can . . . forbid people to speak their English language, but it is clear that they are only blind forgetting human history. What is desired [is] that you get on going there and [organize] . . . and we shall be able therefore to open the eyes of the people, who are today living in darkness. The sun of righteousness, it seems to me, is rapidly springing upon the sons and daughters of Africa and who knows that sooner or later we may hail the dawn of freedom. To accomplish this fact we must act in unionism, breaking all our tribal prejudices . . .

—Clements Kadalie to Isa Macdonald Lawrence, April 4, 1925

During the years between the two World Wars, Africans in Nyasaland and Northern Rhodesia sought in every conceivable constitutional way to better the political, social, and economic order to which they had been subjected. Chilembwe's abortive rising signified the end of a defensive era; thereafter, Africans recognized that the colonial governments had come to stay and that the imposed codes of law were not to be removed easily. Africans tried to work

* From Robert Rotberg, *Rise of Nationalism in Central Africa* (Cambridge, Mass., 1965).

within the colonial context. Using the political concepts and language of their rulers, they unsuccessfully claimed a democratic right to participate in the governing process. At first they wanted no more than to have their collective voice heard in those matters directly affecting the lives and actions of the indigenous population. To this end, those Africans (for the most part clerks, evangelists, and teachers) to whom the white man's ways had become most familiar imitated the settler example by forming associations through which their pleas for reform, and for consideration, could best be expressed.

Among the several widespread manifestations of indigenous protest, the establishment of voluntary associations played the most significant role in the development and the eventual emergence of the avowedly nationalist movements of the 1940's. For more than twenty years the associations sought redress for grievances suffered or allegedly endured by Africans.

From 1920, for example, the North Nyasa Native Association continually urged the government to spend more money on education and, indeed, to raise hut taxes in order to do so. It asked for alterations in the postal regulations so that Africans might not have to apply directly to Zomba for the delivery of parcel-post packages. In 1929, it explained knowledgeably that Africans emigrated to Rhodesia and South Africa because the British government had spent almost no money developing Nyasaland. The association demanded that the government should provide Nyasaland with a good road network in order that Africans might thereby be enabled to export their agricultural produce. If the government refused to provide a decent infrastructure, the members of the association thought that Nyasaland could never hope to develop economically. In another vein, they later tried to persuade the government of the iniquity of a law that penalized intercourse between black men and white women only. But to all these and to other requests the administration turned a deaf ear. And, with regard to the last iniquity, Karonga's district commissioner showed a complete disregard for, or lack of appreciation of, the problem. He wrote: "It is a peculiar thing that almost every highly educated native of the Livingstonia Mission is politically minded and race conscious and always on the lookout for some stigma. At the back of their minds is an intolerance of the Europeans and their creed is 'Africa for the Africans.' " [1]

After 1920, Nyasas elsewhere in the Protectorate followed the example of their brothers in the north and established a number of independent bodies to serve ends similar to those espoused by the first association. At Mumba's suggestion, in 1923, forty Africans organized the Southern Province Native Association with headquarters in Zomba. The main original object of what was to become the most articulate of the many associations was ostensibly "to assist the government in every way, especially by keeping it informed of native public opinion." Like other associations, it expected "to assist the native by representing him in all political matters, [and] by keeping him informed of and explaining the objects of legislations . . . to organize public meetings for the discussion of subjects of general or special interest, and to keep in touch with other similar native associations." [2]

The activities of the Southern Province Association began innocuously; but, as its members gained confidence in their undertaking, their proposals grew more aggressive. In 1924, at a time when the Phelps-Stokes educational commission was visiting the Protectorate, they urged the government to improve the quality of the educational instruction available to Nyasas.

By 1933, educated Nyasas had formed fifteen different associations. Their memberships occasionally overlapped, and a number of individuals each helped both to organize

---

1. S 1/1481/19: The District Commissioner, Karonga to the Northern Provincial Commissioner, January 27, 1931, Northern Rhodesia National Archives.
2. S 1/3263/23: Rules of the Nyasaland (Southern Province) Native Association, December 23, 1923, Zomba archives.

and to administer several groups as adjuncts of their own
professsional careers. Each association had its obvious
leader, whether the Rev. Mr. Yesaya Zerenji Mwasi in
West Nyasa, the Rev. Mr. Charles C. Chinula and the Rev.
Mr. Yesaya Mlonyeni Chibambo in Mombera, George
Simeon Mwase and James Ralph Chinyama in Lilongwe,
Mumba in North Nyasa, Zomba, and later Lilongwe,
Andrew Jonathan Mponda and Charles Jameson Matinga
in Blantyre, or, in Chiradzulu, the American-educated Rev.
Dr. Daniel Sharpe Malekebu, leader of Chilembwe's Provi-
dence Industrial Mission. Educated men all, they sought
concessions, compromises, and recognition from the government. They argued according to the British conventions of
the day or, on occasion, of an earlier era, and contentedly
turned their associations into debating societies. They pur-
posely limited the membership of their associations to the
new elite of Nyasaland, shunned the masses, and refused to
make of their constitutional approach a genuine popular
movement of political change. They patiently awaited the
happy day when the government would begin to deal justly
with Africans and their self-appointed representatives. By
the outbreak of World War II, Nyasaland's many separately
run associations could claim few concessions from the government of the Protectorate. The government still failed to
regard African opinion in a serious light.

Before World War II, associations played a more immediate role in the highly charged racial atmosphere of
Northern Rhodesia than they did in Nyasaland. In Northern
Rhodesia, the conditions of urban life and the pressure and
political ambitions of a comparatively large white settler
population openly and significantly disadvantaged educated
Africans. The latter possessed abundant sources of grievance and, in absolute terms, probably were discriminated
against more persistently than were their fellow Africans in
Nyasaland. In time, therefore, Africans resident in Northern
Rhodesia—many of whom had lived elsewhere—imitated

the example of Nyasas, Southern Rhodesians, and South Africans and formed political organizations.

In Northern Rhodesia, Africans established what were ostensibly welfare societies. The first owed its inspiration directly to Nyasaland. In 1923, Levi Mumba sent a copy of the constitution of the North Nyasa Native Association to Donald Siwale, then a clerk. Together with David Kaunda (the father of the president of Zambia) and Hezekiya Kawosa, he organized the Mwenzo Welfare Association in order to provide a forum where Africans could express their political and social views. A year later, they protested against the heavy tax burden that the government had forced rural Africans to bear.

The first permanent African political body originated in the minds of four or five Nyasa civil servants (at least one of whom had been in communication with Marcus Garvey and had been a member of the Lilongwe Native Association) working in Livingstone, the capital of the Protectorate. In 1928, Isaac Rankin Nyirenda later recalled, the people of Maramba, Livingstone's main African township, expressed little interest in the possible formation of an association. But in 1929, Nyirenda and Edward Franklin Tembo asked the government if they and their friends might form the tentatively entitled "Northern Rhodesia Native Welfare Association" in order both to "help the government to improve the country" and to "deal with matters and grievances affecting the native people." [3]

The vice-chairman of the association, J. Ernest C. Mattako, raised an additional, rather novel concept: "We can get freedom through pulling together in this movement." Six weeks later, the association held a second meeting that was attended by three local chiefs, Sakasipa, Mkuni, and Musokotwani. The last chief aired a number of complaints

---

3. ZA 1/9/45/1: Minutes of meetings of the Livingstone Native Welfare Association, June 9, 1929, April 19, 1930, Lusaka archives. See also Sec/Nat/321, Lusaka archives; *Central African Mail* (October 24, 1964), 38.

against individual European officials and then told the crowd that the white man was "chasing us from our lands where our forefathers died to lands which are strange to us where we are not allowed to cut down trees." They also chase us, he continued, "out of the [district] like dogs."[4] To every proposal and complaint, even those occasionally supported in private by younger officials, the government gave no satisfaction. The governor suggested that his subordinates should ridicule the members of the association and "treat them as errant children."[5]

By this time, however, Africans elsewhere in Northern Rhodesia had begun to form welfare associations. Mattako, a court interpreter, had been transferred to Ndola. There, in the winter of 1930, he joined with Ernest Alexander Muwamba, the trusted head clerk at the Ndola *boma* and a Tonga from Nyasaland (he was also a close relative of Clements Kadalie, the founder of the Industrial and Commercial Workers Union of South Africa[6]) and Elijah Herbert Chunga, another civil servant, to organize an association along lines constitutionally similar to those of Livingstone.

Their initiative worried the officials responsible. Moffat Thomson did not want civil servants to hold office or to participate vocally at meetings. He worried about the reaction of mine owners to the existence and the activities of the proposed welfare society. "The conduct of the Livingstone association," he wrote, urging Mackenzie-Kennedy to deny the Ndola group permission to meet, "fails to show

---

4. ZA 1/9/45/1: Minutes of the meeting of June 9, 1930.

5. Sec/Nat/321: The Chief Secretary (Donald Mackenzie-Kennedy) to Moffat Thomson, February 24, 1931, Lusaka archives.

6. Unbeknown to Muwamba, the Government of Northern Rhodesia frequently intercepted and inspected his correspondence with Kadalie and with his brother I. Clements Muwamba, a Lusaka clerk. Even so, during World War II, Muwamba for a time ran the Serenje *boma* singlehanded and, after leaving Northern Rhodesia, sat in Nyasaland's Legislative Council and served as a member of its Public Service Commission.

any promise of being helpful." [7] Finally, after considerable debate in the highest official circles, the governor and his Executive Council sanctioned the formation of both the Ndola and the newly proposed Mazabuka associations. They placed no restrictions on the roles to be played therein by African civil servants.

During the next two years educated Africans formed five other welfare associations along the line of rail. In Broken Hill, P. J. Silawe, a civil servant transferred there from the capital, attempted to organize a branch of the Livingstone association, but the Protectorate authorities distrusted moves that would encourage African unity, and Silawe contented himself with the establishment of an unaffiliated society. The Broken Hill Native Welfare Association aimed to stimulate "cooperation and brotherly feeling, to interpret to the government native opinion on matters of importance, to encourage the spread of civilization, and to protect and further native interests in general." [8] Later it requested a "proper" school, better treatment in the hospital, the closing of the local beer hall on Sundays, a market, and that the African compounds should be kept clean.

Tonga from Nyasaland organized both the Mazabuka and Lusaka welfare associations. During the first months of their formal existence, both associations condemned the conditions under which Africans were compelled to purchase meat. I. Clements Katongo Muwamba and Henry Mashwa Sangandu, chairman and secretary respectively of the Lusaka Native Welfare Association, averred that the local European butcher refused to sell decent meat to Africans. He either threw it on the floor or refused to allow Africans to see what they were purchasing before they paid for pre-wrapped items. Sangandu wrote that the butcher treated Africans "as though the native was a dog, whereas

---

7. Sec/Nat/322: Moffat Thomson to Mackenzie-Kennedy, July 21, 1930, Lusaka archives.

8. Sec/Nat/324: P. J. Silawe to Moffat Thomson, September 29, 1930, Lusaka archives.

as a human being the natives know what is good to eat." [9]

Members of the Choma and Lusaka associations separately requested the right to farm plots of agricultural land outside the confines of their urban townships. Africans who already called themselves "detribalized" wanted these allotments both in order to grow food for themselves and for sale. They thought that a partial return to the land, and an admittedly compromise marriage of urban and rural ideals, would contribute to the mental and physical "uplift" of towndwellers.

In 1932, the Lusaka and Luanshya associations began a concerted attack upon the mass of discriminatory legislation to which Africans were subjected by the alien white government. They wanted responsible Africans, like all whites, to be permitted to carry guns. Of even greater moment to their members, the associations asked "Why do only Africans need to carry passes in their own country?" [10] They referred to the identification certificates that the government had, since 1927, compelled all Africans to carry when they resided in the towns, and the passes necessary if they wanted to leave their housing compounds after dark. Both associations requested that "Africans of good character" should be exempted from the need to carry identification certificates.

Africans organized themselves into associations even in the rural areas. Abercorn, Kasama, and Fort Jameson each boasted a welfare society before 1933, although the government strictly defined their functions. "It must be clearly understood," the Chief Secretary wrote to the provincial commissioner responsible, "that membership of the association must be confined solely to natives who, though residing in Abercorn, owe no kind of allegiance to any Native Authority there, and who engage in no sort of political

---

9. Sec/Nat/332: Minutes of the meeting of June 3, 1931, Lusaka archives.

10. Sec/Nat/325: Minutes of the Luanshya meeting, September 16, 1932, Lusaka archives.

activity. The association can act as the mouthpiece of natives who are not within the ordinary organization of native society, but there must be no question or possibility of the association becoming either a rival to or a "cell" within the Native Authority." [11]

Despite numerous rebuffs, the various African voluntary associations of Northern Rhodesia and Nyasaland refrained from speaking publicly of self-government and, by 1939, they had alluded only in the most tangential manner to the possibility that Africans might one day be represented in the Legislative Council by persons of their own choice. Their leaders spoke rarely of "freedom" and of the stratagems that might ultimately return the two protectorates to indigenous control. At the onset of the war, they wanted equality of opportunity more than power, and status within the existing society more than its wholesale transformation. Yet, if timidly, their actions kept alive the fires of protest. Associational activity also provided training for future politicians. Through such channels Africans could harmlessly vent their frustrations and exhaust many of the ordinary British methods of effecting change. Although they accomplished little thereby, their formation of and participation in associations filled large, unsatisfied needs. At the time, Central Africans may have lacked the experience or the desire to organize themselves in ways from which they might have derived greater and more lasting benefit. Their associations were, nonetheless, the logical progenitors of the more "modernist," nationalist-minded congresses of a later day.

---

11. Sec/Nat/327: R. S. W. Dickenson (the Chief Secretary) to the Provincial Commissioner (Abercorn), March 9, 1933, Lusaka archives.

The Bukoba African Association
in Tanzania in 1930's

RALPH A. AUSTEN *

The first evidence that the educated elite would challenge the *bakama* for local leadership occurred precisely in those undertakings where the chiefs had proved most unable or unwilling to assert themselves. Thus in 1931 it was Herbert Rugazibwa, former secretary of the Bukoba Union and then clerk of the Bakama Council, upon whom the chiefs depended for their information concerning British East African policy. Similarly, administration efforts to improve Haya standards of coffee production found their only encouraging sign in the establishment of a hulling plant by Klemens Kiiza, former president of the Bukoba Union.[1] Finally, when Nyakato was converted from a central to an agricultural school, the only support for the objections of the local education officer came from the same group of commoners, now reconstituted as the Bukoba branch of the Tanganyika African Association.[2]

Mistrust by the Bukoba traditional chiefs of a popular reform movement attempting to communicate directly with the administration was to be expected in any case, but much that was done by both the African Association collectively

---

* From Ralph A. Austen, *Northwest Tanzania Under German and British Rule* (New Haven, Conn., 1968).

1. Bukoba to DSM, March 10, 1933, SMP 10071.
2. Bakama Council Proceedings, September 14, 1935.

and its individual members tended particularly to antagonize the *bakama*. Even in the dynastic affairs of the kingdoms themselves, the évolués tended to take a line opposed to the existing rulers.

With the exception of a virtually unpublicized demand by Kiiza for a solution to the perennial Bukoba prostitution problem,[3] all the progressive measures advocated by the African Association tended also to challenge the *bakama*. Thus the traditional prohibition on female inheritance— a custom closely connected with the land interests of chiefs —was attacked in provocatively modernist terms. "The Europeans have come to teach us every sort of good custom—a woman has a right to inherit an entire kingdom." [4] Although the chiefs were able to hold their own there, the Provincial Commissioner did respond to a renewed petition against unpaid road labor by ordering that all such efforts would have to be recompensed in the future.[5]

The climax of the African Association's early conflicts with both the *bakama* and the administration's ideas of traditionalism came in maintenance of protests against the closing of the Nyakato Central School. Although the Education Department's primary incentive in reducing its Bukoba commitment had been economy, administrative and agricultural officials immediately responsible for the conversion of the school into a coffee-growing training center saw the measure as a positive step toward the Indirect Rule ideal "to produce a more intelligent type of peasant farmer, who will be content to earn his livelihood from the soil rather than as a pseudo-clerical wage earner." [6]

The African Association had been encouraged to object to such a policy by the Bukoba Education Supervisor, G. N. Eeles, who was himself extremely bitter about the

---

3. Kiiza to editor of *Mambo Leo,* November 6, 1932 (not published), MPMP 438.

4. African Association to Bakama, September 12, 1933, BBUP.

5. P.C. to African Association, July 29, 1935, BBUP.

6. Joint statement, S.N.A., Senior Ag. Off., P.C., March 7, 1933, Nyakato Minute Paper (hereafter NMP) 376.

proposed change.[7] The Association's subsequent petition thus attempted to meet agricultural Indirect Rule doctrine on its own grounds, claiming that English-language training was necessary for proper technical education and that Haya pupils sent to central schools in other districts were rendered "detribalized natives and useless for home life as true Africans." [8]

The conversion of Nyakato Central School into a coffee training center had also been envisaged as an aid to local agricultural improvement through the production of both African staff for local agricultural administration and more enlightened independent growers.[9] At the beginning of the 1935 academic year, however, the majority of the pupils refused to report to the school, complaining that the curriculum placed too much stress on practical agriculture rather than academic work and did not assure graduates of government employment.[10] The Agriculture Department now considered shifting the school's emphasis from academic education to the training of mature Africans already involved in practical agriculture. For the younger graduates of the existing program, a scheme of settlement on hitherto unoccupied land was proposed.[11]

In the hope of encouraging more progressive attitudes within the general body of Bukoba agriculturalists, the administration, in 1932, began investigations into the possibility of establishing some form of local marketing cooperatives similar to the organizations developed among the Chagga coffee growers of Mount Kilimanjaro.

In contrast to the *bakama* and populace of Bukoba, the leadership of the African Association had shown a very

---

7. Eeles to DSM, Feb. 20, 1932, NMP 376; Eeles–African Association correspondence, January 1935, BBUP.
8. African Association to Lake Province Schools Inspector, January 27, 1935, BBUP and SMP 10514.
9. Nyakato to Ag. Dept., May 25, 1933; Senior Ag. Off. to Nyakato, November 28, 1934, both NMP 376.
10. Sr. Ag. Off. to Ag. Dept., February 14, 1935, ibid.
11. Memorandum, Wakefield, February 14, 1935, ibid.

active interest in coffee enterprises. On the basis of a small mechanical huller which Kiiza had been operating since 1928, he and Rugazibwa, in 1935, organized seven hundred coffee farmers into an "African Trade Union." The members delivered their produce directly to Kiiza who—presumedly at advantageous prices—hulled it and made deliveries in bulk to a leading Bukoba merchant.[12]

A request by the Association itself, in 1934, that all licensing restrictions be removed from African coffee traders had been rejected out of hand by the administration; but when, in the following year, local agricultural officers began to see hulling facilities as a key to general local improvement, the positive response of the évolués was more warmly received.[13]

The fuller reorientation of Bukoba coffee policy toward the educated leadership followed the arrival at Mwanza of a new Lake Province Provincial Commissioner, C. MacMahon. With the same energy that had characterized his long tenure in Shinyanga and later work in Musoma, MacMahon immediately determined to attack the Bukoba coffee problem on two fronts. First, the local agricultural officers would revise the cumbersome 1930 coffee rules into a form simple enough to be accepted and enforced by the *bakama*. Second, the District Officer would "endeavor to turn the present African Association into an Agricultural body in the form of a coffee planters Association instead of allowing them to be a political thorn in our sides." [14]

As it turned out, the group of African Association leaders who accepted MacMahon's offer of economic support in return for "abstention from political intrigues" consisted of Kiiza and Rugazibwa, who simply changed the name of the African Trade Union to the Native Growers Association.[15]

---

12. D.O. A.L. Pennington to P.C., July 12, 1935, ibid.

13. MacMichael notes on African Association petition, December 11, 1934, SMP 19957/1; District Ag. Off. to P.C., July 15, 1935, MPMP 976.

14. MacMahon to Ag. Dept., October 12, 1935, MPMP 976.

15. Bukoba District Report, 1935, MPMP 1246.

MacMahon encouraged the establishment of NGA branches
in every Bukoba chiefdom and suggested a loan of £750
from the Central Native Treasury for the purchase and sale
of metal hand hullers.

The financial situation of the Native Treasury prevented
the loan from taking place, and Rugazibwa's suggestion,
that the NGA be given a monopoly of Bukoba coffee trade,
failed to meet with MacMahon's approval.[16] The Provincial
Commissioner's immediate interest in the new organization
lay less in the area of marketing than that of improved cultivation. Nevertheless, in the belief that "we cannot expect
too much from the chiefs at present," his hopes for the NGA
remained high. "The salvation of Bukoba coffee will I
think be in their hands and we must nurse this association." [17]

The membership of the NGA, meanwhile, had increased
to one thousand growers.

MacMahon's most far-reaching ambitions for the NGA
were expressed in his request to have the Bukoba coffee
industry investigated by the Tanganyika Registrar of Cooperatives, R. C. Northcote.

I am sure that any efforts we make to guide the Association
during its infancy will be of great assistance not only to the
coffee industry, but will also enable us to restore confidence
between the Chiefs (Native Authorities) and many of the
educated Bahaya who have lost confidence in the Native
Authorities.[18]

Government confidence in the évolués involved in the
Native Growers Association came to a very sudden end with
the revelations of Northcote's report. "It would be folly to
regard it [the NGA] as a marketing organization," Northcote
pointed out in his opening summary, and went on to recom-

16. MacMahon to DSM, Oct. 18, 1935; D.O. Page to P.C.,
January 13, 1936; MacMahon to D.O., January 23, 1936; NGA to
P.C., January 15, 1936; all ibid.

17. MacMahon to D.O., June 1, 1936, ibid.

18. MacMahon to DSM (n.d. [July 1936]), MPMP 976, p. 233.

mend far different methods for introducing cooperation into Bukoba. The more detailed indictment of the NGA included a dismissal of its proposals for expanding trade on the basis of government loans as "fantastic" and a characterization of Kiiza and Rugazibwa as somewhat unscrupulous profiteers with little interest in the improvement of local agriculture.[19] Independent African evidence seems to support these pessimistic conclusions, and they were regretfully endorsed by the Bukoba District Officer, who foresaw political difficulties in the eclipse of the NGA.[20]

The immediate cause of the unrest that finally broke out in Bukoba during the first two months of 1937 was an attempt by European officers and the *bakama* to introduce the new coffee rules. To the Haya peasants who demonstrated against these laws and resisted, even to the point of taking up arms, the inspection of their plots, the new regulations represented not only an unwarranted interference with their cash coffee cultivation, but also a positive threat to their subsistence banana crop. "We do not need to be taught how to grow coffee or banana trees or to stop from growing anything on our *shambas* [plots] or on our soil." [21]

At the first, relatively mild, signs of disaffection, the administration abandoned a previously disputed aspect of the coffee rules by transferring the powers of crop supervision from the Agriculture Department to the Native Authorities. It was thus hoped that the *bakama* would be forced, against some of their own inclinations, to take responsibility for the rules. To the shock of the administration, however, a mass public meeting held together with the *bakama* at their council headquarters produced the first of several large-scale riots.[22]

19. Northcote to P.C., October 5, 1936, MPMP 1410.

20. Proceedings of NGA meeting, Ibuga (Kianja Chiefdom), January 15, 1936, BBUP; Page, note to Northcote report, MPMP 1410.

21. Anonymous to P.C., February 1937, MPMP 976.

22. Flynn to P.C., February 6, 1937, ibid.; for accounts of other riots see correspondence, February–March 1937, MPMP 1445.

With the subsequent occurrence of similar outbreaks in the three main coffee-producing chiefdoms, the administration was made even more aware than previously of the inadequacy of the *bakama* as an instrument for executing progressive policies. At the same time the educated elite appeared to have fulfilled the worst anxieties of conservative officials. "The agitation against the coffee rules," wrote the provincial commissioner, "was merely a lever used by the African Association against the chiefs and their corrupt subordinates and deputies." [23]

Although the 1937 coffee riots represented the first direct challenge to colonial rule in Bukoba since early German times, the administration experienced little difficulty in dealing with its short-term effects. Thus, although the objections of growers inhibited some of the stipulations of the new coffee rules, the most important government prerogative of inspection rights was gradually imposed upon all parts of the district.[24] Those African Association members, like Justus Bujurwa, who had taken a discernible part in inciting unrest were quickly arrested and jailed for brief periods. The disturbances remained serious only insofar as they challenged the entire basis upon which the British had attempted to build modern African political institutions.

------

23. P.C. to DSM, March 11, 1937, MPMP 1445.
24. MPMP 976, 1410 passim.

The Apostolic Revelation Society:
A Religious Association
in Ghana, 1930's–1950's

G. BAETA *

The headquarters of this society is at Tadzewu in the Keta district of the Trans-Volta Region of Ghana. It is reached by motor road from two points on the main road from the Volta River at Sogankope to Denu, and also from Hevi on the Ho Denu road, being only seven miles from this junction. The founder of the society is Mr. Charles Kobla Nutonuti Wovenu, generally known as Prophet Wovenu, but regularly referred to by his followers as *Mawu ƒe ame* (i.e., man of God). The last name *Wovenu,* meaning literally "He has received mercy," was revealed to the prophet in a dream, in which he was instructed to make it his surname. Here is his own account of himself and of his work:[1]

My father's name is Emmanuel Nutonuti, and my mother's Mikayanawo. Both were pagans when I was born. My

---

* From G. Baeta, *Prophetism in Ghana* (London).

1. This account is a conflation of information personally communicated to me by the prophet in a personal interview and material contained in a little booklet in Ewe by him on the history of his Society from 1939 to 1954: *Apostolowo Fe Dedefia Habobo Nutinya* 1939–1954, Mfantsiman Press Ltd., Cape Coast. As I had read the booklet before the interview, it was possible to ask for further elucidation on certain points.

father afterwards became a Christian, but my mother became a *dasi* (literally wife of a snake, i.e., a priestess of the snake fetish). My father remembers that, about ten years before I was born, a stranger, dressed in a long, white gown, once lodged with him. My mother was then barren and remained so a long time, all medical and magical treatment having failed to help her; indeed I am her only child. Yet this man told my father that she would bear him a son, and that this son's head would stand higher (literally "go further") than my father's.

For this reason when I was born in December of 1918 (the day of the month is unknown), my father greatly disliked me. He thought that somehow my arrival signalized his own death, not knowing that the fortune teller's prophecy merely meant that my religion would be a better one than his. I attended the Government Boys' School at Kibi from 1930 to 1935, living with my uncle, Mr. Alfred Kpodo, who was working in that town. I afterwards came back to my home country to continue my schooling at Anyako, and I finished at the fifth standard under Teacher (now the Reverend) E. A. Banini. I became in turn a Post Office messenger, a policeman, a prison warder, an employee of the Government Department of Agriculture, and of the Mines office at Akwatia.

During my stay at Akwatia from 1935 to 1939 I preached a great deal, holding Bible classes, conducting a singing band, and even teaching literacy in my off-duty hours. I became even more interested in these activities than in the job for which I was paid. All over the district I was well known as a voluntary evangelistic worker. At the outbreak of the Second World War, it was announced that all the employees of the mines would be regarded as conscripted, with the exception of the chief clerks only. This was not to my liking, so I left Akwatia to return to my hometown, Tadzewu.

This town is reputed in the district for its market, to which people come from far-off places. But the inhabitants were very few when I arrived, some 150 to 200 people all told.

The men were mostly farmers, who also tapped palm trees for wine; the women sold palm-wine and various foodstuffs. The inhabitants were all very fond of drumming and dancing, but they used these recreations as occasions for singing mocking and insulting songs about one another, saying very bitter things to one another in pretendedly jocular fashion. In short, it was a vicious form of amusement, from which no good could come. Water was extremely hard to come by in the place. The shallow wells dug in the beds of streams soon dried up, and water had to be fetched by head porterage from distances of from two to nine miles according to the severity of the drought. This difficulty was a major factor in preventing the growth and development of the town. It was surrounded on all sides by thick woods, and sanitation, in particular with regard to the disposal of all kinds of refuse, was at a very low level.

I left Akwatia on the fourth of October 1939 but it was not until the first of November that I got home. Early the following morning, I sent someone round the town with a hand-bell to summon all who would come. There were many children and a few adults. I preached to them, and spoke to the children especially about the advantages of attending school. I asked if they would like to go to school, and they hailed the idea with great delight. On the following day, I had not myself even risen from bed before they began to forgather. There were twenty-four of them, and this was the nucleus of my school. I felt intensely happy, like a man who had at long last found his real life's vocation.

Apart from the school, I undertook some work among grown-ups too. I organized voluntary sanitary overseers to help promote cleanliness in the town; I also started a prayer group, with regular meetings for biblical exhortation and prayer. Although all the members were as yet heathen, I taught them to call on the name of Jehovah the great God, and on the name of Jesus Christ, and soon several among them were able themselves to offer Christian prayers both in public and in private. When I saw how well they were doing, I turned the group into a catechumen's class and had its members baptized when they were ready, by the Rev. Elias W. Tamakloe of the Ewe Presbyterian Church then stationed at Abor. These first Christians formed the mainstay of my work in the succeeding period, and continue to be such until the present day. In addition to my work in church and school I started a dispensary and dressing center. My volunteer helpers and I dressed all sorts of sores, and I gave to the people, free of charge, many of the common patent drugs which they needed, and of which I kept a supply at my own expense. For all other sick I held regular sessions of prayers for healing.

Among many other revelations was one on September 29, 1946, to the effect that I would now have trained certificated teachers for my school. This prophecy came to pass in the arrival, on September 28, 1949, of Mr. A. A. Kuadey, followed soon afterwards by Mr. J. K. Tsa. As the school was still unrecognized by the government, so that no grants were paid towards teachers' salaries, these men had to make do with very meager salaries until 1952, when finally the school was placed on the list of schools encouraged by the government.[2] For what God himself intends to do must needs happen.

Both the town and the congregation also grew by leaps and bounds. There are about 1000 people in Tadzewu today, most of them strangers who have come here somehow or other in connection with my work. Among the aboriginal population Christians now greatly outnumber pagans, and only a few heathen rites are still to be seen being performed publicly. My Society has its own hospital, with accommodation for people who come from distant places for healing.[3] Those with contagious diseases such as

2. The prophet had now conformed to the regulations.

3. This place is not to be conceived as a hospital in the usual sense. It merely consists of a number of huts in which the patients live, looked after by their own people under the supervision of the Society's nurses. These, though not professionally trained, can direct patients to take the drugs being used for them at the proper times, etc., and on the whole nurse the sick in a more enlightened way than their own people are usually able to do.

leprosy, tuberculosis, epilepsy, yaws, various bad skin diseases, and whooping cough are required to live separately. We have had two cases of smallpox that we promptly reported to the District Government Hospital, which immediately took charge of them. We engage in practicing and teaching many useful trades and businesses. Apart from providing the income that we require, these occupations offer opportunities of apprenticeships and gainful employment to many of our young people. I run a poultry farm and vegetable gardens; corn mills and lorry transport; workshops for tailoring, blacksmithy, the maintenance and repair of lorries and bicycles, etc. We have a post office, a printing press and electricity plant of our own. In our Society we support only genuine destitutes, all others have to fend for themselves.

One of the greatest steps forward was taken when God in his mercy permitted me to ordain my own clergy to assist me in his work. On the nineteenth of June 1949 I ordained the first batch of these, seventeen in number, with four "judges." [4] Since then their number has greatly increased, and not only have I benefited from their help, but I have had the joy of knowing that my work cannot now perish, for even if I should die, there are those who will carry it forward.

One remarkable feature of our Society's life is the yearly great festival or "anniversary." It lasts a whole week. Quite early in our history, the members of the Society began to attach great importance to it, and even after seven days of celebrations nobody ever gets tired; always it is only with the greatest reluctance that people finally leave again to return to their own homes. Since 1954, we have organized the anniversaries with such care that each has been grander and better than the preceding one. Our spending for hospitality alone now exceeds £1000 sterling on each occasion, but on the other hand people make generous voluntary

---

4. The 'judges' are men (usually 3 or 4 in number) who are appointed to sit with the prophet and determine all matters threatening the peace, good order and harmony of the community.

offerings, so that a substantial part of the revenue of the Society comes from this source. Each celebration remains the talk of the whole district in which it was held, if not of the entire Trans-Volta Region, for weeks and even months afterwards.

Our workers take no fixed salaries. We all share whatever funds are available from voluntary gifts, whenever it is convenient to do so. We likewise share the foodstuffs from our Society's farms, and at outstations members assist their workers by making and maintaining vegetable gardens for them. We all find that this is ample to meet our needs, and God always provides.

Members of other Christian denominations may join our Society and still retain their membership in their own churches, but we do not accept pagans, Muslims, or other non-Christians. Our instruction period both for adult baptism and confirmation is one year, but in cases of emergency, a person may be baptized after only two weeks of instruction. We recognize and practice infant baptism. In this rite, as in confirmation and the ordination of ministers, we follow the usage of the Evangelical Presbyterian Church, as adapted by ourselves.

We print and distribute our own literature. Our hymn-book is the work of the printing firm of J. J. Augustin Gluckstadt in Germany. It was an unforgettable day of triumph and rejoicing when, at the great anniversary which we celebrated at Papase in 1953, this collection of our Society's own dearly beloved songs and hymns could be put in the hands of members as a beautifully bound book. We have in booklet form the history of our Society from the beginnings till 1954. We print yearly calendars showing the Bible passages to be read by members and to be used for preaching every day of the year, as well as giving statistics and other important information about the current state of the Society. I used to have these printed by the Scottish Mission Press at Accra, but at one stage the Manager told me that the Evangelical Presbyterian Church had raised an objection, so I now have them printed by an independent African firm at Cape Coast.

In 1958 this Society claimed around 50,000 members.[5] Its calendar for that year names 115 towns and villages in which it is represented; in 33 of them it had a school as well as a congregation. The number of ministers given is 55, but I was informed later on in the year that this had risen to 70. Besides 65 school-teachers and three "judges," the following are listed as the official workers of the Society: office clerks, five; herdsmen, four; printers, four (including two women); masons, eight; tailors and dressmakers, five (three women); carpenters, seven; organist, one; nurses, nine (three women); children's nurse, one (woman); laborers, two; cornmill tenders, three (two women); drivers, three; blacksmiths, three; mechanic, one. This gives an indication of the Society's activities.

Under the heading "Other Institutions or Agencies of the Society" the calendar shows: "*1*) Moral Institutes; *2*) The Institute of Marriage Instruction (this is printed in capitals, doubtless to indicate the importance attached to it); *3*) Community Center; and *4*) Trade School." All these are located at the Tadzewu headquarters. I did not see the "Moral Institute." Probably, what is meant is the meetings organized to discuss married life and good behavior in general. The "Institute of Marriage Instruction" is a sort of boarding school for girls, run on lines similar to those of a convent. There were some twenty in residence at the time of my visit, their ages ranging from about 13 to about 18. In charge was an educated, middle-aged widow from an urban area in the district, of very good family and upbring-

5. The membership figure was given me by the prophet; the others are mostly taken from the latest available pocket calendar of the Society. The article in the *African World* states: 'Its active membership has reached a total of more than 60,000, and there are about 150 congregations or stations with primary schools attached, and supervised by 52 pastors of the Society'.

ing; in fact it is she who holds the official position of organist, being an extremely competent and effective accompanist on the harmonium. The girls study all the various aspects of ordinary domestic science and child care, as practiced in the homes of educated but non-professional Africans. All the indications were that they received a good deal of moral exhortation as well. There is not a trade school as such, but several boys living with the boarders of the elementary school or with families in the town learn their chosen trades as apprentices in the various workshops.

The main purpose of the calendar is, however, to give the selected Bible readings for each day of the year, as well as Church statistics, etc. In the preface, the Prophet urges all members to buy copies because he had asked God especially to be directed to choose the most suitable and helpful passages, and because by so doing members would make it possible for him to continue to give them his services.

Blaise Diagne: African Politician
in the Colonial Era, 1914–1930's

G. WESLEY JOHNSON *

Blaise Diagne is an African politician who has been neglected by historians because of the onrush of events in independent Africa. Forty years ago he was famous both in
Europe and Africa as the only African who sat as a member of the French Parliament in Paris. He was known to
many as a statesman of the highest character and motives, to
some as a revolutionary who plotted separatist movements,
and to others as the collaborator of the French colonial
regime. In his own complex way, Diagne was all three of
these during his important and colorful public career.

Diagne's political ability won him many honors during
his tenure as deputy from 1914 to 1934: Under-Secretary of
State for Colonies, High Commissioner of African Troops,
President of the Chamber's Commission on Colonies. At
the same time Diagne was able to bring about political
changes in Senegal and accomplish many lasting reforms
for the benefit of his people. Such an important and interesting man is deserving of closer attention; the lines that
follow are an attempt to sketch the main points about
Diagne, his career, his views, his accomplishments, and his
contributions to African history.

* From G. Wesley Johnson, "Blaise Diagne: Master Politician of
Senegal," *Tarikh,* 1966, No. 2.

Blaise Diagne was born on Gorée island, just off the coast of Dakar, in 1872. His father was Serer and his mother Lebou, but from his early childhood he was looked after by the Creole Adolphe Crespin, who sent him to the Catholic grammar school at Gorée. Blaise did well at his lessons, in fact so well that he spent many days writing letters home to France for illiterate white French soldiers who were quartered on the island.

Because Blaise was a bright student, Adolphe Crespin decided to send him to France to continue his education. He started his studies near Marseille, but soon became homesick in this strange country. He returned to Senegal and enrolled in the secondary school in Saint-Louis, which was then the capital city of the colony of Senegal. Here he apparently did very well, because the Official Journal of Senegal, the government newspaper, lists him as winning first prize in his graduating class of 1890. Blaise then tried unsuccessfully to gain a post in the French customs service, which at this time was still open to qualified African applicants. In 1892, he was finally accepted and sent to Dahomey for training, then on to Gabon and the French Congo. He performed his functions well but ran into trouble with his superiors. He sincerely believed the lessons that he had learned in school about assimilation—that is, if an African was educated, he could expect to be accepted as an equal by the white members of the colonial administration. In theory this was France's ideal, but in practice it was not a reality. Diagne found himself discriminated against and passed over for promotion.

Such a young man, who was highly color conscious, who was trying to reconcile his learning with the inadequacies of opportunity, was bound to create trouble for the colonial administration. He was shipped away to Reunion Island, then to Madagascar and tagged as "an undesirable." He was finally ordered to French Guiana in South America, a backwater of the French empire, where he might look forward to a passive future, far removed from Africa where he might stir up his African comrades. Even so, he found ways to serve as a municipal councillor and participated in Guiana politics to a limited extent.

Meanwhile Diagne married Odette Villain, a young Frenchwoman, and spent his leave time in France. Here he became acquainted at first hand with French politics and decided to take leave of absence from Guiana and try for the most important political office in his home colony of Senegal: deputy to the French Chamber. Since 1848 Senegal had sent deputies to Paris, but they were always either French or Creole. Never had the electorate, which was about 90 percent African, sent an indigenous African to Paris. Diagne decided that he would try his luck. He knew that his future in the customs service would be difficult if he lost, for he would be a marked man.

Returning to Dakar in February 1914, Blaise Diagne made contact with the Muslim leaders, the Lebou chiefs, and most important, the Young Senegalese, a group of young Wolof intellectuals who were smarting under new French restrictions which limited their advance in the administration. They made common cause with Diagne, who won the election by defeating a combined French and Creole group of candidates. For the first time, Senegal had an African leader who was not afraid to speak up, who met the French on equal terms. In the past, Africans had served in minor positions and were known as "yes" men. Diagne now inspired a new generation of Africans to political action.

He called for the incorporation of citizens of the four Old Communes of Senegal into the French army, instead of serving with the colonial troops. This was a popular idea with his voters, who were also pleased with his 1915–1916 laws, which gave them full French citizenship but allowed those who wished to retain traditional law in family matters. Rural Senegalese on the other hand were bitter because of the discrimination. They felt they had borne the brunt of the war burden by sending their sons to the army and that they should have a voice in the political affairs of the colony.

Clemenceau, Prime Minister of France, decided in 1918

to recruit more African troops since they were badly needed on the European battle lines. He called on Diagne and asked him to head a recruiting mission to West Africa. Most observers thought Diagne would not accept, but he did, on condition that hospitals, schools, and medical facilities be improved in West Africa. While this recruitment trip won Diagne great popularity in wartime France it brought disdain from most Africans. Had Diagne become a Frenchman during his four years in Parliament? Had he forgotten his fellow Africans? These were the questions his critics hurled at him. In fact Diagne realized the Africans were likely to be conscripted anyway, and by intervening personally, he secured for them better facilities in the army plus much needed social amenities.

In 1919, after the war was over, new elections were held in Senegal. The returning African veterans formed the nucleus of Diagne's Republican-Socialist Party, the first African political party organized in French tropical Africa. The election was a turning point for Senegal: not only was Diagne reelected deputy by a great majority, but his friends conveniently won the contests for municipal offices and seats on the General Council. Diagne had completely Africanized Senegalese politics within five years of leaving Guiana. What is more, he had done it legally within the framework of free elections and despite immense pressure from French merchants and colonists. Naturally, the French administration was alarmed by Diagne's successes and a "reactionary" governor-general was appointed to govern French West Africa. Diagne would not knuckle under to the old-style paternalistic policy of prewar days: he had tasted real power in Paris, had been treated as an equal by Clemenceau and was an intimate friend of Henry Simon, the wartime Minister of Colonies. Diagne opposed French attempts to whittle away the powers of the political institutions of Senegal; he was called a separatist, a radical, and his name was linked with Du Bois and Garvey and the pan-African movement. Soon Diagne found all his efforts to bring progress to Senegal blocked by French business and government.

Under these circumstances, Diagne changed his tactics. He signed the famous Bordeaux agreements of 1923, a truce between the Diagnists and French merchants. Immediately the young African intellectuals in both France and Senegal cried out that Diagne had sold himself to the French. Indeed, the next year Lamine Gueye, the first African to win a doctorate in law in Paris, organized a coalition of young intellectuals against Diagne. Even so, in 1924, Diagne won easily as deputy and in 1925 was elected Mayor of Dakar. He appointed an assistant to manage the city during his absences in France.

It was inevitable that some of Diagne's lieutenants would become dissatisfied with his increasingly arbitrary rule. They joined with Galandou Diouf and Lamine Gueye to oppose Diagne in 1928 and 1932. The record indicates that but for official French connivance Diouf would have won in 1928 but by 1932 Diouf had become bankrupt and the opposition discouraged. Meanwhile, however, over a dozen magazines and newspapers had sprouted up in Senegal to oppose Diagne and to call for better treatment under the colonial regime. These new intellectuals wanted certain of the advantages of French civilization, but they were emphatic about remaining Senegalese. They thought of themselves first of all as Africans and this is indicated by the editorials and writings from this period. Politics in pre-World War II Senegal were much livelier than is supposed: there were riots, demonstrations, strikes, imprisonment of candidates, enormous political rallies, and impassioned speeches. There was a remarkable measure of freedom of speech, and political rallies were called to explain the positions of various groups.

Social unrest in the 1930's put Diagne on the horns of a dilemma. How to help Senegal? What price collaboration? He masterfully negotiated the first French subsidy for groundnuts, which ensured economic stability for Senegal for the next thirty years. But at the same time he was called upon to represent France at the Geneva labor talks on forced labor—and found himself defending the French colonial policy which weighed so heavily upon Africans outside Senegal. Worn out by international politics, by attempting to reconcile his concern for Africa and his knowledge of what was politic, Diagne died in May 1934.

A political vacuum was created in Senegal. Without his leadership Diagne's party collapsed within a few months. Galandou Diouf emerged as the new deputy, inheriting Diagne's political mantle and continuing his policy of collaboration. Lamine Gueye and the intellectuals went into loyal opposition, arguing for reform. They joined with French socialists in the colony in 1936 to form a Senegalese Popular Front and to prepare the way for post-World War II developments. Thus the political tradition that Diagne started was carried on after him. In a sense, his heirs were the African leaders of 1946 who organized political parties in French Africa and finally came to power after 1960.

Leader-Follower Relationship
in an African Political Party:
The Sierra Leone People's Party

MARTIN KILSON *

The manner in which the leader-follower relationship has
developed in Sierra Leonean parties provides another index
of the nature of power and influence in these parties. From
their beginning the major postwar parties offered membership to all segments of the adult population irrespective
of sex, tribe, religion, etc. All parties required a member
to pay either an initial fee or an annual subscription or both.
For example, the SLPP and the United Progressive Party
(UPP), one of the major opposition parties since 1955, required only an initial fee of 1s. and 2s. respectively; the
People's National Party (PNP), another important opposition party founded in 1958, required both an initial membership fee of 6d. and an additional 6d. annual subscription. The UPP and PNP, unlike the SLPP, also provided for
membership by entire organizations, among which were,
as listed in the UPP Constitution, "Trade Unions, Organizations of Professional Workers, Ex-Servicemen's Associations, Civil Service Associations, Co-Operative and Farmers'
Organizations, etc. . . ." [1] The SLPP, however, was also

* From Martin Kilson, *Political Change in a West African State*
(Cambridge, Mass., 1966).

1. *Constitution of the United Sierra Leone Progressive Party*
(Freetown, 1956), pp. 3–4.

linked to voluntary organizations of one sort or other, largely through interlocking leadership ties. Key leaders in the SLPP were simultaneously heads of sizable voluntary bodies like the Ex-Servicemen's Association, which had a membership over 3,000, and the Sierra Leone Women's Movement, which had a membership of 5,000 women traders, hawkers, seamstresses, etc. Though these organizations did not hold direct membership in the SLPP, they invariably brought many of their followers into the party or implored them to support it in general elections.

In general, Sierra Leonean parties do not actively pursue the enrollment of ordinary members, as do, say, the radical type of African parties like the *Parti Démocratique de Guinée* (PDG), which claimed 1,600,000 members in 1961 out of a total population of 3,000,000. Of the nearly 1,000,000 qualified voters in Sierra Leone in 1961 (out of a total population estimated at 2,250,000, though probably nearer 3,000,000 in fact), only 150,000 were reported as enrolled party members. This comparatively low party membership resulted from, among other things, the absence of a militant nationalist ideology on the part of the major party, the SLPP, the relatively small role of party machinery in the political process, and the tendency of Sierra Leonean parties to activate themselves only in periods of political crisis, after which they revert to relative inactivity. A political crisis of one sort or other was, in fact, invariably associated with the main effort of opposition parties to gain members.

The UPP, for instance, obtained the main body of its members during the tax riots in 1955–1956, at which time the party's leader, Cyril Rogers-Wright, a lawyer-politician, freely placed his legal skills at the service of thousands of tax rioters who confronted the Magistrate's Court. Some peasant rioters so defended by Rogers-Wright responded by joining the UPP; others voted for the UPP candidates in the 1957 General Election in which the UPP gained seven seats in the northern and southwestern provinces, the only

Creole-led party ever to do so.[2] This crisis-based backing for the UPP was, however, merely a transitory gain. Its new peasant following had joined or supported the party only partly out of positive sympathy, being motivated more by a desire to discredit the corrupt system of native administration taxation that had plagued them for some thirty years. By 1958 most of the UPP's supporters in the northern and southwestern provinces had left it; in some instances they had, indeed, requested that the pro-SLPP chiefs whose corrupt administrations had sparked the tax riots be reinstated.[3] It would seem that such peasant ambivalence toward traditional rulers, evident throughout West Africa, constitutes a decisive factor in limiting the capacity of militant or radical parties (which in the Sierra Leone context the UPP was) to penetrate the rural populace.

The PNP also gained much of its membership in the context of a political crisis. The party arose out of a protracted struggle for leadership of the SLPP between Sir Milton Margai and his younger brother, Albert Margai, which reflected a more basic conflict between the older and younger men in the party. (Sir Milton Margai was 62 years old at the time, and Albert was 48 years old.) Upon his failure to wrest leadership from Sir Milton, Albert Margai formed the PNP in mid-1958, largely as an afterthought in which he was prompted by Siaka Stevens, a former minister in the SLPP government who shared Albert Margai's misfortune but was game for, and capable of, battle with the SLPP. In leaving the SLPP, Albert Margai and Stevens carried many of the young supporters of the party with them, especially young clerks, teachers, professionals, and some skilled workers in the hinterland towns like Moyamba, Bo, Port Loko, Kenema, and Sefadu. These elements were never happy in their support of the SLPP, given its large dependence upon chiefs, and seized the opportunity to realign

---

2. See A. G. Simpson, *Report on the Sierra Leone General Election, 1957* (Freetown, 1957), pp. 1–6.

3. Interview with District Commissioner, Kambia, March 1960.

when Albert Margai and Siaka Stevens formed the PNP. Furthermore, these elements later shifted their support to the All People's Congress (APC) which Siaka Stevens founded in mid-1960 after Albert Margai disbanded the PNP to rejoin the SLPP government as Minister of Natural Resources. Shortly thereafter the APC proved itself the most effective party ever to oppose the SLPP, gaining twenty-two of the sixty-four seats contested in the 1962 General Election.[4]

In addition to the voluntary associations—and we have mentioned only a few of them—chiefs and the institutions they control have been even more important in obtaining a popular following for the SLPP.[5] Those peasants and casual wage-laborers in the provinces who supported or joined the SLPP did so largely because their chiefs suggested or required it. Despite their not infrequent rebellious outbursts against chiefly rule, the bulk of the peasants continue to defer to chiefly dictates in matters of authority and politics. The SLPP Propaganda Secretaries responsible for organizing the provinces leave the major part of membership recruitment to chiefs and native administrations.[6] The 1959 report of the SLPP Propaganda Secretary in Kenema District recorded the procedure involved as follows: "No sale conducted by me in this town; at the same time, I appointed Section Chief Alfred Pekawa of Baama, Secretary for Baama town only—the largest and most populous town in the Chiefdom. He was given 150 cards and I fully demonstrated how each card is to be issued out." [7] The report further noted that the staff of native administrations were utilized to distribute party cards.

---

4. Electoral Commission, *Sierra Leone General Election, 1962 Score-Sheet* (Freetown, 1962), pp. 8–12.

5. For data on cooperatives, through which many cash-crop producers were linked to the SLPP through government aid, see *Sierra Leone Protectorate Handbook, 1961* (Freetown, 1961).

6. Interview with A. H. Kabia, SLPP Senior Propaganda Secretary, December 1960.

7. S. M. Kone, *SLPP Propaganda Secretary's Report on Kenema Election, October, 1959* (typescript; Freetown, 1959).

One outcome of this method of recruiting members or supporters was a rather uninspired kind of participation in party activity. Even aside from the lack of adequate party machinery to stimulate member participation, it was unlikely that the people enrolled as party members through chiefs' instigation would express a penchant for serious activity. An SLPP gathering in the rural areas is typically a rather contrived affair; several hundred peasants are herded by a chief into a native court *barri* or some other traditional setting to welcome touring SLPP ministers and other leaders. The dancing, drumming, and singing in traditional idioms characteristic of these gatherings seldom amount to more than merrymaking—a kind of respite from the boredom of village life. A more politically meaningful experience for the rural populace came only in anomic outbursts of one sort or other.

It is notable that though this pattern of member participation has been characteristic largely of the caucus-type parties like the SLPP or the Northern People's Congress in Nigeria—parties, that is, which are linked to the wider populace through the intermediary agency of chiefly bodies— it is increasingly being reverted to by the mass-type parties, or rather what were mass-type parties during the mature period of anticolonial nationalism, like the *Parti Démocratique de la Côte d'Ivoire*, the PDG, and the Convention People's Party (CPP) in Ghana.[8] Once the elite who used the mass-type party to obtain political office succeeded, the tendency has been for them to preempt the process of bona fide political participation by the populace, turning the party instead into a callous instrument of political control (including oppression) and social order. This has often involved a reversion to traditional and chiefly-centered agencies of public gatherings of all sorts, though strictly under the ruling party's auspices. In Ghana, for example, the CPP government has stimulated the revival of many

8. For an excellent study of a mass party, see A. Zolberg, *One-Party Government in the Ivory Coast* (Princeton, N.J., 1964).

public festivals and ritual occasions that had long lapsed.
The Traditional Area Councils receive funds from the government or from the CPP district branches to cover the costs
of such festivals, including in some instances stimulating
drinks. Party representatives appear at these events and
make speeches about the need to be loyal to the president,
the party, and the government. Even the formal political
rallies held in Accra and other urban centers increasingly
entail the format of a traditional public occasion, with local
chiefs and their entourage participating. Their appearance
at such rallies, always in regal splendor, is often taken as a
cue by the crowd for merrymaking; the result is the blunt-
ing of the serious side of political gatherings and the political perception of the masses. In short, the traditional context of popular political participation long utilized by caucus-type parties like the SLPP is increasingly being adopted
throughout African party systems in order politically to
rout the masses.

A final facet of the leader-follower relationship that
should be mentioned is the mode of communicating party
aims and policies. The SLPP, which is the only party dis-
cussed here, reaches its supporters through the same intermediary bodies that secure most of its backing in the first
place. The chiefs and native administrations play the most
important role in this regard, and during elections the SLPP
works almost exclusively through chiefs. In the local government elections of 1959 the SLPP propaganda secretary in Kenema district recorded in his report how he organized campaign rallies through the native administration;
at one such rally in the Gorama Mende Chiefdom, he lec-
tured the people and chiefs "on the importance of the local
election and why a PNP member should not be given any
chance." The selection of candidates was also done through
the native administration, and local sentiment on the choice
of candidates was given great weight. In Wando Chiefdom,
for example, the propaganda secretary recorded that he
"held a meeting in the chief's *barri* with the tribal authority.
I read out the names of the applicants for the election. They

unanimously declared that they would not allow a man staying outside the chiefdom to represent them in the [district] council . . . Section Chief Alfred Pekawa was unanimously appointed . . ." [9]

The national leaders of the party communicate with the masses in the same manner. Sir Milton Margai was particularly keen on this method of conducting his contact with the rural populace; a typical newspaper account of one of Sir Milton's innumerable political tours of the provinces observed: "The Premier, Sir Milton Margai, has met the tribal authority of the Jong Chiefdom (Bonthe District) at Mattru . . . Tomorrow, Sir Milton will visit Gbap, after meeting the chiefs and tribal authorities of Sitia and Bendu-Cha Chiefdoms." [10] Occasionally Sir Milton summoned paramount chiefs to his office in Freetown to discuss party policies and to give them directives on how to disseminate it. In December 1960, for example, he met with twenty-five leading paramount chiefs to inform them of the party's plans for attaining independence from Britain and instructed them how to communicate the information to the masses. "Their duty," he directed, "was to tell all the section chiefs about independence; the section chiefs in turn should educate the town head-men who should explain to the people." [11]

Thus the SLPP's method of informing the rural populace of its policies may be described as a primary communication network; it rests upon the face-to-face contact, inherently coercive, that characterizes traditional relationships between chiefs and peasants. Moreover, this method of political communication is congruent with, and a direct function of, the SLPP's conservative view of modernization —a view which considers as desirable and necessary the integration of as much as possible of traditional authority patterns into the modern sociopolitical system.

The SLPP, however, was required, like other African

9. Kone, *SLPP Propaganda Secretary's Report on Kenema Election, October, 1959.*

10. *Sierra Leone Daily Mail,* October 8, 1959, p. 9.

11. *Shekpendeh,* December 2, 1960, p. 4.

parties, to adopt more explicitly modern channels of communicating its aims and policies to the literate and semi-literate urban population. Here the party relied to some extent upon its formal branches; in 1960–1961 the SLPP had twenty-one organized branches, and those situated in coastal urban centers of Freetown and Bonthe, and in the leading provincial towns like Moyamba, Makeni, Bo, and Kenema, were of some use in channeling party policies.[12] More important than the party branches, however, were its ties to voluntary associations like the Sierra Leone Women's Movement, the Youth Movement, the Cooperative Societies, and the Ex-Servicemen's Association, all of which were bound to the SLPP through interlocking leadership and invariably influenced their thousands of members on behalf of the party. Thus Dr. Karefa-Smart, President of the Ex-Servicemen's Association, was Minister of External Affairs in the SLPP government; Paramount Chief R. B. S. Koker, Secretary of the influential Old Bo School Boys' Association, was Minister without Portfolio; M. S. Mustapha, a leading figure in the Muslim Congress, was Minister of Finance and treasurer of the SLPP; Mrs. Constance Cummings-John, founder and Organizing Secretary of the Sierra Leone Women's Movement, was a Vice President of the SLPP; Madame Nancy Koroma, Mende Tribal Headman in Freetown and head of the Mende Tribal Committee, was a member of the SLPP Executive Committee; and Kandeh Bureh, Temne Tribal Headman in Freetown and founder of several Temne tribal associations, was a member of the SLPP's Executive Committee and Minister of Public Works.

At election time, though on other occasions as well, the interlocking tie between the SLPP and voluntary associations was a crucial factor in the popular backing the party received. The voluntary associations also gave the articulate supporters of the SLPP much more opportunity to initiate

---

12. Interview with R. G. O. King, General Secretary of SLPP, January 1961.

lines of action and policy for the party than did the party branches. And as long as they are not fully absorbed into the party structure—which has been the plight of voluntary associations in the single-party states, especially those with the mass-type party—the voluntary associations in Sierra Leone will provide some democratic initiation at the grass roots. Neither the largely inactive party branches nor the native administrations approximates the voluntary associations in this regard.

It should be noted, finally, that the mass media are also of some importance in channeling the party's aims and policies. Since its formation the SLPP has had two newspapers—the *Sierra Leone Observer* and the *African Vanguard*. The former was founded by Sir Milton Margai two years before the founding of the party, and in 1958, the year the *Sierra Leone Observer* folded, it had a circulation of 1,500 copies weekly. The *African Vanguard*, founded by the liberal Creole politician Laminah Sankoh in 1948 and turned over to the SLPP in 1951, is now the party's only newspaper; it has a biweekly circulation of 3,000. The SLPP also depends upon the British-owned *Sierra Leone Daily Mail* for favorable coverage; it has the largest circulation in Sierra Leone. The total newspaper readership in Sierra Leone was estimated at 40,000 in 1961. It should also be mentioned that the SLPP has access to the government-owned and controlled radio station for political purposes. In 1961 there were 23,000 radio receivers and between 150,000 to 200,000 listeners in Sierra Leone, most of whom were literate and resided in the coastal urban centers and in the provincial towns.

Uses of Power in African Parties:
Nigerian Experience, 1951–1960

*K. W. J. POST **

In 1951 the three major parties were given an opportunity to gain power in a system which was intended to put one group firmly in control in each region. We have seen that this had a powerful attractive effect during and immediately after the elections, with independents and even members of rival parties declaring for the party which seemed strongest. The constitutional changes of 1954 gave more power to the governing parties—removed central control over regional legislation, for example—and so enhanced the power of each party in its own region. In their dealings with their opponents and the ordinary electors, the major parties did not hesitate to insist that they were "the party in power" in their own regions. It was a slogan used as much in the election of 1959 as in previous elections, even though that was a federal, not a regional election. As a result, it was commonly believed that the various parties would use their control of the regional governments to preserve and increase their own power, and the wealth and influence of their supporters. Such a belief was a great incentive to cleave to the party in power, and it undoubtedly helped to keep the parties together after 1951, while their actual organizations were still being developed.

* From K. W. J. Post, *The Nigerian Federal Election of 1959* (Dandon, 1961).

It may be noted that each regional government had grad-ually acquired a number of public boards by 1959 which could be used as a means of dispensing patronage to party worthies. The various housing corporations, information services, cinema corporations, library boards, and printing corporations had their quotas of members who were active politicians. This was made more obvious by the occasional appointment to these regional bodies of party stalwarts from outside the region: in 1959 there was, for instance, an east-ern member of the Western Region Housing Corporation, and a western member of the Eastern Printing Corporation. The first was the Leader of Action Group's Zone A in the East, and the second was President-General of the Zikist National Vanguard, an auxiliary of the NCNC. It was not unknown for a prominent party member to be given a place on one of these boards as compensation for failing to secure nomination in a regional or federal election. A man who had been successively a teacher, a public works department timekeeper, a soldier, a railwayman, and the proprietor of an institute for the healing of the sick through the "psychic sciences" found himself appointed to the cinema corpora-tion. In any case, a politician appointed to one of these bodies would be expected to pay a percentage of his salary to the party.

Control of the regional governments did not give the major parties an opportunity merely to appoint members of public boards; they were also able to influence the decisions of a number of bodies which had very considerable sums of money at their disposal. The marketing boards, which came under the control of the regional governments in 1954, had large reserves, the result of their purchase of cash crops from the farmers at a guaranteed price each season and sale of them on the world market at a price which for a number of years was considerably higher than that paid to the farmer. Various finance and development corpora-tions were empowered to spend money, drawn from these reserves and other sources, on projects designed to increase the economic activity of Nigerians and promote the welfare of the people. In addition to this, the new regional governments were in a position to spend large sums of money, even before 1954, on projects such as roadbuilding. The opportunity for a share in the funds thus disbursed was a powerful incentive to the new men to continue to support the party in power. The Action Group and NCNC thus contained extremes among their members. At the highest level could be found a group of men who might, in fact, lose money by neglecting their businesses or professions for the sake of politics, but who found their reward in the power and prestige of office and in the feeling that they were helping their people. At the local level could be found the small contractor who hoped by showing zeal for the cause to be given work by the local council which his party controlled.

It is impossible to assess how far government boards showed favoritism toward members of the party which controlled them. It was commonly believed in 1959 that this was the case, but widely held beliefs are not necessarily true ones. Nevertheless, there is frequently a close connection between business and politics in modern political systems, and such was the case in Nigeria. As in other countries, it is difficult to isolate these connections in detail, but enough evidence is available to enable us to see some of the connections between governments, parties and private business.[1]

In general any remarks which are made will apply to the South, but not to the North. Enough has already been said about the Northern People's Congress to show that its origins and the social forces which it represented differed in important respects from those of the Action Group and NCNC. There were business interests in the NPC in 1959,

---

1. Much of the information which follows is taken from the returns of public companies kept at the Federal Ministry of Commerce and Industries in Lagos, and published periodically in the *Nigerian Trade Journal*. The author is deeply indebted to Mr. J. D. Nyhart for allowing him to draw on his research files.

but they showed no signs of becoming as dominant as their southern counterparts.

In the South, politicians were often also businessmen and would frequently go into business with one another. In September 1952, for instance, the Aboki Trading Company was formed in Lagos; its directors were Kola Balogun, a lawyer and National Secretary of the NCNC, and F. S. McEwen, a school proprietor and principal, and at that time prominent in the NCNC Youth Association and Lagos politics in general.[2] Again, in April 1955 the Ideal Commercial Syndicate was formed in Sapele. Two of its three directors were Chief Gabriel Ekwejunor-Etchie, a prominent local Action Group leader, and Chief Arthur Prest, Action Group Federal Minister of Communications from 1952 till 1954. When the latter began to move away from the Action Group (he was finally expelled in November 1957), he ceased to be a shareholder and was replaced by a relative of Chief Ekwejunor-Etchie and the Secretary of the Action Group branch in Sapele.[3]

There were not only business connections between individual politicians. The parties themselves were part of rival business and financial structures which existed to make money for the individuals concerned and provide financial backing for the parties. When Dr. Azikiwe returned to Nigeria in 1937, he set out to build up for himself a commercial empire based on the Tinubu Properties Ltd., which speculated in Lagos real estate, and on the *West African Pilot,* the chief organ of the nationalist movement. In 1948 the Tinubu Properties Ltd. became the African Continental Bank, which was re-formed as a public company in June 1950.[4] The directors were Dr. Azikiwe, his father, and his

---

2. McEwen succeeded Balogun as National Secretary in November 1957.
3. At the time of the federal election of 1959 the latter was Organizing Secretary for Action Group in Warri Division.
4. For general information about Nigerian banking at the time when the parties were forming see W. T. Newlyn and D. C. Rowan,

sister; of 111,935 ordinary shares issued by the end of 1954, Dr. Azikiwe held 28,000 and his father, sister, and her two young daughters, 4,000 each.[5] By 1956 Dr. Azikiwe's companies included the Nigerian Real Estate Corporation Ltd., Nigerian Commodities Ltd., Suburban Transport Ltd., African News Agency Ltd., Nigerian Printing Supply Co. Ltd., Nigerian Paper Co. Ltd., the African Book Co., Zik's Enterprises Ltd., the *West African Pilot* Ltd., and Associated Newspapers of Nigeria.[6] As Mr. B. J. M. MacKenna, Q.C., put it in his opening speech as counsel for the Foster-Sutton Tribunal, which was set up in 1956 to examine the affairs of these companies and the African Continental Bank, "The principal use made of the public deposits [in the Bank] was to finance the Zik Group of companies." [7]

By 1955 these companies had lost at least £98,000 and five of them showed deficits over their original capital. In all 56 percent (£321,000) of the Bank's total funds had been loaned to one or other of Dr. Azikiwe's companies, the main function of which was to produce the *Pilot,* his chief political organ. Some £170,770 of these loans and overdrafts had been guaranteed by two Eastern businessmen, L. P. Ojukwu and N. M. Ugochukwu.[8]

Money and Banking in British Colonial Africa (London: Oxford Studies in African Affairs, Oxford University Press, 1954), Chapter V.

5. The information on Dr. Azikiwe's businesses is mainly drawn from the *Proceedings of the Tribunal Appointed to Inquire into Allegations of Improper Conduct by the Premier of the Eastern Region of Nigeria in Connection with the Affairs of the African Continental Bank Limited and other Relevant Matters* (Lagos: Federal Government Printer, 1957). Details of shareholdings in the Bank are in paragraphs 5,525–35, page 205.

6. In 1959 the last group included the *Southern Nigeria Defender* (Ibadan), *Nigerian Spokesman* (Onitsha), *Eastern Sentinel* (Enugu), *Eastern Nigeria Guardian* (Port Harcourt), and the *Daily Comet* (Kano).

7. This view was confirmed by Dr. Azikiwe in his evidence before the Tribunal: see paras. 22,043–22,044, page 826.

8. Details of the position of each company can be found in the

In 1955 the African Continental Bank was insolvent, with a ratio of cash held to customers' deposits of about 8 percent. The Banking Ordinance of Nigeria, which came into force on May 22, 1952, gave all banks three years in which to qualify for a license, which depended on a liquidity ratio of 30 percent. On May 20, 1955, an agreement was made by the Eastern Region Finance Corporation to invest £800,000 in the Bank; the money had come from the Eastern Region Marketing Board, and was part of a transfer of £2,000,000 from the funds of the Marketing Board to the Finance Corporation. At this time, Dr. Azikiwe was Premier of the Eastern Region, and L. P. Ojukwu was Chairman of the Marketing Board. This injection of capital raised the value of the Bank's shares from nothing to 14s. 10d. each, and it was the demand by E. O. Eyo, an Ibibio and an erstwhile lieutenant of Dr. Azikiwe, that this be investigated which led to the setting-up of the Foster-Sutton Tribunal.[9]

This, then, was the complex financial and business substructure upon which the NCNC was based. The various companies and the African Continental Bank were used to finance its newspapers. Dr. Azikiwe used his own personal fortune, made from his business ventures, to help finance the party; at the Jos Convention in December 1952, for instance, he donated £5,000 in cash and revenue-bearing securities to party funds.[10] Alternatively the Bank would make loans to the party for special purposes, like the one of £50,000 at 4 percent interest which was revealed during the proceedings of the Tribunal.[11] Sometimes, however, the relationship would apparently be a purely business one;

---

evidence of Mr. S. P. Wilkins, the chartered accountant who acted on behalf of the Tribunal, more especially paragraphs 5,500–5,524, pages 204–205.

9. See the evidence of Mr. Wilkins, paragraphs 5,190–5,212, page 195.

10. In all £25,000 was raised on this occasion.

11. See the evidence of Mr. Wilkins and E. O. Eyo, para. 5,366, page 200, and paras. 12,925–12,936, page 487. The money was to form a campaign fund for the Western Regional election of 1956.

in 1954, Zik's Enterprises made a profit of about £8,000
from the sale of party buttons to NCNC. Above all, the dangers of mixing politics and business are very apparent. In
1955 the Bank and most of Dr. Azikiwe's businesses were
virtually bankrupt, and had to have a large transfusion from
Eastern Government funds, which fortunately for the party
were controlled by the NCNC, in order to restore them.

The financial position of the party and the businesses in
1959–1960, the year in which the NCNC was called upon
to make its greatest effort to win power at the center, was
obscure. In his report to the Annual Convention held in
Lagos on September 10 and 11, 1960, the National Secretary, F. S. McEwen, confirmed the shaky financial state of
the party. Between January 1957 and July 1960, that is in
the period which included the federal election of 1959,
the NCNC had spent approximately £1,200,000. In the
same period its income "from all sources" had "not ex-
ceeded" £500,000.[12] The position of the party would
have been even worse had it not been able to draw on the
credit of the African Continental Bank, a credit which
from May 1959 was that of the NCNC-controlled Eastern
region government. In that month the Eastern Minister of
Finance announced that the Bank had been completely
taken over by the Eastern Region Development Corporation.[13] The Chairman of the Corporation, L. P. Ojukwu,
was to be Chairman of the Bank, and F. S. McEwen the
Acting General Manager.

The Action Group was also based upon a group of banking and newspaper concerns, the National Bank of Nigeria
Ltd., the Amalgamated Press of Nigeria Ltd., and Allied
Newspapers Ltd. The Amalgamated Press published the
main party organ, the *Daily Service,* and in October 1959
launched the new *Sunday Express.* Allied Newspapers was
a company set up in February 1959 to publish a chain of
newspapers which the Action Group was establishing in all

---

12. F. S. McEwen, *NCNC on the March* (NCNC National Headquarters Bureau of Information and Publicity, n.d.), page 14.
13. *Daily Times,* May 7, 1959.

three regions.[14] Its Managing Director was Editor-in-Chief of the *Daily Service*.

The National Bank was one of the oldest Nigerian banks. It was incorporated in Lagos as a private company in February 1933, with a nominal capital of £10,000. In September of the same year the Mutual Aids Society, a loans company, was incorporated with it. By 1951 it was banker to the Federal Cocoa Marketing Board (since superseded by Regional Boards) and had accounts from the United Africa Company, Elder Dempster, G. B. Ollivant, and other expatriate enterprises. Its paid-up capital in that year was £38,220, deposits amounted to £870,540 and loans, advances, and other accounts totalled £762,170.[15] Thus in 1951 it differed from the African Continental Bank in being an enterprise run according to purely commercial principles and with a large number of shareholders, most of them with small blocs of shares. From 1951, however, it became associated with Action Group. Two of its six directors in 1959 were Dr. Akinola Maja, for many years a leading Lagos businessman and known in the Action Group as "Father of the Party," and Alhaji S. O. Gbadamosi, the party's Federal Treasurer. The biggest single shareholder was the Western Region Marketing Board, which the Action Group Government had directed to invest £1,000,000 in the Bank in October 1955.[16] The next largest holding was that of a Lagos moneylending firm, with 27,470 shares. The balance sheet of the National Bank for 1958–1959 indicated the total assets £16,070,916 and the profit for the year as £43,851. The years since

---

14. This group included the *Mid-West Echo* (Benin), *Eastern Observer* (Onitsha), *COR Advocate* (Uyo), *Middle Belt Herald* (Jos), *Northern Star* (Kano), and the *Bornu People,* published in Jos but intended for Bornu. In addition there was the *Nigerian Tribune* (Ibadan). This was published by the African Press Limited, which existed before the Action Group, until July 1st, 1959, when it was transferred to the Allied Newspapers group.

15. Newlyn and Rowan, op. cit., pages 106–107.

16. In April 1961 the government of Western Nigeria took full control of the National Bank.

1951 thus showed a considerable increase in the Bank's business.

One of its interests was in the Amalgamated Press. Among the shareholders of this Action Group publishing company, according to its latest returns in 1960, were Obafemi Awolowo and S. L. Akintola, who together owned a block of 1,000 shares. T. A. Odutola and Akinola Maja were also shareholders, along with such original members of the party as Akanni Doherty, A. A. Akinsanya, and S. O. Shonibare. The major shareholder, however, was the National Bank, with 53,700 shares, the result of loans to the company of £45,000 in 1954 and £115,000 in 1956.[17] Like its NCNC counterpart, the Amalgamated Press ran at a loss; by 1959 it had apparently lost £158,950 altogether. The Action Group was fortunate in having a bank connected with it whose credit was strong enough to enable the party's major newspaper to appear despite this handicap.[18]

We have now seen that each major southern party was supported by a bank, which in particular was responsible for keeping the party's main newspaper alive, and that each bank had in the past received a very substantial injection of public money from government agencies, the respective governments being controlled by the different parties. This raises the whole intricate question of the use made by each party of the funds of the various Regional Marketing Boards, Finance Corporations, and Development Corporations. Constant allegations of favoritism and corruption were a normal part of Nigerian political life, but never proved.[19] The Foster-Sutton Tribunal provided the one in-

17. Of the thirteen other shareholdings, one was that of the Service Press, which was absorbed by the company in 1953, the five non-Action Group directors being dropped (the sixth was Akinola Maja). Another was held by Chief Akintola in his own name alone. A third was held by Mrs. Awolowo.

18. In August 1960, the Amalgamated Press entered into partnership with Roy Thomson, the owner of newspapers in Canada and Great Britain, and replaced the *Daily Service* with the *Daily Express*.

19. In April 1960, for instance, Chief T. A. Odutola was awarded

stance of an investigation into the use of such funds, and it
concluded that the action of the NCNC government in putting public funds into the African Continental Bank was
not a desirable one. This did not prevent Dr. Azikiwe from
winning a massive majority at the election he called in the
Eastern region shortly after the report of the Tribunal appeared.

Without going into the vexed question of morality, it
may be concluded that there was a general failure in Nigeria to distinguish between public, party, and private financial interests, and that this gave the parties the opportunity
to increase their own strength in a number of ways. One
last example of the relationship between private enterprise,
public money, and political profit may be given. This was
the series of loans made by the Western Region Marketing
Board to the National Investment and Properties Co. Ltd.,
a real estate and construction company formed in Lagos in
April 1958. The four shareholders, with 25,000 shares
each, were Akinola Maja, S. O. Gbadamosi (Action Group
Federal Treasurer), S. O. Shonibare (Action Group Federal Publicity Secretary), and Alfred O. Rewane, Chief
Awolowo's political secretary. The loans totalled £2,300,-
000, the share capital of the company being nominally
£100,000. Among other ventures, the company provided
the £20,000 to set up the new Action Group newspaper
chain, Allied Newspapers, in February 1959.

Business, then, added another dimension to politics in
Nigeria in 1959. It created new interests and relationships,
new allegiances and obligations. It helped to bind together
the major parties more closely, to attract to them the support of people who hoped thus to advance their business
careers.

£1,000 damages by a Lagos High Court in a libel action against
the *West African Pilot* and its editor. It had been alleged that his
loans from the Western Region Development Board had been
given for political reasons.

An African Party at the Grassroots:
The Convention People's Party
in Larteh Town in 1960's

DAVID BROKENSHA *

Larteh has political links with various authorities, and
a brief description of their organization may help to clarify
the relationship. First, the Akwapim Local Council is one
of 154 similar councils in Ghana. Councillors, who are unpaid, are elected for three-year periods, nowadays mostly
with CPP support: Kubease and Ahenease elect one councillor each. Chiefs may be councillors, and in 1961–1962
the *mamponghene* was the Chairman of the Akwapim Local Council. The local council operates fairly efficiently,
raising revenue mainly by levying rates, deciding on policy
through its committee system, and spending £80,000 per
year on health, education, sanitation, markets, etc. It has
judicial functions, and also supports Akwapim Traditional
Council by making an annual grant of £5,000.

The grant of £5,000 helps to pay the allowances of
chiefs—the *benkumhene* receives £240 per annum, the
kubeasehene £180 per annum. The traditional council is
composed of chiefs and elders from the whole state, and
concerns itself with matters of protocol, relations between
chiefs, and settlement of disputes arising from alleged

---

* From David Brokensha, *Social Change at Larteh, Ghana*
(London, 1966).

breaches of custom. Although most of its discussions are remote from the pressing national concerns of the day, the traditional council still has prestige, and its deliberations, if they affect Larteh directly, are eagerly followed.

Relations with other states are normally conducted by either the local council or the traditional council, but in some circumstances Larteh may engage in direct negotiations. This happened over the "Shai Lands Case," which concerned a large tract of land in the plains below Accra which has been in dispute intermittently for eighty years. Briefly, the claim of the people of Larteh-Ahenease is that they have a traditional right to these lands, which the Shai people occupied during the early cocoa migration days when Larterian attention was elsewhere. A series of court cases culminated in a 1962 judgment in favor of Ahenease, declaring the lands to be part of Akwapim stool-property. The *omanhene* watched the proceedings with interest, but initiative came from Ahenease. Many people had spent several years, and hundreds of pounds of their own money, to support the legal proceedings, because it was generally felt that the possession of the lands, which have little economic importance, was essential to raise the prestige of Ahenease. There was a strong feeling that it was incumbent on a loyal son of Ahenease to do what he could to restore ancient rights, so as to please the ancestors and "raise the name" of the town.

In the early years of the century the Basel missionaries were alarmed at the growth of political activities: ". . . societies call themselves temperance unions, usually with a core of lapsed Christians, and soon become agitators and political revolutionaries, with banners of Nationalism and Ethiopianism" (*Annual Report,* Basel Mission, 1908). However, little political activity on a national scale occurred at Larteh until the 1920's, when both the *benkumhene* and *kubeasehene,* as well as many other Larterians, became active members of the Aborigines Rights Protection Society. By 1949, branches of both the Convention People's Party (CPP) and the United Gold Coast Convention (later

the United Party) were established in Larteh. The latter
disappeared when it became apparent that the CPP was
firmly established, another example of Larteh accommodation to events.

In 1959, the Kubease people broke away from the Larteh
branch of the CPP and formed their own branch on the
grounds that they were accustomed to have separate institutions and that they had been overshadowed by the Ahenease people. Despite attempts by party officials to maintain one branch, local separatist tendencies were too strong,
and separate branches were formed in each town. Although
separate meetings are always held, it is customary to invite
some of the leaders, both traditional and new, from the

Table 1
Analysis of Larteh-Kubease CCP *Committee* (*1963*)

	Sex	Age	Educa-tion[1]	Membership of church[2]	Office held in CPP
1	M	67	TT	P	Chairman
2	F	45	S	P	Secretary
3	M	59	M	A	Treasurer
4	M	49	S	O	—
5	M	56	TT	P	—
6	M	53	Lit.	—	—
7	M	43	M	P	—
8	M	55	M	M	—
9	M	56	Lit.	P	—
10	M	32	M	P	—
11	F	55	P	P	—
12	F	30	M	A	—

Notes:
 [1] Lit. = Literate in Twi; P = Primary Schooling; M = Middle Schooling;
 S = Secondary Schooling; TT = Teacher Training.

other branch to attend any important CPP rally. Despite the intense rivalry such invitations are accepted and there is at least superficial cordiality. Several traditional leaders are members of the CPP Committee; an analysis of some of the principal committees shows the multiple membership of the leading citizens, and also illustrates that Larteh values, to which these leaders owe their positions, are of equal importance to external ones. The Kubease branch for a time had as its chairman a staunch young CPP man, who had the full support of the party but who was forced to resign in 1963 after a series of complaints which included his alleged pride and his not being "a proper Larterian," as his mother was an Ewe: in his stead the Committee elected a reliable older man, a cousin to the chief. (See Table 1 for an analysis of CPP Committee membership at Kubease.)

Occupation	Member Town Development Committee	Traditional office	Other
Retired: now farms		A "royal"	
Housewife		Wife to *kubeasehene*	
Local Council levy-collector	Yes	Linguist	
Pastor	Yes		Member Health Committee
Headmaster	Yes		Member Health Committee; Presbyter
Goldsmith and farmer		Linguist	
Driver	Yes		
Farmer			Local Councillor
Driver			
Tailor and farmer	Yes		Presbyter
Cloth trader	Yes	A "royal"	
Seamstress			

[a] Presbyterian; O = African Orthodox; A = Anglican; M = Methodist

. . .

The ascendancy of Larteh values may be more specifically illustrated by an account of a particular ceremony, a CPP rally held at Kubease on Sunday, June 4, 1961. The occasion was similar in most respects to other rallies. Special invitations, which included the program, were printed and distributed two months before the rally:

Program
Sunday, June 4, 1961

Mass Rally And Harvest
in Aid of Kwame Nkrumah Trust Fund

Larteh Kubease Branch of CPP

PART I

1. Town Procession   1:00 P.M.
2. Assembly at the Kubease Plaza   2:00 P.M.
3. Arrival of Invitees   2:15 P.M.
4. Song "Yen Ara Arase Ni"   Brass Band
5. Opening Prayer by Rev. Clegg of
        Methodist Church
6. Pouring of Libation by Osofo Agyekum

PART 2

1. Introduction of Chairman by Miss Kate Agyemfra
2. Object of Meeting—Branch Chairman
3. Address: K. Asante-Sakyi, M.P.
4. Music: Brass Band
5. Address: District Commissioner Akwapim
6. Address: Nana Kubeasehene
7. Music: Kubease Adenkum Band
8. Address: Nana Ankobeahene
9. Address and Distribution of Membership Cards by the
        Regional Commissioner, Eastern Region
10. Song: Presbyterian Singing Band
11. Appeal for Funds by Comrade E. W. Ofori
12. Vote of Thanks: Comrade Anno-Nyako
13. Light Refreshment and Music: Brass Band
14. Prayer and Benediction: Rev. Fr. Erskine

National Anthem

The program was followed, although a little later than announced: some of the "invitees" arrived at 5:00 P.M., and proceedings really started at about 3:30 P.M. There were some substitutions: Rev. Erskine of the Anglican church took the place of the Methodist minister; the Regional Commissioner was represented by his deputy secretary; Comrade Madame Botsio, the wife of a Cabinet Minister, who had been declared chairman, sent Madame Hannah Cudjoe, the Chairman of the National Day Nursery Movement who is also a prominent CPP member, in her place.

The meeting was held in the half-completed plaza in Kubease, the seating arrangements being of interest; the chief and elders occupied the raised dais, while the CPP leaders erected their own platform at a lower level. Visiting chiefs from Mampong, Amanokrom, and Adukrom sat with the *kubeasehene,* and other visitors sat with the distinguished guests. The organizers were constantly taking away chairs from those considered of less importance to give to later but more distinguished arrivals, without any protest being made.

Several features of the program deserve comment and explanation, as they typify the accommodation of Larteh to new institutions. First, the chief not only occupied a prominent place in the plaza but was accorded respect by most of the speakers. Although the regional commissioner's representative did make adverse comments on the small number of CPP members, 212 party cards were distributed, and the chief and others were told that a larger membership was expected. The chief was the first to receive his card at the distribution, followed by the *ankobeahene,* the *mankrado,* and the priest of Akonedi.

The *Sea Never Dry* Brass Band was, inevitably, in attendance, as no Kubease function is complete without them. On this occasion they arrived late and were not up to their usual form, it being said that they had played first at a funeral and were rather tipsy, and that several of the best bandsmen had not come. There was competition between them and the chiefs' drummers, who drummed out the chiefs' war songs from time to time despite protests by the master of ceremonies.

At most Larteh public ceremonies an opening prayer is given by a Christian minister, and this is usually followed, as on this occasion, by the pouring of a libation to the gods and ancestors; the pourer of the libation was the chief priest of Akonedi. Later in the ceremony the Presbyterian choir participated. The minister from the African Orthodox church was present, as is usual on Kubease public occasions. (The African Orthodox church was originally founded in Larteh in 1936 as part of the Marcus Garvey movement.)

Speeches were made in the prescribed order, preceded by the beating of the double gong-gong, and were all in Twi, not Guan. This was to be expected at such a meeting, when important non-Larterians were present, but at domestic rallies, such as one to mark, informally, the twenty-fifth anniversary of the *kubeasehene* on the stool, on April 24, 1963, one hears only Guan. Further, the CPP discourages any localism, and therefore would not welcome the use of a minority language such as Guan. The M.C. had earlier that day appeared as a presbyter in church, indicating that he saw no contradiction in the two roles.

This microcosm of one particular political party at Larteh-Kubease neatly illustrates the peculiar processes of accommodation, and also some of the difficulties faced by the CPP in its task of unification and modernization of political institutions. The CPP has stated that "the institution of chieftaincy will assist in the preservation of all that is best in our traditional culture" (1962 Program: *Work and Happiness*) and has reiterated this support subsequently. Yet at the same time the CPP discourages, as a national party must, any particularism or excessive local preoccupation which chieftaincy might support, and also continues the process of eroding the military, administrative, judicial, and political functions of chiefs. From the viewpoint of Larteh, there is still a strong sentimental attachment to chiefs, and the problem is to continue this while also supporting the CPP.

The rally illustrates the subtle way in which the compromise is reached. The CPP, as organizers of the meeting and as representatives of the government, are accorded respect, but so are all the other components of Larteh society. The chief and his elders and his drummers, the visiting chiefs, the shrine officials, Christian ministers, local councillors, the doctor, headmaster, merchants, cocoa farmers, and scholars, the leaders of women's groups and of the drivers—these and many more all have their part to play in the ceremony. And the merry notes of the *Sea Never Dry* Brass Band intervene from time to time, competing with the insistent drums of the *kubeasehene* to remind everyone that this is a Larteh occasion as well as a national political rally.[1]

---

1. Table 1 analyzes the Kubease CPP Committee membership, showing that it represents many traditional and contemporary institutions.

Influence and Control in an African Party:
Case of the Tanzanian African
National Union in 1960's*

HENRY BIENEN

In 1965, major constitutional changes were made in TANU. Prior to 1965, TANU had been defined by *T.A.N.U., Sheria na Madhumuni ya Chama* (literally, Law and Intentions of the Association). The constitutional arrangements for the party had been essentially the same since 1954, although the intentions of TANU as stated in the preamble to the constitution had been modified after it was clear independence would be granted.[1]

The organization of TANU has been based on territorial units (see Figure 1). However, functional or "place-of-work" TANU branches also exist, and are increasing in numbers. Policemen have joined TANU as a police branch; TANU branches have been started in the military; and there are TANU branches that are coterminous with pilot agricultural projects.

TANU has both elected and appointed officials, and different TANU organs are made up primarily of elected or ap-

* From Henry Bienen, *Tanzania: Party Transformation and Economic Development* (Princeton, 1967).

1. Nyerere is said to have modeled TANU's first Constitution along the lines of the Constitution of the Convention People's Party in Ghana.

Fig. 1: *The TANU and Government Pyramid*

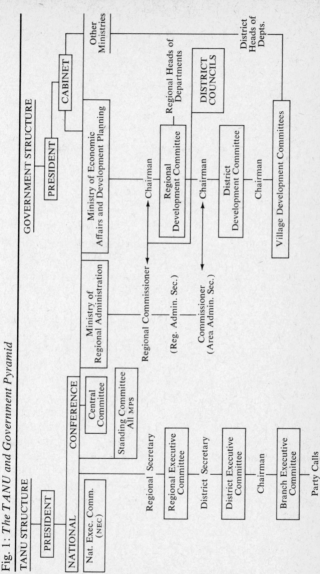

Table 1
Formal Links Between TANU and Government

1) The leader of the party is both President of Tanzania and President of TANU.

2) All Members of Parliament are delegates to the National Annual Conference and members of regional and district executive committees of their constituencies.

3) The President and members of the National Assembly constitute a Standing Committee of the TANU National Annual Conference.

4) Regional commissioners (appointed by the President) are *ex officio* TANU regional secretaries. They act as:

    a) *Ex officio* Members of Parliament.

    b) Members of the National Executive Committee.

    c) Delegates to the National Conference.

    d) Chairman of the regional development committee.

    e) "Proper Officer" for supervising the district councils.

    f) Responsible for sending official reports to the various ministries.

5) Area commissioners are TANU district secretaries, chairman of the district development committee, and non-voting delegates to the National Conference.

6) The TANU district chairman is chairman of the district council.

7) The TANU branch chairman is chairman of the village development committee.

pointed members. The National Conference with its elected President and Vice President, and the National Executive Committee (NEC) are elected bodies, though both have *ex officio* members; the Central Committee and the National Headquarters members are appointed or *ex officio*; regional, district, branch, and cell organizations have both elected and appointed members.[2] The distinction between elected and appointed TANU officials is an important one, which existed even before TANU formed the government. From the moment TANU began appointing officials in the regions and districts (1958–1959), the elected and appointed hierarchies became potentially competing systems of political power. However, there is no simple bifurcation here: some individuals hold both elected and appointed posts; some elected as well as many appointed officials hold both government and TANU jobs; some elected and some appointed

---

2. Cells have been a very recent innovation in TANU.

TANU people operate only at the districts and regions, whereas others also come to national institutions and take part in deliberations in Dar es Salaam. For example, in the past, one man could be district secretary of TANU and thus an area commissioner and head of government in his district; at the same time, he might be a regional chairman of TANU and come to the NEC in that capacity. There are a number of possible overlappings, and thus the relationships between elected and appointed officials cannot be neatly drawn in terms of two separate parallel hierarchies.

When we speak of a regional or district chairman of TANU, we refer to the chairmen of the TANU executive committees at those levels. The chairmen of the executive committees are elected by the Annual Conference of the regions and districts. Membership in the regional conference is given in Table 2.

The size of a regional conference varies depending on the number of districts within the individual region. There are seventeen regions altogether, most of which have three or four districts, but Mtwara region has six and Mara region has two at the extremes. The regional conference now meets in ordinary session once every two years immediately before the National Conference's own session, and its business consists largely of electing the new regional chairman, nominating an MNE who must be approved by the National Annual Conference, and electing the regional executive committee.

The regional executive committee is supposed to be convened four times a year. It is made up of all *ex officio* members of the regional conference plus a delegate elected at the regional conference to be an executive member for each district. The four members elected from the district to sit on the regional conference are not members, but aside from them, the membership is the same as the regional conference. As an executive body, the regional executive committee is too scattered to play a major role in TANU or government affairs. TANU work in the regions is handled by the regional working committee and the district executive

Table 2
Membership in the Regional Conference

Regional chairman
Regional secretary
Members of the regional working committee (These include the aforementioned regional chairman and regional secretary plus four people appointed by the regional chairman. Usually the regional secretary is equal to or more important than the chairman in the appointments. The TANU deputy regional secretary is often a member of the working committee.) [a]
All Members of Parliament resident in constituencies in the region
All members of the National Executive Committee resident in the region
All district chairmen in the region
Five delegates elected from each district [b]
A representative from each of the affiliate organizations
A representative from each of the party sections
Members of the regional executive committee (The regional executive committee includes all members of the regional conference except the five delegates elected from each district to the conference. It also includes all district secretaries of TANU in the region —that is, the area commissioners—and one person from each district who is elected at the regional conference to be the elected regional executive committee member.) [c]

[a] The appointed working committee members have no vote. They are the only representatives now specifically designated as being without the vote. In the past, MPS and MNES who were on the conference by virtue of their residence in the region had no vote unless they were also elected delegates.

[b] Prior to the 1965 changes, two members came from each district.

[c] In the past, district secretaries were listed as regional conference members in their own right. Now they are included by virtue of their membership on the regional executive committee. They have no vote at the regional executive committee meetings. Working committee members are without vote there too.

and district working committees. The regional executive committee's major function involves determining the candidates for TANU regional offices—that is, most of its energies go into electing a chairman, a new executive committee, and an MNE.

The regional conferences are involved in handling representation and succession functions. Just as American national parties come to life as national entities—and in fact identify themselves as existing at the national level—when they choose candidates, so the TANU regional party organi-

zations come to life and identity. This parallel can be carried
even further. With some few exceptions, the strongest
American party organizations exist as party machines in
urban areas. These machines were based originally on ward
organizations, and it was precisely at this level that the most
frequent elections were held for the most numerous offices.
Similarly in Tanganyika it is at the district level—not the
regional or branch level—that TANU organizations are most
vigorous and visible. And it is at the district level where the
most numerous elections take place, both in terms of number of offices to be filled and in terms of frequency of
elections.

National TANU bodies do not determine the individuals
who hold elective TANU office in the regions and districts.
Prior to 1965, candidates for the National Assembly were
nominated by district organizations. Although the NEC
could disapprove them, it did so only once in the 1960
election. In 1965, the NEC intervened to disallow one of the
two candidates selected by a TANU district conference primary for nomination as TANU candidate for National Assembly in 15 cases out of 91 constituencies (or 182 opportunities).

The tables show that some individuals have been very
successful in perpetuating themselves in office. Furthermore,
not all turnover is a result of electoral defeat; some of the
regional chairmen and MNE have been appointed to government posts and did not stand for reelection.[3] Appointment
to government posts did not automatically disqualify one
from holding elective TANU office. Some of the regional
chairmen and MNE tried to keep their TANU posts even
after they became commissioners. They were able to be
both chairman of MNE and commissioners as long as they
resided within the region where they were elected to TANU
office. However, in practice, a regional chairman or an MNE

---

3. Thus regional chairmen P. S. Muro, S. Mtaki, and R. Tambwe
became regional or area commissioners in 1962 and did not run for
TANU elected office.

would hold his post although he became a regional or area commissioner outside his region.[4]

When we consider the nature of the regions themselves, it may seem surprising that individuals can have long tenures as regional chairmen or MNE. Regions are entirely artificial, administrative demarcations. Under the colonial regime, nine provinces had been set up; the independent Tanganyika government first restyled these provinces as regions, and then in 1962–1963 increased the number of regions to 17.[5] This increase in number was designed to make administration more efficient and rule from a regional center feasible.

The regions, as drawn, are not natural economic demarcations. While many have a large majority of one particular tribe, all regions are multi-tribal.[6] Furthermore, we have seen that Tanganyika tribes are not centralized political entities. Thus tribal-regional leaders do not characterize Tanganyika's political life, as they do Uganda's.[7] The regions

---

4. E.g., as of September 1965, two MNE were area commissioners: H. Kiluvia and M. Kalemaga. The former was posted outside his region, the latter within it. As of March 1965, three MNE were area commissioners; all three—Kissokiy, Laicer, and Kalemaga—were within their regions. Kissokiy is an interesting case: he has been an MNE and a six-time TANU regional chairman. He moved out of Mbeya region for a short period in 1964 when he was an area commissioner of Iringa district. This district is contiguous to districts in Mbeya region. He retained his chairmanship even when he was out of the region (the residency requirement was not strictly applied, apparently), but returned shortly thereafter to Mbeya region and became area commissioner of Mbeya district.

5. The original regions of Tanganyika were: West Lake, Lake, Northern, Tanga, Central, Western, Southern Highland, Southern, and Eastern. The 17 regions are now called West Lake, Mwanza, Mara, Kilimanjaro, Arusha, Kigoma, Tabora, Tanga, Dodoma, Shinyanga, Coast, Mtwara, Morogoro, Iringa, Ruvuma, Mbeya and Singida.

6. E.g., although Kilimanjaro region has many Chagga and Mwanza region is predominantly Sukuma, both regions include many non-Chagga or non-Sukuma.

7. There are leaders in Uganda who claim, with some success, to represent not only their own tribe but also other tribes. They are "northern" leaders. The fact that Uganda is divided into districts

do not provide a base for national political power. Individuals find it hard to consolidate political power at the regional level. Factionalism within TANU at the district and sub-district levels affects elections for regional leaders because of the way delegates to the regional conference are chosen. Thus not only does the dual hierarchies of elected and appointed officials give two bases of support, but it is difficult for individuals who have achieved high electoral position to dominate the electoral process in the future. Within a region, there are a number of bases from which individuals can try to influence the selection of elected regional TANU officers. This can be seen by looking again at the membership in the regional conference (see Table 2). The list itself does not tell us whether or not the different categories of membership constitute viable power bases. In practice, they do.

From 1961 to 1965 many of the M.P.'s felt that they had an independent political base by virtue of being already elected to office. Until 1965, it was not known how "open" an election could take place for a new National Assembly. M.P.'s mended fences but primarily they looked to the NEC and the President for approval of their performance. As it turned out, the district TANU conferences were crucial to the continued holding of office by M.P.'s because the TANU district conferences nominated two candidates and most of the nominated candidates were approved by the NEC to stand as the only legal candidates under a TANU banner for the 1965 election. But immediately after independence, M.P.'s felt secure in the local political positions. Increasingly, they were appointed to government posts: at the beginning of December 1964, 37 out of 98 M.P.'s held office as ministers or junior ministers; in addition, ten M.P.'s were regional commissioners, three were area commissioners, and one was Deputy Speaker. Others served on or

---

and kingdoms in a federal-type structure has given such leaders a framework to operate within. And the framework has called forth tribal-regional leaders.

were chairmen of bodies like the Mwanachi Company which was linked to TANU, or the Worker's Investment Company which was linked to government but were not state concerns. Prior to 1965, these government officials looked to Dar es Salaam, not to their constituencies for continuation in office.

SELECTED BIBLIOGRAPHY

Bretton, Henry L. *The Rise and Fall of Kwame Nkrumah.* New York, 1966.

Burke, Fred G., and Stanley Diamond. *The Transformation of East Africa.* New York, 1966.

Coleman, James S. *Nigeria: Background of Nationalism.* Berkeley, 1958.

Cowan, L. Gray. *Local Government in West Africa.* New York, 1958.

Davidson, Basil. *The African Genius: An Introduction to African Cultural and Social History.* Boston, 1969.

Emerson, Rupert. *From Empire to Nations.* Cambridge, Mass., 1960.

Hodgkin, Thomas. *Nationalism in Colonial Africa.* London, 1956.

Lloyd, P. C. *Africa in Social Change.* London, 1967.

Morgenthau, Ruth S. *Political Parties in French-speaking West Africa.* Oxford, 1964.

Perham, Margery. *The Colonial Reckoning.* London, 1961.

Wallerstein, Immanuel. *Africa: The Politics of Independence.* New York, 1961.

Zolberg, Aristide. *One-Party Government in the Ivory Coast.* Princeton, N.J., 1964.

Index

About the Authors

W. W. CLARIDGE—formerly official historian in the British Foreign Office, now deceased.

W. MALCOLM HAILEY—member of the British Colonial Service who undertook several major surveys of British colonial administration.

R. GRIFFETH—Professor of History, University of California, Los Angeles.

C. WESLEY JOHNSON—Professor of History, Stanford University.

RICHARD PANKHURST—Professor of History, Haile Selassie I University, Addis Ababa, Ethiopia.

R. DELAVIGNETTE—formerly colonial governor in Upper Volta, French West Africa.

GEOFFREY GORER—British anthropologist and writer.

ELLIOTT SKINNER—Professor of Anthropology, Columbia University.

MARTIN KILSON—Professor of Government, Harvard University.

MARGERY PERHAM—Fellow of Nuffield College, Oxford University.

BRIAN WEINSTEIN—Professor of Government, Howard University, Washington, D.C.

ROBERT ROTBERG—Professor of History and Political Science, Massachusetts Institute of Technology.

CRAWFORD YOUNG—Professor of Political Science, University of Wisconsin.

DAVID BROKENSHEA—Professor of Anthropology, University of California, Santa Barbara.

RALPH AUSTEN—Assistant Professor of History, University of Chicago.

KOFI BUSIA—Prime Minister of Ghana and formerly Professor of Sociology, University of Ghana.

A. L. EPSTEIN—formerly Research Fellow, Rhodes-Livingstone Institute, Lusaka, Zambia.

HENRY BIENEN—Assistant Professor of Politics, Princeton University.

KENNETH POST—Professor of Politics, University of the West Indies.

C. C. BAETA—Professor of Religion, University of Ghana.

HANS DEBRUNNER—formerly missionary in Ghana.

About the Editors

WILFRED CARTEY, born in Port of Spain, Trinidad, in 1931, was graduated from University College of the West Indies in Jamaica, and holds a Master's Degree and a Ph.D. from Columbia University, where he is Adjunct Professor of Comparative Literature at the African Studies Institute. He is also currently Professor of Comparative Literature at the City College of New York. Among the numerous prizes and grants he has been awarded is a Fulbright Travel Grant, from 1955–1959, to study Afro-Antillian and Latin American Literature. In 1967 Dr. Cartey was Visiting Scholar at the University of Legon, Ghana.

Dr. Cartey lectures and writes widely on African and Black literature, and contributes to numerous journals and magazines here and abroad. In addition, he is Literary Editor of *African Forum,* and the author of two books, *Islands in the Sun* and *Whispers from a Continent,* the latter published by Random House in 1969. Dr. Cartey is also the editor of an anthology of African literature, and the author of *Black Images,* both to be published later this year.

MARTIN KILSON received a Bachelor of Arts Degree from Lincoln University in Pennsylvania, and holds a Master's Degree and a Ph.D. from Harvard University, where he is currently Professor of Government. From 1964–1965 Dr. Kilson was a Visiting Professor at the University of Ghana.

Dr. Kilson has contributed numerous articles on African politics and Black Studies to periodicals such as *Dissent, World Politics* and the *Journal of Modern African Studies.* He is the author of *Political Change in a West African State* and another book *Chiefs, Peasants and Politicians: Grassroots Politics in Ghana,* which will be published later this year. In addition, Dr. Kilson has co-edited two books, *À Propos of Africa: Sentiments of American Negro Leaders Towards Africa, 1815–1950* with Adelaide Cromwell Hill and *Political Awakening of Africa* with Rupert Emerson.